the new
MEAT
LOVER'S
cookbook

the new MEAT LOVER'S cookbook

JANEEN A. SARLIN
AND DIANE PORTER

Macmillan • USA

MACMILLAN

A Simon & Schuster Macmillan Company

1633 Broadway

New York, NY 10019

A catalogue record is available from the Library of Congress.

ISBN: 0-02-860393-1

Manufactured in the United States of America

10   9   8   7   6   5   4   3   2   1

Design by Kevin Hanek

*For J. Troy Schrock, my Dad,
my unmeasured love and gratitude
for teaching and encouraging me to love life
as well as meat.*

contents

Acknowledgments

Tons of love and gratitude to Diane Porter, my co-author, whose good humor, practical knowledge, attention to detail, expertise at deciphering my rough drafts, and ability to meet every deadline led to the creation of this book.

Pounds of thanks to her husband, Donald Porter, a keen wordsmith, whose patience, palate, and delicious humor will never be forgotten.

Quarts of kudos to Judith Weber, our agent, who suggested this book at just the right time, brought Diane and I together in no time, stood by us patiently time and again—the results . . . a book on a timely subject.

Buckets of appreciation to my faithful students, loyal friends, and supportive family who were trusted testers and sometimes unknowingly the tasters for these recipes.

Bushels of love and thanks to Roger and Marcheta Tate, fellow Hoosiers and good friends, who produce the best veal I've ever eaten.

Ounces of thanks to Lisa Donahue, a fellow Aries, who introduced me to Cervena venison long before I wrote this book.

Heaping pints of appreciation to Justin Schwartz, our editor, whose even-tempered disposition carried all of us through the turmoil of hammering together a book.

Overflowing gratitude to Susan Sloan for her assistance with the final manuscript.

Stacks of thanks to all the farmers, ranchers, packers, meat bards, steak houses, and butchers; all members of the food chain that produces the excellent quality of lean meat that is affordable and available today.

And finally, Diane and I send an infinity of love and kisses to our children, Katherine, Victoria, Scott, and Paige, for being who they are, and for their love, patience, and undying support of their working moms.

INTRODUCTION

On a recent flight to Chicago I was seated next to an attractive, tall, slim, and healthy-looking woman in her thirties. She was reading a popular health-oriented magazine, and on its cover I saw the lines:

GO AHEAD EAT AN EGG
IT WON'T KILL YOU

She saw me glance at it and said, "Isn't that a relief! I've mostly given up eggs, but every time I eat one I feel a little guilty and scared."

What's to become of us if we react to food this way—needing to be reassured that an egg won't kill us! I'm health conscious, but I have little tolerance for remarks like the one made recently by a friend with whom I was out to dinner. I'd ordered a grilled steak, and when it arrived, she muttered, "Heart attack on a plate."

Of course I'm not advocating unbridled bingeing on slabs of roast beef so big they hang over the edge of the plate. But I love meat. I grew up on it, and I plan to continue eating it in healthful ways. That's what this book is about: eating moderate portions of nutritious low-fat meats—cooked with little if any added fat—but with large dollops of flavorful spices and seasonings. I say, relish the hearty Braised Lamb Shanks (page 99) on a cold day in January, indulge in the Modern Steak au Poivre (page 130) for a special dinner, and savor the Southwestern Grilled Pork Tenderloin (page 184) on a balmy summer night. All these can be part of a healthy diet.

Ee-I-Ee-I-O

Ever since my early childhood on a Midwest dairy farm, I've been a meat-lover. We ate what we raised, both livestock and garden vegetables, with beef and pork being the cornerstones of our meals.

We ate meat at least twice a day, and often at every meal. For breakfast we had eggs with bacon, homemade sausages or pan-fried steaks, and tons of fresh fruit and cereal. For lunch at school, I almost always devoured a meat sandwich. Dinners, served in the middle of the day, might feature a slow-cooked beef stew, mashed potatoes and gravy, vegetables from the garden, a green salad, fresh fruit, dessert, and milk for everyone. For the evening meal, called "supper," we dined on sautéed pork chops, homemade applesauce, fried potatoes with onions, cabbage salad or a green salad, fresh fruit, dessert, and milk.

Poultry was served twice a week, but never fish. So meat it was, day in and day out. Roasts, stews, chops, steaks—we never grew tired of it.

We were all involved in raising the animals, which were fed a special corn diet to fatten them for our family table. Dad butchered them, and Mom and Grams cooked them. As a curious little girl, I watched and questioned Dad while he butchered a steer or a hog that hung from the elm tree beside the granary. He described in detail the anatomy of the animal as he cut it, never laughing at my endless questions, patiently identifying and explaining its inner parts.

Life on the farm flowed naturally with the rhythms of the seasons and our love of the land.

The Modern Me

If I ate today the way I did when I was young, I'd weigh twice what I do. Yes, there are still times I indulge with gusto, feasting on a large steak or a high-fat meal. However, if I overeat one day, I work out longer at the gym the next and then cut back on what I eat for the following week, having large breakfasts of low-fat cereal and fresh fruits, salads for lunch, and light dinners. Over a week's time, my diet balances out.

Most of the time I eat everything in moderation, including sweets. I control my portions—usually three to four ounces of meat per serving—and complete the menu with cooked vegetables as well as large green salads, which isn't all that different from what Mom did years ago. I prefer high-quality, low-fat cuts of meat like filet of beef, pork tenderloin, ground sirloin, Cervena venison, veal scallops from the leg, and well-trimmed loin lamb chops. I've replaced the extravagant amounts of butter I used years ago with small amounts of olive oil.

I think of myself as a country-modern cook, someone steeped in the Midwestern corn belt yet influenced by major urban chefs. I love today's emphasis on exotic flavors and international spices, yet I'm passionate about the food of my youth. The recipes in this book reflect this mix.

I've come a long way from the 17-year-old girl who won a four-year college scholarship for being the Betty Crocker Homemaker of the Year with my Double-Stuffed Pork Chops. I live in the Big Apple and run a catering business and a cooking school; I write a syndicated food column; and several years ago I wrote *Food from an American Farm*, a cookbook that celebrates the food of my childhood.

A New Meat-Lover's Cookbook

In this book I've taken a new look at meat. Over the past 20 years my cooking of meat has steadily evolved. Today, for example, instead of frying in two inches of lard, I film a nonstick skillet with vegetable oil or dust a very hot, well-seasoned cast-iron skillet with salt and sear the meat. I even use a microwave to speed up the cooking time or to finish the cooking of the finest dishes. My Doctored Beef Broth (page 279) fills in fine for most dishes when I don't have the time to make homemade stock. I recognize that unlike my mother and grandmother, most women can't spend all day in the kitchen.

How often I've heard the complaints "If I have to look at chicken again, I'll just scream" and "My husband is a meat-and-potatoes man; he's not happy with my cooking anymore."

A story I love, because I think it's true for so many of us, comes from a hard-working Milwaukee schoolteacher, wife, and mother who came to one of my classes. After class she said, "Janeen, I don't know what to do. I try to feed my family healthy foods, chicken, pasta, and lots of vegetables. But my husband grumbles all the time and says he misses the pork chops and beef stews I used to make, and why can't I cook like that anymore? Worse, he says why can't I cook the way his mother used to? When he goes out he orders a huge steak, or we both take the kids to McDonald's and I feel guilty. This doesn't make sense."

I agree that it doesn't make sense. My answer is to serve moderate-size portions of deliciously cooked, healthful, low-fat cuts of meat at home. Chances are your family won't feel the need to pig-out on the high-fat stuff when they're out.

"There Are No Secrets in Cooking, but Let Me Tell You a Few"

I've used this line for years in my cooking classes. There are no secrets, but over the years I've learned and developed techniques and tricks. In this book I'll share many of mine, like the following simple ones:

- *How to make a fast and foolproof filet of tenderloin every time.*
- *How to use spicy dry rubs that add flavor without fat or calories.*
- *How to turn defatted broths and natural juices into wonderful sauces.*

Another "secret" no recipe can tell you, is the precise time it takes to cook a piece of meat or to reduce a stock. One steak is a bit thicker than another. This time the fire's a touch hotter. One pot has a thicker bottom; another, a tighter-fitting cover. The diameter of one pan is larger than another, shortening the time it takes to reduce a sauce. When you cook, stay alert and use your best judgment.

I believe in buying the finest cuts of lean meat, the freshest and best-quality fruits and vegetables, and superior condiments. Mediocre ingredients lead to mediocre results. Contrary to what most people believe, when you eat the tastiest meals, you eat less. You're satisfied, delighted with the food, and not overeating in search of a taste sensation that has eluded you.

My last "secret" for now—whether using this cookbook or any other—is to take all instructions with a grain of salt. It's not necessary to follow a recipe to the letter. You don't have to use the precise quantities or even the same ingredients that are called for in recipes. Be inventive! Use what you have on hand, substitute a spice you love for one about which you feel so-so, and have fun. You'll change from thinking of yourself as someone who cooks to someone who *is* a cook.

Not All Red Meat Is High in Fat

Many of us believe that all meat is high in fat. Not true. For instance, filet mignon has about 12 grams of fat for a 4-ounce serving. That's less than the fat in a tablespoon of olive oil.

Even lower in fat is a 4-ounce serving of leg of lamb. It has about 8 grams of fat, which is less than 2 teaspoons of oil, 1 ounce of most hard cheeses, or $1/4$ cup of ordinary tuna salad. Four ounces of top sirloin has only 6.5 grams of fat. Pork tenderloin, veal cut from the leg, and chicken breast with the skin removed all have about the same amount of fat—5 grams for a 4-ounce portion.

Of course, there are cuts of meat that are high in fat—pork spareribs, breast of veal, and ground chuck—and it's wise to avoid them.

Use your eyes—they'll tell you how fatty the meat is. Examine the meat for marbling, those streaks of fat running through it, and avoid those pieces. Look to see how much fat you'll have to cut away. Examine the packages of ground meat in your supermarket's meat case. Observe how much more fat is in ground chuck than in ground round. Notice that ground sirloin is leaner still. Place a package of lean ground sirloin next to a package of ground chuck or a package of what supermarkets call "ground beef" (usually made from a mixture of cheap beef cuts) and compare the colors. The high-fat meat will be much lighter than the low. Those white flecks you see are fat.

You may have noticed how much leaner today's meat is than it was a decade ago. Livestock is now raised differently and butchers trim away more of the fat, so the meat is significantly leaner. (More about this in the first chapter.)

Cooking Meat in Low-Fat Ways

Other than deep-frying, no method of cooking meat inherently adds much fat. In these recipes I use lean cuts of meat, and the little fat I do add is olive or canola oil, both highly touted in today's health-conscious world.

Grilling is a low-fat way to cook. As the meat cooks, the fat melts from the meat into the fire.

Sautéing, cooking over high heat for a short time, can be done with minimal oil. Using a nonstick pan, you need only a teaspoon or two of oil to brown garlic or shallots, even less if the oil's sole purpose is to brown the meat, in which case only a film is needed. Because the fat cannot drip away, I'm careful when I sauté to use especially lean cuts and to trim away any fat the butcher hasn't.

For pan-searing, no fat is needed. Typically, a well-seasoned cast-iron or other heavy skillet is heated until very hot and then sprinkled with a pinch of coarse salt. The chop or steak is added to the pan and quickly seared to seal in its juices.

A note about using nonstick skillets. While I recommend cooking and even searing meat in them, some research indicates the possibility that harmful, odorless fumes occur when you heat nonstick skillets or dry-cook (pan-searing and sautéing) over high heat. An alternative to nonstick skillets is to simply spray an ordinary skillet with vegetable oil.

Most roasts require no added fat, although you may film the roasting pan with oil and sear the meat before roasting it.

Stews can be low in fat or loaded with it. By using lean meat and skimming off any fat that rises, you ensure a low-fat, healthful stew.

Ground meats are as low or high in fat as the meat from which they're ground. If you use lean meats, you won't have a problem. Be wary of hamburgers and other ground-meat dishes in restaurants. These tend to be made with high-fat cuts because fatty meats are less expensive and the fat keeps the meat moist.

Even pâtés can be low in fat. By using egg whites, bread soaked in milk, or a mixture of yogurt and oatmeal instead of fat to moisten and bind the meat, you can have all the flavor of a rich pâté without the fat.

Some Final Words

So having said all this about fat, why haven't I included nutritional breakdowns—such as calories, fat grams, and sodium counts—with my recipes? There are two reasons, the most important of which is that the breakdowns I've seen are often so inaccurate as to be ludicrous. Mistakes creep into them. How on earth can you figure how much oil a chop absorbs from a marinade or how much fat has dripped from a grilled steak? Have you chilled the stew and removed all the fat, or merely skimmed the top, leaving some behind?

The other reason is that I don't think of food as numbers to be added and analyzed. Hey, I'm a chef, not a nutritionist. I don't weigh meat before I cook it, and certainly not afterward. If I want to know the weight after cooking, I eyeball it; a 3- to 4-ounce piece of meat is roughly the size of a deck of cards. And while I'm careful to eat very little salt, I haven't the slightest desire to calculate the sodium content of everything I eat. For those who are interested, I suggest you purchase a book like *The Corinne T. Netzer Encyclopedia of Food Values* (Dell Publishing, 1992).

Another word about salt. I know that many of us have cut back. I use very little in my catering business. Clients don't notice any lack of flavor because in its place I use plenty of herbs and pepper. Most of the recipes in this book are low in salt. However, if you want to eliminate it, go ahead. Taste and correct the seasonings with additional herbs and pepper.

The portion sizes in this book will appear generous by today's standards, skimpy by old-fashioned ones. Consider the other dishes you're serving when you decide how many people a pound of meat will serve. If you want to serve a judicious portion of meat and have your guests walk away from the table satisfied, serve additional dishes like interesting vegetables, big salads, and a healthful dessert. For a family meal I usually serve at least a salad, a starch, and a cooked vegetable. For company I add an appetizer and a dessert. If you serve only a steak and a salad, guests will eat a lot more steak than if you add a baked potato and steamed broccoli. In other words, use your judgment.

For me, "Eating well is the best revenge!"

Bon appétit!

GLOSSARY

Here is a short list of the cooking terms about which I am most often asked:

BRAISE (v)—To brown and then cook meat in a small amount of liquid over low heat for a long period of time.

BUTTERFLY (v)—To split a piece of meat down the center, cutting almost but not completely through. The two halves are then opened flat to resemble an open book or a butterfly shape.

CASSEROLE (n)—A heavy enameled pot, such as those made by Le Creuset, with a tight-fitting lid, ideal for cooking stews and covered roasts in an oven; also, the dish baked in a casserole.

CHIFFONADE (n)—Leaves, such as lettuce, spinach, and basil, cut crosswise into thin ribbons.

CILANTRO (n)—A pungent herb, also known as fresh coriander and Chinese parsley, commonly used in Mexican, Indian, and Chinese cooking.

DEGLAZE (v)—To add a small amount of liquid (usually wine or stock) to a pan, then to heat and scrape up the flavorful browned bits of meat or vegetable that have stuck to the bottom of the pan. This mixture becomes a sauce or the foundation of one.

DEMI-GLACE (n)—A thick, rich reduction of stock, espagnole sauce (a traditional brown sauce), and wine used to enrich a sauce, or to act as the base for many sauces.

FILM WITH OIL (v)—To add only enough oil to create a coating over the bottom of a pan. If the pan is tilted, there should be no accumulation of oil.

FLAMBÉ (a)—A French word (in English, "flamed") to describe a dish in which a small amount of liquor, such as brandy or port, is drizzled over the meat and ignited.

GRILL (v)—To cook on a heavy metal grate set over hot coals or other direct heat.

JULIENNE (v)—To cut into matchstick-size pieces

NAP (v)—To cover a piece of meat with a thin glaze or a thick sauce.

NONREACTIVE COOKWARE (n)—Bowls and cooking pans that will not cause changes in the food from such chemically active ingredients as lemon juice, tomatoes, vinegar, and wine. Stainless steel, glass, ceramic, and nonstick cookware are examples of nonreactive materials.

PARCHMENT PAPER (n)—A grease- and moisture-resistant heavy paper used for baking and lining pans; it will not burn in a hot oven.

ROAST (v)—To bake a large piece of meat in an uncovered pan. This dry-heat method of cooking concentrates the meat's flavor and produces a crusty, brown exterior and a tender, moist interior. (n)—The meat cooked in this manner.

SAUTÉ (v)—To cook for a short period in a pan over high heat using a small amount of fat.

SCORE THE EDGES (v)—To slash the edges of steaks and chops every couple of inches so the meat doesn't curl as it cooks.

SEAR (v)—To brown the surface of meat rapidly over high heat without added fat. Often done in a well-seasoned cast-iron skillet with a pinch of salt.

SILVER SKIN (n)—The shiny, silvery-white membrane that surrounds many roasts.

STIR-FRY (v)—To cook small pieces of food rapidly for a short time in a small amount of oil while constantly tossing the food.

STUD (v)—To insert flavorful or aromatic items, such as cloves or slivers of garlic, into the surface of the meat.

WELL-TRIMMED MEAT (n)—Meat from which all the separable fat, gristle, and silver skin has been removed.

ZEST (n)—The aromatic rind, without the bitter white pith, of citrus fruit.

THE MEAT WE EAT

First You Find a Butcher

I tell my students to buy their meat either at a reputable meat market— what we used to call a butcher shop—or at a supermarket that has its own butcher. If you buy your meat at the supermarket, as most cooks do, you may assume you can buy only what's in the meat case. Not so. Many supermarkets have butchers right in the store who are glad to help you.

Most are friendly, willing to cut meat to your request and eager to share their knowledge. I've even met a few who enjoy sharing their family recipes. Ask questions. You may be surprised how much help you'll get.

Know Your Meat

Shop only where you can buy meat that is good quality, fresh, and well trimmed. Buy the best cuts you can afford, particularly if the meat is to be roasted, grilled, or sautéed. Look for sales of expensive cuts. Make sure the meat is fresh, not too heavily marbled with fat, well trimmed, and evenly cut—it's hard to properly cook a steak that's ½ inch thick on one end and 2 inches thick on the other.

If you buy meat from the meat case, examine the label. Not only does it describe the kind of meat, the price per pound, the weight of the meat, and the cost, but it also tells you both the primal (i.e., wholesale) and retail cuts of the meat. For example, "Lamb Loin Chops" tells you the kind of meat (lamb), the primal cut (loin), and the retail cut (chops); "Beef Top Round Steak" details the kind of meat (beef), the primal cut (round) and subprimal cut (top round), and the retail cut (steak).

In addition, many packages carry nutritional breakdowns on their labels. Recently at my local market I noticed the ground beef was labeled 74% lean, the ground chuck 80% lean, the ground round 85% lean, and the ground sirloin 90% lean. Let's be clear: 74% lean means 26% fat; 90% lean, 10% fat.

There's a big difference between 26% fat and 10% fat! Read the labels—they often tell you a lot.

After many years I've come to a conclusion that at first blush appears paradoxical: The most expensive cut of meat often turns out to be the most economical. With less fat, gristle, and bone, expensive cuts often give you more lean meat per dollar than the less expensive cuts.

Regardless of whether you choose beef, veal, pork, or lamb, select lean cuts, trim away the fat before cooking, and serve moderate portions.

Keep It Fresh

Living in a large city, I have the luxury of shopping at the butcher's most days, so I don't often freeze meat. However, to make last-minute meals, I do keep hamburgers in the freezer for up to 2 weeks. The U.S. Department of Agriculture guidelines suggest that ground meat or meat cut up for stew can be frozen for up to 3 to 4 months, larger cuts of beef for 6 to 12 months, lamb for 6 to 9 months, pork for 4 to 6 months, and veal for 4 to 8 months, but I prefer to use frozen chops and roasts within a month. If I had a chest freezer, I would feel comfortable freezing meat for longer periods. A chest freezer used for long-term storage isn't opened with the frequency of a small unit attached to a refrigerator, so its temperature can be trusted to stay uniformly low, keeping the meat in excellent condition for many months.

Whether meat is to be stored in the refrigerator or freezer, it must be well wrapped. If it's already wrapped in butcher's paper when you bring it home, don't unwrap it. Wrap over the butcher's paper with plastic wrap, place the package into a zipper-lock bag, squish out the air, and zip it shut.

If the meat comes in a Styrofoam tray wrapped in plastic—the way it does in every supermarket I know—remove the meat and wrap it tightly, first in plastic wrap and then in heavy freezer paper, sealing the ends well with freezer tape, and place it in a zipper-lock bag. Always mark on the bag or the wrapping paper the date the meat was purchased.

By using heavy freezer paper and wrapping the meat several times, you prevent freezer burn. When you thaw the meat, it will look fresh and will taste almost as good as fresh.

Fresh meat should be stored in the coldest part of the refrigerator and for only a short time. I usually limit this to 1 day for ground meat, 2 for small cuts, and no more than 3 for roasts—unless I am aging beef (see page 12).

From the Freezer to the Pan

While it's possible to thaw meat safely in a microwave or in cold water, I prefer to take the meat out of the freezer the night before and thaw it overnight in the refrigerator. This is both the safest way to thaw meat and the one in which the meat loses the least moisture. Do not defrost meat at room temperature, as the outside thaws before the inside, and the risk of bacteria multiplying is too high to chance. If you're desperate—you forgot to take out the steaks and your in-laws will arrive in 30 minutes—defrost them in a microwave following the manufacturer's directions or put the sealed zipper-lock bag in cold water to defrost the meat.

Unless I am marinating meat for an hour or less, I marinate it in the refrigerator. I put the meat into the marinade (or if it's veal, into milk) while it's only partially defrosted, accomplishing two jobs at once.

For safety, I never leave raw meat at room temperature for more than an hour.

Beef

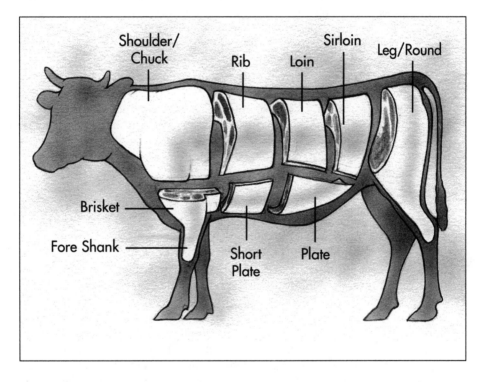

When most Americans think of red meat, they think of beef, the quintessential American meat. With beef, more than the other meats, there's a striking difference in the amount of fat between one cut and another. I prefer the lower-fat beef cuts for taste as well as for nutritional reasons.

The filet of beef is my all-time reliable standby for dinner parties and catering events, and filet mignon is my favorite steak. Some chefs claim the filet lacks deep-meat taste, but to me its subtle flavor and buttery texture more than compensate.

I like T-bone and shell (also known as strip) steaks, both cut from the short loin. I also enjoy an occasional rib-eye steak, a boneless steak cut from the rib section of the loin. Rib-eyes, however, tend to have more marbling, making them fattier than the other steaks I cook. All of these tender steaks are ideal for fast, dry-heat cooking, that is, grilling or sautéing.

Some tougher cuts, like round steak, flank steak, and top sirloin, can be cooked quickly if they are first marinated. Other tough cuts, like brisket, require slow, moist-heat cooking to make them tender.

In response to the consumer's concern about fat in beef, ranchers now raise leaner breeds of cattle, feed their cattle more grass and less corn, and send the animals to market younger, before they grow fat. Butchers trim cuts more closely, resulting in significantly leaner beef than a decade ago.

Beef is often graded, but not always. Prime, choice, and select are the three grades that reach the consumer. Prime meat has the best texture and color but also the most fat. Ironically, it's the moist juiciness of the fat that we associate with the best beef. Most prime beef is used in fine restaurants, although some is available through butchers.

All the beef recipes in this book have been tested with choice, since this is the grade overwhelmingly sold in supermarkets and used today by home cooks. By cooking a choice steak properly, as recommended in these recipes, you will end up with tender, mouth-watering steaks without the extra fat and cost of prime meat. Select is the leanest of the three grades but doesn't have the flavor or texture of prime and choice.

Fresh beef will be red, and its fat white, not yellow. It's easy to see how much fat is in beef. Avoid well-marbled pieces and choose those with little fat around the edges.

You can make a wonderful rib roast at home if you first age the roast. When meat is aged by a butcher or in the warehouse, it's stored for 3 to 6 weeks at low humidity and a temperature in the mid-30s. Because the rib roasts I buy are often not sufficiently aged for my taste, I age them at home. The way I do this is called "dry-aging," which means the meat is left uncovered to age and dry in the refrigerator.

To age a roast, I trim it of all excess fat, leaving only the thinnest film of fat over the top. Then I place the roast, fat side up, on a rack in a pan. I put it, uncovered, in the back of the refrigerator—where it stays cold even when I open the refrigerator door—for at least 24 hours, preferably for 3 to 5 days. I do nothing further. Just before roasting, using a sharp knife, I shave off the dried ends of the roast. It's not necessary to shave the top because it has a thin film of fat that has kept the meat from drying out. Then I proceed with my recipe. Aged beef is tastier, more tender, and tends to cook faster than beef that hasn't been aged.

Lamb

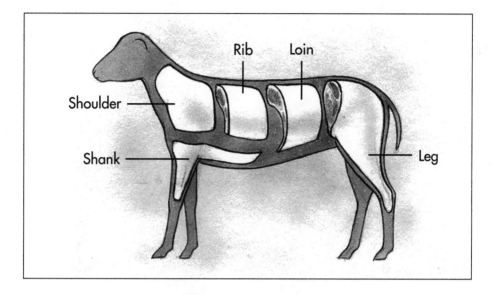

Lamb comes from sheep less than a year old, and most of our lamb is from animals about 6 months old. Due to improved breeding, today's lamb is lean, tender, and flavorful. Retail cuts are trimmed so that little fat remains.

Lamb is graded as "prime" and "choice" for the quality of the meat, not its fat content. Most of today's lamb is choice.

Lamb has never been popular in America. Personally, I love lamb now, but like many of my generation, I hated it as a child. Mom occasionally received "lamb chops" as a gift from our neighbor. It was actually mutton, the meat of older sheep. The meat was tough, and the unpleasant, overpowering odor that filled the house as it cooked left me prejudiced against lamb for many years.

It was only after I moved to New York that I tasted lamb at its best, and it was love at the first juicy bite. I came to adore rare lamb chops, I discovered delightful ways to season leg of lamb, and I was captivated by rack of lamb!

I often make a lean leg of lamb for guests and clients. My favorite cut of lamb, however, is a whole rib called a rack of lamb or when formed into a circle and tied, a crown roast. It's an expensive cut, and perfect for a formal event. Be sure to have the butcher trim it well. While this cut is not as lean as the leg or the loin, I doubt anyone will eat it often enough for the difference to matter. Most lamb I see in the market is lean, but the ground lamb sold in the supermarket is usually fatty. I recommend that you buy a lean cut and have the butcher grind it for you.

While lamb chops often cost more than steak or pork chops, they do go on sale. A whole leg can be a bargain, and most butchers will cut it to your specifications, giving you a roast, steaks, and lean ground meat.

Pork

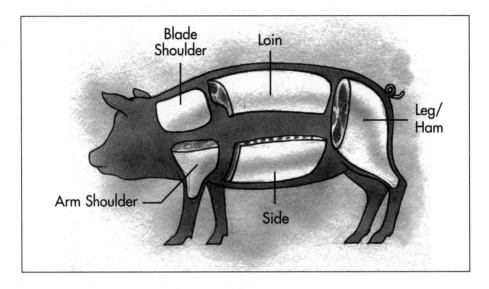

The pork industry has effectively gotten the word out—pork is "the new white meat." Today some cuts of pork are nearly as low in fat as skinless chicken and lean fish.

Try a pork tenderloin or a center-cut loin chop. Be sure to remove any separable fat surrounding the chop. Notice how little marbling there is. Since these cuts of pork are low in fat, be careful not to overcook them—they easily dry out.

I like to cook pork so that there is still a bit of pink inside. Some of you may be more comfortable cooking it until the meat is cooked through and the juices run clear. That's fine, but make sure to stop the cooking as soon as the pork is cooked through. As with all meat, the most accurate way to judge when it's done to your liking is with a meat thermometer.

My favorite cut of pork is the loin. A whole pork loin can feed an army and I rely on it for a large buffet.

Pork chops remind me of the farm meals I grew up on. They're ideal for informal family dinners, or when set afire, like Pork Chops Flambé, they're perfect for a fancy dinner.

Pork tenderloin is one of the darlings of the '90s. Again I warn you not to overcook it or it will be dry and tasteless instead of mild-tasting and fork-tender.

Two-thirds of the pork in this country is sold processed. While I still love a ham on Easter Sunday and use Cindy's Best Baked Italian Sausage (page 246) for a buffet or as an hors d'oeuvre, on a daily basis I limit my consumption of bacon, ham, and sausage because of their high sodium content.

For the best ham, talk to your butcher. Some hams are much lower in fat and far superior in taste than others. I never buy ham that has water pumped into it. Buying a ham is one situation in which you can't tell much by examination and must rely on your butcher to guide you to a good-quality brand.

Veal

Because veal comes from young animals, there is little fat on most cuts and no marbling. The best veal comes from calves less than 3 months old, but most of the veal in supermarkets comes from animals 4 to 5 months old. Some would argue that this is "baby beef," not really veal, but because the Department of Agriculture has not set a standard defining veal, growers and processors can call it veal. This meat is darker and its texture less delicate than that from a younger animal.

Look for pale-pink, fine-textured meat with no marbling. Even at a good butcher shop it is often hard to find top-quality veal. The best veal is called "special-fed veal," and it comes from young calves fed a unique liquid diet.

I soak veal overnight in milk, which draws out the blood. If you soak it in milk, you'll end up with veal that is white and tender, even if the veal you start with is cut from an older animal. Remember, though, that it will never be as succulent and delectable as top-quality veal.

Be sure veal scallops are cut from the leg. Scallops cut from the shoulder don't match those from the leg in either taste or tenderness.

"Stewing veal" is sometimes available at a reasonable price at supermarkets, but look carefully to be sure the meat is lean and not full of connective tissue.

Veal leg and loin are expensive, but they are the only cuts I find worth using. There's no waste, they're very lean, and the meat is finely grained and delicate.

Venison

When I was a child, the men brought venison (deer) home from their hunts. After Dad butchered the deer, Mom marinated the steaks for 2 to 3 weeks and the roasts for a month.

Today's store-bought venison is farm raised, the meat tender and mild, with little of wild deer's gamy flavor. Venison is available through many local butchers, some supermarkets, and by mail order (see page 170).

Because of its low fat content and a mild taste that lends itself to creative seasonings, chefs have recently developed imaginative new venison recipes.

Chops cut from the leg or the loin can be seared and cooked quickly as you would lamb chops or steak. Venison is most tender when served rare or cooked very, very slowly.

THE FAITHFUL ROAST

*J*ust as every woman needs a "little black nothing" to fall back on when she has "nothing to wear," every hostess needs within her cooking repertoire those effortless core recipes around which she can always assemble an outstanding dinner.

Regardless of the occasion, you're never out of fashion with a roast as the center of a meal. Roasts are always in impeccable taste for a party, whether it's dinner for 8 or a wedding for 200. Classic, elegant, and when you know the simple art of cooking them, close to foolproof.

Any roast can be dressed up for a white-tie dinner party or made casual for the family. Like that "little black nothing," much of the effect lies in presentation and accessories.

For the most luxurious affair: First, fillet of sole encircling salmon mousse, masked with an herbal green sauce and trimmed with grilled-pepper coulis. Then Braised Fruit-Stuffed Loin of Pork (page 58), served with a potato gratin and a mélange of baby vegetables. Followed by a salad of mesclun and sliced pears dressed with champagne-mustard vinaigrette and Roquefort on the side. Capped off by poached pears with fresh raspberries, chocolate sauce, and crème fraîche, accompanied by espresso.

For a family gathering: Open with Braised Fruit-Stuffed Loin of Pork with mashed potatoes and steamed broccoli. Next, a salad of sliced fresh tomatoes and sweet onions. End with a dessert of frozen yogurt or ice cream with chocolate sauce.

In my family Sunday dinners often brought a standing rib roast adorned with Whipped Horseradish Sauce (page 30); a fancy ham announced Easter; and whenever Aunt Ruby came over, Mom served a loin of pork dressed with apples and prunes.

Little is simpler than making a roast. Except for ham, which lends itself to the sweet spiciness of cloves, any roast can be studded with garlic, bedecked with freshly ground black pepper, and simply baked until done.

I use a meat thermometer to tell me when the meat is cooked to my taste. For an accurate reading, it's important that the thermometer not touch bone or fat. If, as I do, you use an instant-read meat thermometer, it's easy to take readings in several places in the roast. To obtain the most accurate reading with an ordinary meat thermometer, thrust it into the thickest part of the meat. The temperature of the roast rises between 5 degrees and 10 degrees after it is removed from the oven.

The following are the temperatures I use:

Beef

120°F for rare
125° to 130°F for medium rare

Lamb

125°F for rosy rare
130°F for medium rare
140°F for medium

Pork

155° to 160°F

Veal

150° to 155°F

I tie all my roasts, even if they're not stuffed. Tying keeps boneless roasts well shaped, and well-shaped roasts look more stylish and cook more evenly. When roasts with bones (like a standing rib roast) are tied, the meat stays firmly attached to the bones.

I use a slip knot. For those of you who knit—or at least remember how to—it's like casting on a big, fat needle. Slip knots are faster than tying individual knots and cutting the string each time, but it doesn't matter which method you use, as long as the string is tied tightly around the middle of the roast every couple of inches.

A stuffed filet of beef or loin of pork is elegant and dressy enough to impress both guests and clients, and it's a snap to prepare. I cut a deep slit about three-quarters of the way through lengthwise down the meat and let the sides fall open like a book. I lay the stuffing down the center, lift the sides up, and tie them back together with kitchen string. It's really that easy.

These days string is often made of polyester instead of cotton. Be sure to use cotton kitchen string, also called butcher's twine, because polyester melts in a hot oven.

Fast or Slow Roasting

The argument continues. Supporters of slow roasting say the meat shrinks less and comes out perfect every time. True, but I prefer to cook the roast at a high heat, which turns the outside a rich crusty brown while keeping the inside juicy and tender.

Five Recommendations for Roasting Meat

1. *Start with the meat at room temperature or the outside of the roast will be too well done before the center is cooked to the desired degree of doneness. If you do start with a cold roast, it will take longer to cook than my suggested times.*

2. *Using an instant-read meat thermometer, take readings in several places in the roast. For the most accurate reading using an ordinary meat thermometer, thrust it into the thickest part of the meat, not touching bone or fat.*

3. *Take the roast from the oven slightly more rare than the final result you want because the roast will continue to cook as it rests.*

4. *Allow roasts to rest before slicing. This magically keeps the juices where they belong, inside the roast.*

5. *If you are serving someone who will eat only well-done meat, I suggest you cook the roast to medium and then briefly dip the slices for that diner in simmering juices or gravy to rid them of their pink centers, which is what most people who want their meat well done dislike.*

What to Do When It's Gone Wrong

An overcooked roast is like an out-of-style dress—a cover-up is in order, or at least some new jewelry to jazz it up.

If you slip up, I suggest sautéing some mushrooms with a splash of wine, adding the pan juices, and embellishing the roast with the sauce spooned over the slices. Or quickly sauté some vegetables, heap them on top of the sliced roast, and act as if you had intended to serve it this way. At the very least, add demi-glace (page 273) to the pan juices to make a rich dark sauce with which to veil the sliced meat.

This year at my end-of-summer Labor Day party in Bridgehampton on the east end of Long Island, I overcooked my sister Joan's wonderful Arizona Orange and Garlic Roast Loin of Pork (page 56), which had been marinating for 2 days in herbs, spices, garlic, and red wine.

In the early afternoon I'd gone to the beach for a walk and a swim, and losing track of time, I left the roast in the oven too long. It looked perfect and smelled great, so I didn't bother to check the temperature but simply let it rest on the counter while I showered and changed for dinner. As soon as I sliced it, I groaned.

I quickly fashioned a shallot vinaigrette, lightly cloaked the meat with it, and decorated the platter with sprigs of fresh parsley.

My guests came back for seconds and thirds with comments like, "Hey, this is great!" "Can I have the recipe?" and "It's so tender and moist!" Now I wouldn't think of serving this succulent loin of pork on a buffet without The Great Cover-up Vinaigrette (page 57).

Roasts

BASIC ROAST FILET OF BEEF

MIAMI-STYLE FILET OF BEEF WITH TROPICAL SALSA

WATERCRESS PESTO–COATED FILET OF BEEF

BALSAMIC FILET OF BEEF

**SUNDAY BEST STANDING RIB ROAST WITH
WHIPPED HORSERADISH SAUCE**

OVEN-ROASTED DEVILED COUNTRY RIBS

MOSAIC VEGETABLE FLANK STEAK

ROAST LEG OF LAMB PROVENÇAL

MEDITERRANEAN STUFFED LEG OF LAMB

MINT-STUFFED LEG OF LAMB

SAGE, GARLIC, AND CHIPOTLE PEPPER ROAST LEG OF LAMB

CROWN ROAST OF LAMB WITH PECAN AND BULGUR STUFFING

MINTED MUSTARD RACK OF LAMB

PORK RIB ROAST WITH ARTICHOKE-LEEK SAUCE

GREEN PEPPERCORN PORK ROAST

ROAST LOIN OF PORK WITH ORANGE-CRANBERRY STUFFING

ROAST LOIN OF PORK WITH KILLER MUSTARD SAUCE

ARIZONA ORANGE AND GARLIC ROAST LOIN OF PORK

BRAISED FRUIT–STUFFED LOIN OF PORK

ROAST PORK WITH MUSTARD–CORIANDER SEED CRUST

MUSTARD PORK TENDERLOIN

MARTHA'S TRADITIONAL BAKED HAM

TAILGATE HAM

EASTER SUNDAY HAM

WOODLAND-STYLE ROAST LEG OF VEAL

TOMATO-BRAISED VEAL ROAST

SPINACH-STUFFED ROAST VEAL

ONION-DUSTED ROAST BEEF AND PORK

BASIC ROAST FILET OF BEEF

Makes 8 servings

Some folks refer to this cut as beef tenderloin; others, including me, call it filet of beef. The average untrimmed filet weighs about 7½ pounds; after my butcher trims the fat, it's 4 to 4½ pounds. At home I remove the side strip that runs along the tenderloin and use it to make a staff meal, a stew, ground meat, or Simple Broth from Filet (page 278).

Although it's perceived as expensive, as a caterer I find this tender piece of beef economical. Once it's trimmed, there's no waste; preparation time is uncomplicated; and roasting time is fast and foolproof. It always looks good on the plate, and I can dress it up with various sauces or serve it as is. The meat is lean, it tastes great cold as well as hot, and it's easy to transport to the site of the party. You guessed it—I love it!

Filet is the only roast I make that I cook for precisely the same amount of time each and every time—25 minutes. It's the exception that proves the rule that you need to use your judgment and that each piece of meat cooks differently.

Use this recipe as a guide. If you want to add herbs, rub them on the filet before roasting. If you want an exotic filet of beef, stud the meat with slivers of garlic, sun-dried tomatoes, or anchovies.

The secret to a perfect beef filet is to wrap it as it comes out of the oven, first in parchment paper and then in several sheets of newspaper. I learned this trick many years ago from an English butler I met at a tailgate party at a Princeton-Yale football game. He claimed that only the Wall Street Journal *would do, but I've found the* Minneapolis Star Tribune *works just as well!*

1 whole untrimmed filet of beef, 6 to 7 pounds

1 to 2 tablespoons fresh coarsely ground black pepper

1. Trim the meat of all visible fat, silver skin, and connective tendons. Remove the side strip (which runs along the whole tenderloin) and use it for broth or sauce.

2. Rub the filet with pepper. Fold the thin tail end under and tie with cotton kitchen string at 2- to 3-inch intervals. Let the filet stand at room temperature for at least 30 minutes before roasting.

3. Preheat the oven to 500°F.

4. Put the filet in a low-sided roasting pan and place in the oven. Reduce the heat to 450°F and roast for exactly 25 minutes.

5. Remove the filet from the oven and place it on parchment paper. Wrap it, tucking in the sides of the parchment paper as you roll. Roll the wrapped filet in several thicknesses of newspaper and let it rest for at least 20 minutes. Unwrap the filet, remove the strings, and slice according to desired thickness.

The filet of beef is now ready to serve as is, with or without sauce, hot, cold, at room temperature, almost any way.

After unwrapping and removing the strings, steady the filet with a two-pronged fork. Holding the carving knife perpendicular to the meat, cut across the grain into slices.

If you want a simple *au jus* sauce, heat the roasting pan on top of the stove over high heat and deglaze it by adding ¹/₂ cup Simple Broth from Filet (page 278) and scraping up any bits of meat that are stuck to the bottom of the pan. Strain the pan juices into a saucepan and bring to a boil. (You may, if you wish, add ¹/₃ cup red wine.) Reduce the liquid over high heat until it yields approximately ¹/₃ cup. Taste and correct the seasonings. Spoon over the filet slices.

MIAMI-STYLE FILET OF BEEF WITH TROPICAL SALSA

Makes 8 or more servings

The garlic, curry, cumin, oregano, onion, and jalapeño peppers combine with the sherry and lime juice in a seasoning paste that imparts a unique flavor to the filet. It reminds me of the many happy dinners I ate at a lovely little Cuban restaurant during one sunny winter vacation I spent in Miami.

This is one of my standard summer buffet offerings, as I can roast the meat early in the day to free up the oven for other uses. By dinnertime my kitchen is cool and comfortable.

Often I serve this at room temperature along with the Tropical Salsa and a cilantro-scented rice pilaf into which I've stirred some spicy black beans.

Seasoning Paste

2 cloves garlic, minced

1 tablespoon curry powder

1 teaspoon ground cumin

1 medium onion, minced

2 jalapeño peppers, seeded and minced

1/4 cup dry sherry

1 teaspoon dried oregano

Juice of 1 large lime

1 to 2 teaspoons olive oil

1 well-trimmed 3- to 3 1/2-pound filet of beef, tied (see Basic Roast Filet of Beef, page 22)

1 recipe Tropical Salsa (recipe follows)

1. To make the seasoning paste, combine the garlic, curry powder, cumin, onion, peppers, sherry, oregano, and lime juice in a small bowl. Add just enough olive oil to form a paste.

2. Rub the filet with the seasoning paste and set it aside at room temperature for 30 minutes to 1 hour.

3. Preheat the oven to 500°F.

4. Put the filet in a low-sided roasting pan and place it in the oven. Reduce the oven temperature to 450°F and roast for exactly 25 minutes. Remove the filet from the oven and place it on parchment paper. Wrap it, tucking in the sides of the parchment paper as you roll. Roll the wrapped filet in several thicknesses of newspaper and let it rest for at least 20 minutes. Unwrap the filet, remove the strings, and slice according to desired thickness.

The filet can be prepared hours ahead and refrigerated. Bring it to room temperature before carving. Serve with the Tropical Salsa.

With all meat, other than ground, I first pat it dry with paper towels so that when I season or marinate it, the meat better absorbs the flavors. The meat browns better as well.

TROPICAL SALSA

Makes 8 or more servings

Use any fresh, ripe tropical fruit such as kiwi, papaya, or melon. I like to begin with a mango because of its creamy consistency; then I add other fruits to complement the mango and tickle the taste buds.

Leftover salsa can be served with a grilled veal chop, chicken breast, or fish. Sometimes for lunch I whisk in some fresh lime juice and a bit of extra-virgin olive oil and use this salsa as a dressing over a salad of fresh greens, leftover strips of the filet, and black beans.

1 mango, peeled and chopped

¼ pineapple, peeled and chopped

3 nectarines (unpeeled), chopped

½ cup finely chopped red onion

¼ cup minced fresh cilantro

Juice of 1 lime

1 serrano or jalapeño pepper, seeded and minced

Pinch of salt

Freshly ground black pepper, to taste

Combine all the ingredients in a bowl and set aside for 2 hours at room temperature.

WATERCRESS PESTO–COATED FILET OF BEEF

Makes 8 to 10 servings

Watercress is a natural palate cleanser, and I almost always use a sprig of it to garnish the plate whenever I serve beef.

The peppery watercress pesto seasons the meat so that the flavors spread throughout the filet before it is roasted. As the meat cooks, the filet is automatically basted with the pesto. Serve year-round with oven-roasted potatoes and a green vegetable for a simple and elegant entree.

If you're lucky enough to have leftovers, the filet makes a fabulous cold sandwich, topped with a sprig of fresh watercress, of course.

1 well-trimmed 3- to 3¹/₂-pound filet of beef, tied

2 tablespoons Watercress Pesto (recipe follows) or store-bought pesto

1. Place the filet in a low-sided roasting pan. Spread the Watercress Pesto or other pesto over the top and set aside for 30 minutes to 1 hour to allow the meat to absorb the flavors. Or refrigerate for up to 6 hours and remove from the refrigerator 1 hour before roasting.

2. Preheat the oven to 500°F.

3. Place the filet in the oven and reduce the oven temperature to 450°F. Roast for exactly 25 minutes.

4. Remove the filet from the oven and place it on parchment paper. Wrap it, tucking in the sides of the parchment paper as you roll. Roll the wrapped filet in several thicknesses of newspaper and let it rest for at least 20 minutes. Unwrap the filet, remove the strings, and slice according to desired thickness.

Be sure to check your oven temperature every few months. An inexpensive oven thermometer will do. Probably more roasts have been ruined because the oven wasn't the temperature shown on the gauge than for any other reason.

WATERCRESS PESTO

Makes approximately 2 cups

Combine watercress, parsley, and basil with garlic and olive oil to create a pesto that is terrific on more than just filet of beef.

While not technically a "pesto," as it lacks nuts and cheese, I often use this peppery mixture in place of basil pesto. I always keep some on hand for tossing together last-minute meals. In addition to appearing in Watercress Pesto–Coated Filet of Beef and Grilled Pesto Burgers (page 210), this pesto shows up frequently in my soups and on pasta.

2 cups watercress leaves (approximately 1 to 2 large bunches)

3/4 cup fresh basil leaves

1 cup fresh parsley leaves

4 to 6 cloves garlic, coarsely chopped

1 cup olive oil

Freshly ground black pepper

Put the watercress, basil, and parsley in the bowl of a food processor. Add the garlic and process until finely chopped. With the processor running, add the olive oil in a steady stream through the feeding tube to form a paste. Scrape down the sides of the bowl, taste, and add pepper to taste. Refrigerate for up to 2 weeks or freeze for up to 6 months.

Tasty Tip

Store the pesto in a plastic container. Cover with a 1/4-inch layer of olive oil to prevent air from turning the pesto dark.

BALSAMIC FILET OF BEEF

Makes 8 servings

This dish was inspired by a fellow foodie, Lynne Rossetto Kasper, a soulmate I respect and admire for her contribution to the food profession. At a tasting and lecture she gave in the early 1980s, which educated and elevated my palate, Lynne taught me about balsamic vinegar. She introduced me to the unique and exotic flavors of Emilia-Romagna.

Buy the best balsamic vinegar you can afford. Compare it to the cheaper balsamic vinegar on your shelf. See what I mean? And what a difference it makes in the final quality of this dish! If you must use commercial balsamic vinegar, blend in a little brown sugar to cut its acidity. If using a good-quality, aged balsamic, drizzle a bit over the filet just before serving and invite me for dinner.

Marinade

¼ cup olive oil

¼ cup balsamic vinegar

**1 tablespoon chopped fresh oregano leaves or
1 teaspoon dried**

6 to 8 sprigs fresh rosemary or 1 tablespoon dried

Freshly ground black pepper

1 well-trimmed 3- to 3½-pound filet of beef, tied

Freshly ground black pepper

1. To prepare the marinade, whisk the oil, vinegar, oregano, rosemary, and pepper together in a small bowl.

2. Rub the filet with black pepper. Place in a large nonreactive pan and pour the marinade over the filet. Marinate for 1 hour at room temperature or up to 24 hours in the refrigerator. Bring the filet to room temperature before roasting.

3. Preheat the oven to 500°F.

4. Remove the filet from the marinade and reserve the marinade. Pat the meat dry with paper towels and place in low-sided roasting pan. Place the filet in the oven and reduce the temperature to 450°F. Roast for exactly 25 minutes.

5. Remove the filet from the oven and place it on parchment paper. Wrap it, tucking in the sides of the parchment paper as you roll. Roll the wrapped filet in several thicknesses of newspaper and let it rest for at least 20 minutes. Unwrap the filet, remove the strings, and slice according to desired thickness.

6. If you have an excellent-quality balsamic vinegar, simply drizzle a bit of it over the filet (and discard the marinade). Otherwise, bring the marinade to a boil and simmer for 5 minutes. Spoon the marinade over the filet. Arrange slices of filet on a platter, garnish with the rosemary sprigs, and serve.

SUNDAY BEST STANDING RIB ROAST WITH WHIPPED HORSERADISH SAUCE

Makes 4 servings

When I was growing up on a Minnesota dairy farm, we often had standing rib roast at Christmas or for an important Sunday dinner. (We always entertained on Sunday.) The aroma wafted its way to the door as a hearty welcome. We could hardly wait to sit down to dinner!

If you have the luxury of a friendly butcher, ask him to cut the meat from the bones of the rib roast, place it back on the bones, and tie it to keep the meat in place while it cooks. This makes carving the roast as easy as pie.

If you're having more than four for dinner, add one additional rib for every two additional people and increase the seasonings proportionately. Ask for the loin end of the rib roast; it's less fatty.

For a memorable indulgence, serve the roast with Whipped Horseradish Sauce.

2 tablespoons dried tarragon

1 tablespoon freshly ground black pepper

1 1/2 teaspoons salt

1 well-trimmed 4 1/2-pound 2-rib beef roast with bones, aged (page 12), and tied

2 large onions, sliced

1 recipe Whipped Horseradish Sauce (recipe follows)

1. Grind the tarragon, pepper, and salt together and rub this mixture into the sides and top of the roast. Let the roast stand for 1 hour.

2. Preheat the oven to 450°F.

3. Place the onions in a roasting pan. Set a rack over the onions and place the meat on it. Roast for 10 minutes. Reduce the oven temperature to 325°F and roast for another 50 minutes or until a meat thermometer reads 125° to 130°F for medium rare or the roast is done to your taste.

4. Remove the roast from the oven and let it rest for 20 minutes before carving. To carve, remove the string and (if the butcher hasn't done it already) cut along the rib bones to sever the meat from the bones. Carve the meat across the grain into thick slices.

After untying the meat from the bones, slice the meat across the grain into thick slices.

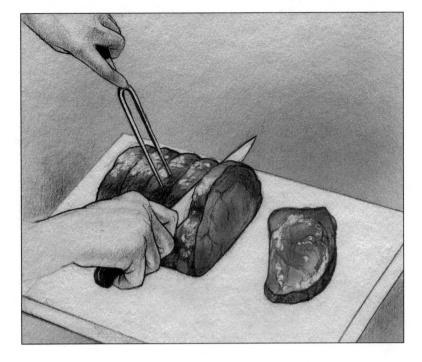

Tasty Tip

I often add vegetables like onions, carrots, and celery to the roasting pan (whether or not I plan to serve them) because they infuse the meat with their aromas and flavor the pan juices, making a big difference should I decide to use these juices to make a simple sauce.

While I might eat the vegetables myself or serve them to family members, for guests and clients I discard them. Although tasty, they're brown, limp, and overcooked.

WHIPPED HORSERADISH SAUCE

Makes about 1½ cups

Here is a real crowd pleaser that takes no time to prepare. If you don't want to use heavy cream, use sour cream instead. The sauce will have a different taste and consistency, but it's nonetheless delicious.

P.S. Don't poke your nose in or over the bowl of the food processor when it stops—or your sinuses will be as clear as a bell and the top of your head will spin while you cry!

Pinch of salt

Pinch of white pepper

½ cup heavy cream

½ cup peeled and grated fresh horseradish

Splash of vinegar, preferably apple cider

Pinch of sugar

1 tablespoon Dijon mustard

Add the salt and pepper to the cream and whip until stiff. Stir in the horseradish, vinegar, sugar, and mustard. Taste and correct the seasonings.

If fresh horseradish is not available, substitute ½ cup well-drained prepared horseradish for the fresh horseradish, vinegar, salt, and sugar.

OVEN-ROASTED DEVILED COUNTRY RIBS

Makes 8 servings

My hat's off to the butchers of America. They've cleverly found a way to cut lean, meaty, boneless beef ribs to suit our modern way of eating. In the Midwest you will find packages called country beef ribs in the meat section of every supermarket. This new cut is just making its way to the East Coast.

This easy "shake and bake" recipe is an updated version of an old recipe that I taught 20 years ago in my first summer session of Cooking With Class. There's no need to throw out your old short rib recipes just because you no longer use the fatty cut. Simply substitute country beef ribs.

³/₄ cup all-purpose flour

1 tablespoon paprika, preferably hot Hungarian

¹/₂ teaspoon salt

1 teaspoon freshly ground black pepper

3 cloves garlic, minced

2 to 2¹/₂ pounds lean, boneless country beef ribs

1 cup Grey Poupon mustard

1 tablespoon brown sugar

1 cup dry bread crumbs

¹/₃ cup chopped fresh parsley

1. Preheat the oven to 325°F.

2. Put the flour, paprika, salt, black pepper, and garlic in a zipper-lock bag and shake to blend. Drop the ribs into this seasoned flour and shake to coat.

3. Place the ribs on a rack in a roasting pan and bake for 1¹/₂ hours. Remove and cut into individual portions. Cool to room temperature.

   The boneless ribs can be prepared up to this point up to 2 days ahead and refrigerated. Return to room temperature before continuing.

4. Preheat the oven to 425°F.

5. Mix the mustard with the brown sugar. Using a clean brush, paint the ribs generously with the mustard mixture. Mix the bread crumbs with the parsley and roll the mustard-painted ribs in the crumb mixture.

6. Place the ribs on a baking pan lined with aluminum foil. Bake until brown and crispy, approximately 45 minutes.

Tasty Tip

I love the subtle nuances of Hungarian paprikas. If you can find them, try both the sweet and the hot. (I'm partial to the hot one in this recipe.) Otherwise, use your regular paprika. The dish will still taste great.

MOSAIC VEGETABLE FLANK STEAK

Makes 10 servings

This butterflied flank steak is stuffed with fresh spinach, cooked carrots, red onions, parsley, and oil-cured olives. It's then rolled up, seared, and oven-braised in red wine and broth until tender. As appealing to the eye as it is to the mouth.

Marinade

1 cup full-bodied red wine

3 tablespoons olive oil

2 cloves garlic, minced

1 tablespoon fresh thyme leaves or 1 teaspoon dried

2 well-trimmed 2-pound flank steaks, butterflied

8 to 9 whole carrots, peeled

1 bunch spinach (about ½ pound), trimmed, washed, and spin dried

1 large red onion, sliced into thin rings

½ cup oil-cured black olives, pitted and chopped

1 small bunch fresh parsley, chopped

½ to 1 teaspoon salt

1 teaspoon freshly ground black pepper

1 tablespoon fresh thyme leaves or 1 teaspoon dried

1 tablespoon balsamic vinegar

1 tablespoon oil

1 cup full-bodied red wine

2 to 3 cups beef broth, preferably Homemade Beef Stock (page 276) or Doctored Beef Broth (page 279)

1. To prepare the marinade, combine the wine, oil, garlic, and thyme in a large nonreactive pan. Add the flank steaks and marinate, covered, in the refrigerator for at least 6 hours or overnight.

2. Steam or cook the carrots in water until almost tender. Cut into thin lengthwise strips and set aside.

3. Remove the steaks from marinade, pat them dry, and discard the marinade. Spread the spinach leaves across the "open" steaks. Lay the carrots on top of the spinach going across the grain of the meat in two parallel rows. Scatter onions, olives, and parsley over the top. Season with salt, pepper, and thyme. Sprinkle with the balsamic vinegar.

4. Roll up the flank steaks with the grain, tucking the vegetables in as you go. Tie with cotton kitchen string.

5. Preheat the oven to 350°F.

6. In a large flameproof casserole with a tight-fitting lid, heat the oil to sizzling over high heat. Sear the stuffed flank steaks, turning a quarter of the way each time, for 3 to 4 minutes on each side. Add the wine and as much of the beef broth as needed to come one-fourth to one-third of the way up the sides of the steaks. Cover tightly and place the casserole in the oven. Bake for 45 minutes to 1 hour, until tender.

7. Remove the casserole from the oven. Transfer the flank steaks to a serving platter and let them rest for 15 to 20 minutes. Skim any fat from the pan juices and boil them until they are reduced to $^1/_2$ to $^3/_4$ cup. Taste and correct the seasonings. Slice the steak and serve with the pan juices.

Tasty Tip

This flank steak is just as good cold. Refrigerate it in its cooking liquid for up to 2 days. When ready to serve, slice and serve it with a spicy sour-cream sauce made of 1 cup of low-fat or nonfat sour cream, $^1/_3$ cup freshly grated or prepared horseradish, 2 tablespoons prepared mustard, and a pinch of freshly ground black pepper.

ROAST LEG OF LAMB PROVENÇAL

Makes 8 to 10 servings

This is one of my favorite recipes for leg of lamb. My students give me a hard time whenever I say "my favorite." They remind me that I've said the same thing about other roasts! Although it's generally true that my favorite food is the one that I'm either eating or preparing, this lamb has a special place on my palate not only because of its complex flavors but because it's easy to make. The herbs, vegetables, and oven do all the work.

I love the assortment of dried herbs called herbes de Provence, *which reflects the cooking of the south of France. The mixture can be found in the spice section of most supermarkets. However, a classic leg of lamb is seasoned with rosemary, so feel free to substitute it in this recipe.*

As the lamb cooks, the seasoned juices flavor the vegetables, creating a one-dish meal that works as a family meal as well as a dinner-party dish. Add a salad and a roasted potato for each person, and dinner is complete.

1 medium eggplant, peeled and thinly sliced

Coarse salt

Seasoning Paste

4 large cloves garlic, minced

1 small bunch fresh parsley, chopped

1 tablespoon freshly ground black pepper

1 heaping teaspoon *herbes de Provence*

1 to 2 tablespoons olive oil

1 well-trimmed 5- to 6-pound leg of lamb

Vegetable oil to film roasting pan

6 tomatoes, peeled and chopped

1 green bell pepper, chopped

2 medium onions, thinly sliced

2 medium zucchini, thinly sliced

1. Sprinkle the eggplant with salt and let it stand for 30 minutes. Rinse off the salt under running water. Drain well and pat dry with paper towels.

2. To make the seasoning paste, coarsely chop together the garlic, parsley, black pepper, and *herbes de Provence*. Add enough olive oil to make a paste. Score the lamb and spread it with the paste. Set the lamb aside for 30 minutes to 1 hour.

3. Preheat the oven to 425°F.

4. Film a large roasting pan with oil and lay the eggplant in it. Scatter the tomatoes, green pepper, onions, and zucchini over the eggplant. Set the lamb on top of the vegetables.

5. Roast for 20 minutes. Reduce the oven temperature to 350°F and continue to roast until a meat thermometer registers 125° to 130°F for medium rare, about 45 minutes, or until the lamb is done to your preference. Remove the lamb from the oven and let it rest for 15 minutes before carving. Spread the vegetables on a serving platter and place the sliced lamb on top.

In the unlikely event that *herbes de Provence* is unavailable where you live, you can simulate the mixture with equal portions of dried basil, fennel seed, lavender, marjoram, rosemary, sage, summer savory, and thyme.

MEDITERRANEAN STUFFED LEG OF LAMB

Makes 10 to 12 servings

Even though this recipe seems intimidating, it's worth the effort. I once served this dish at a wedding reception of 125 people. We made the stuffing three days ahead, stuffed the boned-out lamb the day before, and seared it early on the morning of the wedding. At the wedding we finished roasting the meat. I accompanied the meat with Gratin Dauphinois, *a French version of scalloped potatoes. The lamb was such a hit that I now often make it for the dinner parties I cater.*

If I can't convince you to put the effort into stuffing this leg of lamb, at least spread the seasoning paste on a butterflied leg of lamb, let it marinate for 30 minutes to an hour at room temperature, and grill or broil it for 12 minutes a side for rare and 15 minutes a side for medium rare. Let it stand 10 to 15 minutes before carving.

Seasoning Paste

**2 tablespoons minced fresh rosemary or
  2 teaspoons dried**

3 to 4 cloves garlic, minced

1 to 2 teaspoons freshly ground black pepper

1 teaspoon olive oil

**1 well-trimmed 5- to 6-pound leg of lamb, boned
  and untied**

Stuffing

1 large onion, finely chopped

1 small bunch fresh parsley, minced

2 small roasted peppers, chopped

2 large tomatoes, peeled, seeded, and chopped

2 cloves garlic, minced

**1 1/2 teaspoons minced fresh rosemary or
  1/2 teaspoon dried**

1/2 cup pitted and chopped oil-cured black olives

1 tablespoon capers, chopped

¹/₄ teaspoon salt

¹/₂ teaspoon freshly ground black pepper

1 to 2 tablespoons olive oil

1 carrot, coarsely chopped

1 onion, coarsely chopped

1 stalk celery, coarsely chopped

¹/₂ cup full-bodied red wine

1¹/₂ cups beef broth, preferably Doctored Beef Broth (page 279)

1. Make the seasoning paste by mixing together the rosemary, garlic, black pepper, and olive oil. Rub the lamb inside and out with the seasoning paste. Place the lamb, smooth side down, in a large pan and set aside for 30 minutes to 1 hour.

2. Prepare the stuffing by mixing together the onion, parsley, roasted peppers, tomatoes, garlic, rosemary, black olives, capers, salt, and black pepper. Add enough olive oil to bind.

3. Spread the stuffing on the lamb to within an inch of the edges. Roll the lamb up and tie securely with cotton kitchen string. Tuck any stuffing that leaks out back in as you tie.

   The lamb can be prepared up to a day ahead, covered, and refrigerated. Remove from the refrigerator 1¹/₂ hours before roasting.

4. Preheat the oven to 450°F.

5. Place the lamb on a rack in the roasting pan. Scatter the carrot, onion, and celery around the bottom of the pan. Roast for 15 to 20 minutes. Reduce the oven temperature to 350°F and continue to roast about 45 minutes longer, until a meat thermometer registers 125° to 130°F for medium rare, or the lamb is done to your preference.

6. Remove the lamb from the oven and turn the oven off. Place the lamb on a serving platter and let it rest for 15 minutes before carving.

7. While the lamb is resting, heat the roasting pan on top of the stove and deglaze it by adding the wine and scraping up any bits of meat stuck to the bottom. Skim any fat from the pan juices. Pour these juices and vegetables into a saucepan and add the broth. Cook over high heat until the sauce is reduced to approximately 1 cup. Strain out the vegetables and serve the sauce alongside or over the meat.

MINT-STUFFED LEG OF LAMB

Makes 8 to 10 servings

Each spring, at the first sign of fresh mint, I ask a few of my closest friends over for a sumptuous dinner at which I serve this lamb with fresh mint sauce and orzo.

Have your butcher remove all but the shank bone from the leg of lamb, saving the small scraps of lamb to be ground. With only the shank bone left intact, this leg of lamb is easy to carve, and the presentation is indeed grand.

The stuffing is made from sautéed garlic, parsley, fresh mint, and Madeira wine added to the ground lamb your butcher saved for you.

1 well-trimmed 5- to 6-pound leg of lamb, partially boned

1 clove garlic, cut in slivers

Salt

Freshly ground black pepper

Stuffing

1 teaspoon olive oil

2 cloves garlic, minced

1/2 cup chopped fresh parsley

1 cup chopped fresh mint

1/4 cup Madeira wine

1/2 to 3/4 cup ground lamb (from boning scraps)

1 carrot, coarsely chopped

1 onion, coarsely chopped

1 stalk celery, chopped

Fresh Mint Sauce (recipe follows)

1. With the tip of a sharp knife, make 1- to 1½-inch-deep holes on all sides of the lamb and insert the slivers of garlic. Rub the outside of the lamb with salt and pepper. Set aside.

2. To prepare the stuffing, heat the oil in a nonstick skillet over medium heat. Cook the chopped garlic, parsley, and mint until the parsley

wilts, 2 to 3 minutes. Add the wine, turn the heat to high, and allow the wine to reduce for a minute or two. Cool to room temperature before stirring in the ground lamb.

3. Stuff the leg of lamb with the ground lamb mixture. Close the opening with metal skewers or sew up using cotton kitchen thread.

   The lamb can be prepared to this point up to 1 day ahead and refrigerated. Bring the lamb to room temperature before roasting.

4. Preheat the oven to 450°F.

5. Put the carrot, onion, and celery in the bottom of a large roasting pan. (See Tasty Tip on page 31.) Put a rack in the pan and place the lamb on it. Roast for 15 minutes. Reduce the oven temperature to 350°F and continue to roast for about 50 minutes, until a meat thermometer registers 125° to 130°F or the meat is done to your preference. Allow the meat to rest for 15 minutes before carving. Serve with Fresh Mint Sauce.

Grip the shank bone with a napkin in one hand and lift so the leg is on a slight angle. Holding the carving knife almost parallel to the meat, cut the meat into thin slices.

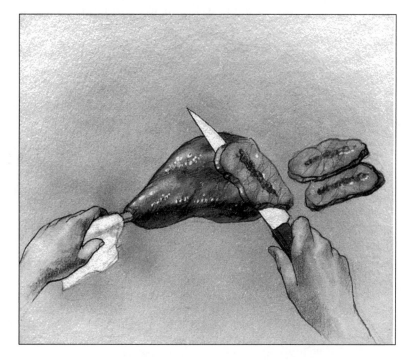

FRESH MINT SAUCE

Makes about 1 cup

This refreshing sauce is good with grilled or pan-seared lamb chops as well as the Mint-Stuffed Leg of Lamb. It also doubles as a quick marinade for lamb and chicken.

3/4 cup chopped fresh mint leaves

2 1/2 tablespoons sugar

2/3 cup white wine vinegar

1/3 cup water

1/2 teaspoon salt

Ground white pepper

Bring all ingredients to a boil in a nonreactive saucepan. Reduce the heat and simmer for 15 to 20 minutes. Taste and correct the seasonings.

The sauce can be prepared up to 3 days ahead and refrigerated. Reheat just before serving.

SAGE, GARLIC, AND CHIPOTLE PEPPER ROAST LEG OF LAMB

Begin one to three days in advance

Makes 8 to 10 servings

The idea of marinating lamb in milk comes from Wayne Nish, executive chef and owner of March, a restaurant in New York City.

However, the notion of marinating meat in milk was not new to me. My great-grandmother used buttermilk to tenderize venison; Mom soaks beef liver in milk overnight to tenderize and draw out "that strong flavor"; and I soak veal in milk overnight to keep it a pale pink. Aside from tenderizing, milk is a good medium to infuse meat with extra flavor.

In this recipe the combination of garlic, dried sage, and chipotle pepper adds a subtle smoked taste to the lamb that eliminates the "gamy flavor" many folks dislike.

1 well-trimmed 5- to 6-pound leg of lamb

Milk for soaking lamb, about 1 quart

1 fresh poblano or other hot pepper, cut in half

1 chipotle pepper (see Tasty Tip below)

5 cloves garlic, sliced

1 tablespoon dried sage

1 onion, sliced

One to three days ahead

1. Put the leg of lamb, poblano pepper, chipotle pepper, garlic, and sage in large nonreactive dish. Add enough milk to come halfway up the leg of lamb. Cover with plastic wrap and marinate in the refrigerator for 1 to 3 days, turning the lamb daily.

Before roasting

2. Preheat the oven to 450°F.

3. Remove the lamb from the marinade and pat it dry with paper towels. Strain the garlic and peppers from the milk and set aside. Discard the milk.

4. Line the bottom of a roasting pan with the onion and set the lamb on top. Roast until the lamb is brown, about 25 minutes. Reduce the oven temperature to 350°F. Add the reserved peppers to the roasting pan and scatter garlic on and around the lamb. Continue to roast about 30 to 40 minutes longer, until a meat thermometer registers 125° to 130°F, or the lamb is done to your preference. Remove the lamb from the oven and let it rest at least 15 minutes before carving. Serve with the pan vegetables alongside.

Tasty Tip

Chipotle peppers are actually smoked jalapeño peppers. Because of their increasing popularity, you may be able to find them at your market. Otherwise, they are readily available at Hispanic markets, in specialty food stores, and by mail (see Penzey's Ltd., page 283).

CROWN ROAST OF LAMB WITH PECAN AND BULGUR STUFFING

Makes 5 to 6 servings

Make this roast for lamb connoisseurs. It's an expensive cut but worth it. I usually count two ribs per person, but for real lamb lovers I allow three. If you have doubts about tying the rack together, ask your butcher to trim and tie it for you. Remember, meat cooks faster with the bones in because they conduct the heat. I cover the ends of the chops with foil once they're brown, and then I adorn them with white-paper frills for the final presentation.

The stuffing is made of bulgur, wheat that's been steamed, dried, and crushed. Popular throughout the Middle East, bulgur is frequently used in pilafs and stuffings. To it I've added pecans, vegetables, and herbs for a rich, flavorful accompaniment to the lamb. Uncork one of your finest red wines and bon appétit!

2 well-trimmed racks of lamb, tied together at both ends to create a "crown"

Freshly ground black pepper

Stuffing

1½ tablespoons olive oil

1 medium onion, finely chopped

½ cup finely chopped celery

½ pound finely chopped mushrooms

1 cup bulgur

1¾ cups beef broth, preferably Homemade Beef Stock (page 276) or Doctored Beef Broth (page 279)

1 teaspoon dried sage

1 teaspoon dried thyme

½ teaspoon salt

¼ teaspoon freshly ground black pepper

½ cup finely chopped pecans

1. To make the stuffing, heat the oil in a casserole. Sauté the onion, celery, and mushrooms over medium-high heat until the onion is golden brown. Add the bulgur and sauté for 2 to 3 minutes, stirring frequently. Add the broth, sage, thyme, salt, and pepper. Cover and simmer until the liquid is absorbed and the bulgur is tender, about 30 minutes. Stir in the pecans. The stuffing can be prepared up to 1 day ahead, covered, and refrigerated. Reheat it before filling the crown roast.

2. Score the outside of the "lamb crown" and rub with pepper. Set aside for 1 hour.

3. Preheat the oven to 475°F.

4. Place the lamb in a roasting pan and roast for 10 to 15 minutes to brown.

5. Remove the lamb from the oven and fill the "crown" with about 2 cups of stuffing. Cover the ends of the chops with aluminum foil to keep them from burning. Return the filled "crown" to the oven and continue to roast for about 20 minutes more, until a meat thermometer registers 125° to 130°, or until the lamb is done to your preference. Allow to rest for 10 minutes before carving.

6. Slip white paper frills on the ends of the chops. Cut into one-rib portions, allowing 2 to 3 per person. Serve atop several spoonfuls of stuffing.

The remaining stuffing can be baked separately in a baking/serving dish alongside the lamb for guests who want seconds. Or you can cover the stuffing, refrigerate, and keep it for up to 3 days to serve alongside another lamb dish, grilled steak, or pork chops.

Any ingredients you combine with raw meat should be at room temperature. Likewise, when stuffing a roast, the stuffing should be at room temperature. This prevents the accidental heating of the meat, which creates the ideal conditions for bacterial growth—and food poisoning.

MINTED MUSTARD RACK OF LAMB

Makes 2 to 3 servings

In my family, birthdays are celebrated at home and the birthday person writes the menu for dinner. On mine, I always order a mustard rack of lamb done medium rare, the ultimate dining experience.

In this recipe the mint leaves impart a fresh, distinctive flavor to the mustard, garlic, soy sauce, and pepper paste. As an easy-to-make indulgence for an intimate dinner party, serve with green beans and a couscous pilaf studded with pine nuts and raisins. Afterward, bring in the birthday cake, the candles ablaze, and celebrate!

Seasoning Paste

¼ cup Dijon mustard

2 teaspoons soy sauce

3 cloves garlic, finely minced

½ cup chopped fresh mint leaves, plus whole mint leaves for garnish

1½ tablespoons freshly ground black pepper

1 to 2 teaspoons brandy, approximately

1 well-trimmed rack of lamb (7 or 8 chops)

1. In a small bowl, mix together the mustard, soy sauce, garlic, mint leaves, pepper, and enough brandy to form a paste.

2. Coat the rack of lamb with the paste and set it aside at room temperature for 1 hour or refrigerate for up to 24 hours. Bring to room temperature before roasting.

3. Preheat the oven to 475°F.

4. Place the lamb on a metal rack set in a roasting pan. Roast for 20 minutes. Reduce the oven temperature to 400°F and continue to roast for about 15 minutes, until a meat thermometer registers 125° to 130°F, or the lamb is done to your preference. Allow the lamb to rest at room temperature for 10 minutes before carving. Garnish with fresh mint.

Carve the meat between the rib bones into individual portions.

PORK RIB ROAST WITH ARTICHOKE-LEEK SAUCE

Begin one day in advance

Makes 8 servings

In the late '70s I created this recipe with heavy cream in the sauce for a private dinner party of five couples at my cooking school. As usual, I deglazed the pan with wine. One man joked that since his wife had started taking cooking classes with me, she used wine instead of soap to wash the dishes!

You can substitute chicken or beef broth for the wine to deglaze the pan. Ginger, sage, dry mustard, and garlic impart an intriguing flavor to this pork as it marinates. The timeless combination of pork, artichokes, and leeks is updated by sautéing the leeks and lemon-coated artichoke hearts and adding them to the natural juices rather than to a rich cream sauce.

Accompany this dish with old-fashioned mashed potatoes.

Dry Rub

1 tablespoon salt

2 teaspoons freshly ground black pepper

1 teaspoon ground ginger

2 teaspoons dried sage

1 teaspoon dry mustard

2 cloves garlic, minced

1 well-trimmed 4½- to 5-pound pork rib roast

Vegetable oil to film pan

1 carrot, chopped

1 stalk celery, chopped

1 medium onion, chopped

2 or 3 leeks, white part only, cut in 2-inch lengths and julienned

1 tablespoon butter

Pinch of salt

½ teaspoon freshly ground black pepper

Pinch of crushed red pepper flakes

Two 14-ounce cans artichoke hearts, drained and cut in quarters

Juice of 1 lemon

½ cup white wine

One day ahead

1. To prepare the dry rub, mix together the salt, pepper, ginger, sage, mustard, and garlic. Rub this mixture into the pork. Place the pork in a nonreactive bowl, cover, and refrigerate overnight. Allow the pork to return to room temperature before roasting.

2. Preheat the oven to 350°F.

3. Scrape off the dry rub from the meat and discard. Film a large flameproof casserole with oil and sear the meat over high heat for 3 to 4 minutes on each side. Remove from the heat and add the carrot, celery, and onion. Cover and place in the oven for about 1 hour. Uncover and continue to roast for about 20 to 30 minutes, until a meat thermometer reads 155° to 160°F. Remove the pork from the oven and let it rest for 20 minutes before carving.

4. Meanwhile, cook the leeks in butter in a skillet, stirring, over medium-low heat until they are translucent, 6 to 8 minutes. Add the salt, pepper, and red pepper flakes.

5. Toss the artichoke hearts in a bowl with the lemon juice. Allow them to soak for 5 minutes, then drain well. Add the artichoke hearts to the leeks and heat until the artichokes are just warmed through.

6. Add the wine to the casserole and bring to a boil. Cook over high heat, stirring occasionally to scrape up the bits of meat that are stuck to the bottom of the pan. Strain out the solids and discard them. Skim off any fat from the pan juices and return the clear juices to the casserole. Add the artichokes and leeks. Taste and correct the seasonings. Slice the pork and serve with the sauce alongside.

GREEN PEPPERCORN PORK ROAST

Makes 10 to 12 servings

This loin of pork is seasoned with garlic, coriander, cinnamon, ginger, nutmeg, cardamom, and green peppercorns combined with Madeira wine and a touch of olive oil, then roasted on a bed of diced carrots, onions, and celery. You get a sweet and spicy pork roast that needs only crispy oven-browned potatoes for a festive company dinner.

Serve the roast hot, or for a summer buffet, serve it at room temperature with potato salad.

Seasoning Paste

2 to 3 teaspoons canned green peppercorns, rinsed and drained

1 large clove garlic, minced

¹/₂ teaspoon ground coriander

¹/₂ teaspoon ground cardamom

¹/₂ teaspoon ground cinnamon

Pinch of ginger

Pinch of nutmeg

¹/₄ teaspoon salt

¹/₂ teaspoon freshly ground black pepper

1 tablespoon Madeira wine

1 to 3 tablespoons olive oil

1 well-trimmed 3- to 4-pound boneless loin of pork

1 carrot, diced

1 medium onion, diced

1 stalk celery, diced

1 cup beef broth, preferably Homemade Beef Stock (page 276) or Doctored Beef Broth (page 279)

1. Preheat the oven to 375°F.

2. To prepare the seasoning paste, put the green peppercorns, garlic, coriander, cardamom, cinnamon, ginger, nutmeg, salt, pepper and wine into the bowl of a food processor. Puree until smooth. Add only enough olive oil to make a paste.

3. Using a knife with a sharp point, make 1- to 1½-inch-deep holes in the meat. Spread the spice mixture over the pork loin, packing it into the holes, and set it aside for 30 minutes to 1 hour.

4. Place the carrot, onion, and celery in the bottom of a roasting pan. (See Tasty Tip on page 31.) Set a rack over the vegetables and place the pork on it. Add the broth to the bottom of the pan. Roast for about 1½ hours, or until a meat thermometer registers 155°F. Allow the roast to rest for 15 minutes.

5. Strain the vegetables from the pan juices and discard. Skim the fat from the pan juices and bring them to a boil over high heat. Cook until reduced to a thick glaze, about 10 minutes. Slice the pork and nap with the glaze.

ROAST LOIN OF PORK WITH ORANGE-CRANBERRY STUFFING

Makes 10 to 12 servings

This magnificent roast is festive at holiday time. I like to serve it for Christmas dinner for more than one reason: to be precise, for six reasons.

1. Cranberries and oranges are at their prime in December.

2. I can prepare it beforehand. Three days before the dinner I marinate the roast; one day before, I stuff it and tie it together.

3. On Christmas day I only need to sear it and put it in the oven.

4. The aroma greets the guests at the door and announces "Merry Christmas."

5. I arrange the roast on a bed of curly chicory, and as it's sliced, the colors of Christmas are revealed.

6. It makes 10 to 12 servings, and any leftover tastes great on Christmas night after the kids are in bed.

Marinade

1/2 cup orange juice

2 tablespoons vegetable oil

1 large clove garlic, minced

1 tablespoon grated fresh ginger

Freshly ground black pepper

1 well-trimmed 3- to 4-pound boneless loin of pork, untied

Stuffing

1/2 cup fresh cranberries

Zest of 1/2 orange, blanched, dried, and cut in slivers (see Tasty Tip, page 111)

1 small tart apple, peeled and chopped

1/4 cup brown sugar (or more, to taste)

1 tablespoon chopped crystallized ginger or pinch of ground ginger

Freshly ground black pepper

½ cup orange juice

Splash Triple Sec, Grand Marnier, or other orange liqueur

1. Prepare the marinade by combining the orange juice, oil, garlic, ginger, and pepper. Slice the pork down the center about three-fourths of the way through, so that it falls open like a book. Place the pork in a shallow, nonreactive pan and pour the marinade over it. Set aside for 1 hour at room temperature or cover and refrigerate for up to 3 days. Return to room temperature before roasting.

2. Prepare the stuffing by combining the cranberries, orange zest, apple, sugar, ginger, and pepper in a small bowl.

3. Preheat the oven to 375°F.

4. Remove the pork from the marinade, reserving the marinade, and pat the meat dry with paper towels. Stuff with the cranberry mixture and tie securely with cotton kitchen string. Pour the marinade into a small saucepan and bring to a boil over high heat. Once it boils, remove from the heat and set aside.

5. Place the pork on a rack in a roasting pan and roast until it's brown, 15 to 20 minutes. Reduce the oven temperature to 350°F and continue to roast about 1½ hours more, until an instant-read thermometer registers 155° to 160°F. Baste occasionally during the last hour of roasting with the reserved marinade. Remove the roast from the oven and transfer to a platter. Allow to rest 15 minutes before slicing.

6. Skim the fat from the pan juices. Add the orange juice and bring to a boil. Cook, stirring occasionally to scrape up the bits of meat that are stuck to the bottom of the pan. Cook over high heat to reduce the liquid until it lightly coats the back of a metal spoon, about 5 minutes. Add a splash of orange liqueur. Taste and correct the seasonings.

When I can get them, I like to use the bones to create a rack for boneless roast. The bones add flavor to the pan juices and conduct the heat so well that the roast cooks a little faster.

ROAST LOIN OF PORK WITH KILLER MUSTARD SAUCE

Makes 12 or more servings as part of a main-course buffet,
24 servings as part of a cocktail buffet

Living in a large metropolitan area and having a summer home on Long Island, I've gathered many friends. I created this recipe as part of a buffet for a large summer cocktail party.

Just before the party started, I decided I needed a sauce for the meat. Using what I had on hand, I whisked together several mustards and served them in a carved-out purple cabbage. The guests slathered it on the thin slices of pork. My family named it Killer Mustard Sauce and the name's stuck.

I prefer to use dried rubbed sage for the seasoning paste, but fresh is fine. If you grow your own sage, line the serving platter with branches of it and arrange the sliced pork attractively on the beautiful green bed. Serve the meat at room temperature.

Seasoning Paste

1 tablespoon salt

2 teaspoons freshly ground black pepper

1 teaspoon ground ginger

2 teaspoons rubbed sage

2 teaspoons dry mustard

3 cloves garlic, minced

2 tablespoons olive oil, approximately

1 well-trimmed 3- to 4-pound boneless loin of pork, tied

Killer Mustard Sauce

½ cup Dijon mustard

½ cup grainy mustard

3 to 4 tablespoons dry mustard

1 tablespoon whole yellow mustard seed, crushed

2 to 3 tablespoons olive oil

1. Prepare the seasoning paste by mixing together the salt, pepper, ginger, sage, dry mustard, garlic, and enough olive oil to bind the seasonings together.

2. Rub this paste into the meat, cover, and set aside for 1 hour or refrigerate for 6 to 24 hours. Return the meat to room temperature before roasting.

3. Preheat the oven to 375°F.

4. Set the pork, fat side up, on a rack in a large roasting pan. Reserve any excess seasoning paste that falls from the meat. Roast until the pork is brown, 15 to 20 minutes. Reduce the oven temperature to 350°F and continue to roast approximately 1½ hours, until a meat thermometer registers 155° to 160°F. Baste during the last hour with the pan juices and the reserved seasoning paste. Remove the roast from the oven and let it rest at least 15 minutes before slicing.

5. While the pork is roasting, prepare the mustard sauce by combining the Dijon mustard, grainy mustard, dry mustard, mustard seed, and oil. Serve in a small bowl alongside the sliced pork.

Vary the mustard sauce with vinegar, black pepper, crushed red pepper flakes, sugar, or horseradish, depending on your whimsy and the other dishes on your buffet table.

ARIZONA ORANGE AND GARLIC ROAST LOIN OF PORK

*Makes 16 to 20 servings for dinner,
40 or more as part of a buffet*

At least once a year I visit my sister Joan in Arizona. Her backyard has orange trees, and rosemary is one of the many fresh herbs growing along the walk to her front door. We often decide at the last minute to have a few friends over for dinner.

I created this easy-to-make, slow-roasted loin of pork so we could enjoy a walk at sunset while dinner baked in the oven. During the last hour we popped whole heads of garlic and baking potatoes into the oven alongside the meat. We dressed the baked potatoes by squeezing the soft roasted garlic onto them as a butter substitute.

Serve hot as an entree or at room temperature with The Great Cover-up Vinaigrette for a buffet.

1 well-trimmed 6- or 7-pound boneless loin of pork, tied

2 large cloves garlic, cut in slivers

1 or 2 sprigs fresh rosemary or 1 1/2 teaspoons dried

Zest of 2 oranges, blanched (see Tasty Tip, page 111)

Pinch of salt

1 teaspoon freshly ground black pepper

1 recipe The Great Cover-up Vinaigrette for serving at room temperature (recipe follows)

1. Preheat the oven 350°F.

2. Using a knife with a sharp point, make 1- to 1 1/2-inch-deep holes in the pork and insert the slivers of garlic.

3. Bruise the rosemary with the flat side of a knife. Mince the rosemary and orange zest together. Add the salt and pepper and mix well. Rub the pork with this mixture, being sure to push some of it into the slits alongside the garlic. Cover and set aside for 1 hour or refrigerate for 6 to 24 hours. Return the pork to room temperature before roasting.

4. Place the pork on a rack in a large roasting pan. Roast about 2½ hours, or until a meat thermometer registers 155° to 160°F. Let the roast stand for 15 minutes before slicing.

THE GREAT COVER-UP VINAIGRETTE

4 shallots, peeled and cut in half

⅓ cup fresh parsley leaves

2 tablespoons Dijon mustard

⅓ cup red wine vinegar

⅔ cup olive oil

1 teaspoon salt

1 teaspoon freshly ground black pepper

¼ teaspoon sugar

Place all the ingredients in the food processor and process until the shallots and parsley are minced. Can be stored in the refrigerator for several days.

BRAISED FRUIT–STUFFED LOIN OF PORK

Makes 10 servings

Pork with fruit is an ageless combination. To a historical Danish combination of prunes and apples I've added nutmeg and mace.

Plumping or steeping dried prunes and apricots in port adds a rich flavor to the sliced-apple stuffing and keeps the meat moist as it cooks. The sauce is a deep ruby-red color with an unmatchable flavor.

Heaping 1/2 cup pitted prunes (about 6 ounces)

Heaping 1/2 cup dried apricots (about 6 ounces)

3/4 cup port

Seasoning Mixture

1 teaspoon salt

1/2 teaspoon freshly ground black pepper

1 teaspoon freshly grated nutmeg

1/2 teaspoon ground mace

1 well-trimmed 3- to 4-pound boneless loin of pork, untied

1 medium Granny Smith apple, peeled, cored, and sliced

Vegetable oil to film roasting pan

1 to 2 cups Homemade Beef Stock (page 276) or Doctored Beef Broth (page 279)

2 tablespoons red currant jelly, approximately

1. Put the prunes, apricots, and 1/2 cup of the port into a small saucepan. Simmer for a couple of minutes, until the fruit swells but has not begun to cook.

2. To make the seasoning mixture, combine the salt, pepper, nutmeg, and mace. Cut the pork loin lengthwise about three-fourths of the way through. It should fall open like a book. Rub the inside and outside of the pork with half of the seasoning mixture. Cover and set aside for

1 hour at room temperature or refrigerate for 6 to 24 hours. Return the pork to room temperature before roasting.

3. Mix together the plumped prunes and apricots with the apple and place down the center of the pork. Bring the sides of the roast up and tie every couple of inches with cotton kitchen string. Rub the outside of the pork roast with the remaining seasoning mixture.

4. Preheat the oven to 350°F.

5. Film a large roasting pan with oil. Brown the pork on all sides over medium-high heat for 3 to 4 minutes on each side. Add enough broth to cover the bottom of the pan to a depth of 1/2 inch.

6. Cover the pan and roast until the meat is tender, approximately 1 1/2 hours, or until a meat thermometer registers 155°F. Place the roast on a platter and let stand for 15 minutes before slicing.

7. Pour off any excess fat from the roasting pan. Heat the roasting pan on top of the stove over high heat and deglaze it by adding the remaining 1/4 cup of port and scraping up any bits of meat that are stuck to the bottom of the pan. Pour the cooking juices through a fine-mesh strainer and discard any bits and pieces left in the strainer. Cook the strained juices for a few minutes to reduce them. Stir in the currant jelly. Taste, and if you want a richer sauce, add more jelly. Slice the roast and pass the sauce alongside.

ROAST PORK WITH MUSTARD–CORIANDER SEED CRUST

Makes 10 servings

I hope you'll try this crunchy, crusted pork loin, but don't substitute ground mustard or coriander or you'll lose the full intensity of this fabulous roast.

Toasting coriander and mustard seeds in a dry skillet until they become aromatic heightens their flavor. The subtlety of coriander blends with the sweetness of cardamom, the pizzazz of mustard, and the bite of freshly ground black pepper.

I would serve brown rice pilaf and tiny green peas to complete the dinner.

Dry Rub

2 tablespoons yellow mustard seed

1 tablespoon coriander seed

1 tablespoon coarse salt

1 teaspoon ground cardamom

2 tablespoons freshly ground black pepper

1 well-trimmed 3- to 4-pound boneless loin of pork, tied

3 cloves garlic, cut in slivers

Vegetable oil to film roasting pan

1 carrot, chopped

1 onion, chopped

1 stalk celery, chopped

1 to 1½ cups beef broth, preferably Homemade Beef Stock (page 276) or Doctored Beef Broth (page 279), or white wine

1. To make the dry rub, toast the mustard and coriander seeds in a dry skillet over medium-high heat, stirring frequently, until fragrant, 2 to 3 minutes. Cool the seeds. Combine them with the salt, cardamom, and pepper and crush to a coarse texture.

2. Using a small knife with a sharp point, make 1- to 1$^{1}/_{2}$-inch-deep holes in the pork and insert the slivers of garlic. Rub the pork with the dry rub, being sure to push some of it into the slits alongside the garlic. Set aside for 30 to 60 minutes or refrigerate overnight wrapped in plastic wrap. Return the pork to room temperature, still wrapped, before roasting.

3. Preheat the oven to 375°F.

4. Film the bottom of a heavy roasting pan with oil and brown the pork on all sides over medium-high heat on top of the stove, 3 to 4 minutes each side. (Use the strings to turn over the meat so that you don't dislodge the seasonings.) Add the carrot, onion, and celery and brown them for a few minutes. Add the broth, cover, and roast in the oven for 1 hour.

5. Remove the cover and continue to roast until the pan juices run clear or until a meat thermometer reads 155°F, about 30 minutes more. Remove the meat to a serving platter and allow it to rest for 15 minutes before slicing. See page 62 for the slicing illustration.

6. Pour off the excess fat from the roasting pan. Heat the roasting pan on top of the stove over high heat and deglaze it with the remaining $^{1}/_{2}$ cup of wine or broth, scraping up any bits of meat that are stuck to the bottom of the pan. Pour the pan juices through a strainer into a saucepan and discard the vegetables. Bring the juices to a boil and cook until reduced by half, about 5 minutes. Taste and correct the seasonings. Serve the sauce alongside the pork roast.

*Cut the meat across
the grain into slices.*

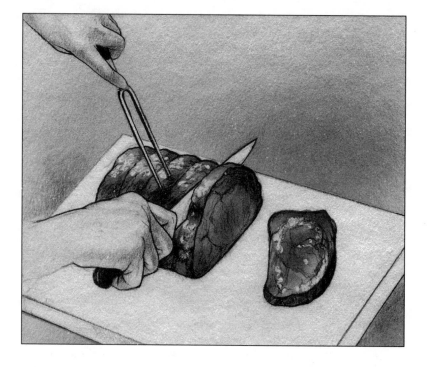

MUSTARD PORK TENDERLOIN

Makes 4 to 5 servings

Nothing could be easier than smearing a robust grainy mustard (for this dish I prefer one with whole seeds and horseradish) over seasoned tenderloin and roasting it on a bed of onion and celery. The meat juices flavor the vegetables and turn them into a tasty side dish.

I confess I sometimes make this roast tenderloin just so I can use it for a dinner sequel, a.k.a. leftovers.

While the meat is in the oven, cook some fettuccine and dress it with olive oil, garlic, and fresh herbs. In less than an hour you'll have a complete meal. Festive and fast!

2 pork tenderloins, about 1 1/2 pounds total

1 to 2 teaspoons freshly ground black pepper

1 1/2 tablespoons grainy mustard, approximately

1/2 onion, sliced

2 stalks celery with leaves, coarsely chopped

2 carrots, sliced (optional)

1/2 cup white wine

1. Preheat the oven to 450°F.

2. Season the tenderloins with pepper. Using a table knife, spread the mustard over the tenderloins.

3. Line the bottom of a baking pan with the onion, celery, and carrots if desired. Set the mustard-coated pork on the vegetables and pour the wine around it.

4. Roast the pork approximately 20 to 25 minutes, until a meat thermometer reads 155°F. Let the pork rest for 10 minutes. Slice it and serve with or without the vegetables.

MARTHA'S TRADITIONAL BAKED HAM

Makes 20 servings with leftovers

Since learning this trick from Martha Smith, a friend and a fine Southern cook who is also my right hand in my catering business, I wouldn't dream of baking ham any other way. Steaming the ham first allows the fat to be released and the distinct clove flavor to penetrate throughout the meat. Glazing both sides of the ham gives each serving some of the sweet, crusty glaze everyone loves to eat.

When my children were in college and invited a crowd to the beach house for the weekend, I prepared this for the first night's dinner. It gave me leftovers for the late-night eaters, cubed ham to brown for an omelet in the morning, slices for grilled cheese with ham for lunch, plus enough to add to a pan of scalloped potatoes for another dinner—as well as for a chef salad for me a day or so later. When you're down to just the bone, make a big pot of pea soup. All in all, you can't beat ham—it's good down to the last oink!

1 ready-to-eat ham, about 15 pounds

Whole cloves

Glaze

3 cups light brown sugar

1 cup Dijon mustard

1 tablespoon dry mustard

1 to 2 tablespoons orange juice

1. Preheat the oven to 325°F.

2. Cut away any skin and excess fat that surrounds the ham. Score the ham, cutting ½ inch into the meat, in a diamond pattern on all sides, including the bottom. Stud the ham with cloves where the lines intersect and place the ham, fat side up, on a rack in a large roasting pan. Pour 1½ to 2 cups of water into the bottom of the pan, making sure the water does not touch the bottom of the ham. Cover the ham with aluminum foil and secure the foil around the edges of the pan. Place the ham in the oven and allow it to steam for 2 hours.

3. Meanwhile, prepare the glaze by combining the brown sugar, Dijon mustard, dry mustard, and enough orange juice to form a paste just thin enough to spread.

4. Remove the ham from the oven. Raise the oven temperature to 350°F. Turn the ham over and spread the glaze over the bottom of it. Return the ham, uncovered, to the oven and let it bake until the glaze is golden brown, about 45 minutes.

5. Remove the ham from the oven again and turn it over. Spread the remaining glaze over the top of the ham. Return the ham to the oven and continue to bake until the glaze on the top is done and a meat thermometer registers 140°F, about 45 minutes more. Allow the ham to rest for at least 20 minutes before carving.

Grasp the shank bone with a napkin. Holding the carving knife almost parallel to the meatiest portion of the ham, make long, smooth horizontal slices. (Discard the first slice.) When you reach the bone, turn the ham over and carve the other side.

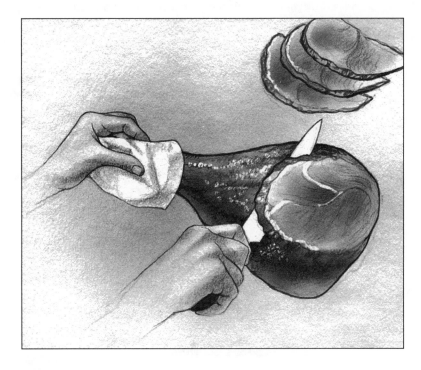

For extra zip, add the zest of 1 orange to the glaze.

TAILGATE HAM

Makes 20 servings with leftovers

Nowadays there are Land Rovers and 4-by-4s that have plenty of space to take a card table to tailgate parties. However, the first time I had a tailgate party at a University of Minnesota football game, we didn't think about tables. I opened the tailgate of my Chevrolet station wagon, covered it with a borrowed plaid blanket, and served my buffet.

Because beer was all the budget allowed, I steamed and glazed the ham with it. My grownup version has bourbon in the glaze.

Add assorted breads, two or three jars of mustard, pickles, potato salad, carrot sticks, celery stalks, cherry tomatoes, steamed broccoli and cauliflower florets—and don't forget the brownies.

Often my clients want this ham as the center of an autumn buffet. I serve it with small baking-powder biscuits, squares of jalapeño-pepper and rosemary-scented corn bread, a chunky applesauce, cranberry chutney, and spicy mustard, and a big salad.

1 ready-to-eat ham, about 15 pounds

12 ounces beer

Glaze

1 cup dark brown sugar

1 cup light brown sugar

1/2 cup grainy mustard

1 tablespoon dry mustard

2 tablespoons bourbon

1. Preheat the oven to 325°F.

2. Cut away any skin and excess fat that surrounds the ham. Score the ham, cutting 1/2 inch into the meat, in a diamond pattern on all sides, including the bottom. Place the ham, fat side up, on a rack in a large roasting pan. Pour the beer into the bottom of the pan. Cover the ham with aluminum foil and secure the foil around the edges of the pan. Place the ham in the oven and allow it to steam for 2 hours.

3. Meanwhile, prepare the glaze by combining the dark brown sugar, light brown sugar, grainy mustard, dry mustard, and bourbon.

4. Remove the ham from the oven. Raise the oven temperature to 350°F. Turn the ham over and spread the glaze over the bottom of it. Return the ham, uncovered, to the oven and let it bake until the glaze is a deep, rich brown, about 45 minutes.

5. Remove the ham from the oven again and turn it over. Spread the remaining glaze over the top of the ham. Return the ham to the oven and continue to bake until the glaze on the top is dark brown and a meat thermometer registers 140°F, about 45 minutes more. Allow the ham to rest for at least 20 minutes before carving.

The reason I score ham 1/2 inch deep into the flesh, instead of scoring only the fat, is to enable the flavor of the glaze to penetrate deep into the ham.

EASTER SUNDAY HAM

Makes 20 servings with leftovers

My family tradition dictates this ham be served on Easter Sunday along with Cheddar-topped scalloped potatoes, deviled eggs, steamed fresh asparagus, a green salad, and a fruit salad. Lemon meringue pie or fresh coconut cake was the usual dessert.

Glazing the already browned crust creates a picture-perfect, sweet coating over the spicy flavors beneath.

1 ready-to-eat ham, about 15 pounds

Whole cloves

1 1/2 to 2 cups apple juice

Spicy Crust

1 1/2 cups dried unseasoned bread crumbs

1/3 teaspoon freshly ground black pepper

1/3 teaspoon ground cloves

1/3 teaspoon freshly grated nutmeg

1/3 teaspoon ground ginger

1 teaspoon dry mustard

1 small jar (about 8 ounces) apricot jam

2 tablespoons rum, approximately

1. Preheat the oven to 325°F.

2. Cut away any skin and excess fat that surrounds the ham. Score the ham, cutting 1/2 inch into the meat, in a diamond pattern on all sides, including the bottom. Stud the ham with cloves where the lines intersect and place the ham, fat side up, on a rack in a large roasting pan. Pour 1 1/2 to 2 cups of apple juice into the bottom of the pan, making sure the juice does not touch the bottom of the ham. Cover the ham with aluminum foil and secure the foil around the edges of the pan. Place the ham in the oven and allow it to steam for 2 hours.

3. Meanwhile, prepare the Spicy Crust by combining the bread crumbs, pepper, ground cloves, nutmeg, ginger, and dry mustard.

4. Remove the ham from the oven. Raise the oven temperature to 350°F. Spread the bread-crumb mixture over the top of the ham. Return the

ham, uncovered, to the oven and let it bake until a crust forms, 15 to 20 minutes. Remove the ham from the oven.

5. Thin the apricot jam with a little rum and spread it over the spicy crust. Return the ham to the oven and bake for approximately 1½ hours more, or until the glaze has set and a meat thermometer registers 140°F. Allow the ham to rest for at least 20 minutes before carving.

WOODLAND-STYLE ROAST LEG OF VEAL

Begin one day in advance

Makes 8 servings

I love to tromp through the woods and hunt for mushrooms and herbs, but I rarely have time for it. I let someone else hunt them or I call my trusted mushroom purveyor, Delices De Bois, and have wild mushrooms delivered to my kitchen door. If wild mushrooms aren't in your budget, fresh white mushrooms are just fine. Serve this roast with risotto and peas.

For a catered elegant dinner party I serve this with a risotto that's perfumed with porcini mushrooms, extra-fancy petit pois tossed with baby carrots, and tiny patty pan squash.

> 1 well-trimmed 3-pound boneless top-round veal roast, tied
>
> Milk for soaking veal, about 1 quart

Dry Rub

> ½ teaspoon freshly ground black pepper
>
> 1½ teaspoons dried chervil
>
> ½ teaspoon rubbed sage
>
> ¼ teaspoon salt

> Vegetable oil to film casserole
>
> 1 tablespoon butter
>
> 1 pound fresh mushrooms (oyster, shiitake, portobello, button, or a combination), sliced
>
> Pinch of salt
>
> Freshly ground black pepper
>
> 2 bunches scallions (white and light green parts), chopped
>
> 1 clove garlic, sliced
>
> 1 small bunch fresh parsley, chopped

WOODLAND-STYLE ROAST LEG OF VEAL

Begin one day in advance

Makes 8 servings

I love to tromp through the woods and hunt for mushrooms and herbs, but I rarely have time for it. I let someone else hunt them or I call my trusted mushroom purveyor, Delices De Bois, and have wild mushrooms delivered to my kitchen door. If wild mushrooms aren't in your budget, fresh white mushrooms are just fine. Serve this roast with risotto and peas.

For a catered elegant dinner party I serve this with a risotto that's perfumed with porcini mushrooms, extra-fancy petit pois tossed with baby carrots, and tiny patty pan squash.

1 well-trimmed 3-pound boneless top-round veal roast, tied

Milk for soaking veal, about 1 quart

Dry Rub

1/2 teaspoon freshly ground black pepper

1 1/2 teaspoons dried chervil

1/2 teaspoon rubbed sage

1/4 teaspoon salt

Vegetable oil to film casserole

1 tablespoon butter

1 pound fresh mushrooms (oyster, shiitake, portobello, button, or a combination), sliced

Pinch of salt

Freshly ground black pepper

2 bunches scallions (white and light green parts), chopped

1 clove garlic, sliced

1 small bunch fresh parsley, chopped

ham, uncovered, to the oven and let it bake until a crust forms, 15 to 20 minutes. Remove the ham from the oven.

5. Thin the apricot jam with a little rum and spread it over the spicy crust. Return the ham to the oven and bake for approximately 1½ hours more, or until the glaze has set and a meat thermometer registers 140°F. Allow the ham to rest for at least 20 minutes before carving.

1 teaspoon rubbed sage or 1 tablespoon minced
   fresh sage leaves

2 juniper berries

8 whole black peppercorns

1 cup white wine

2 cups beef broth, preferably Beef and Mushroom
   Broth (page 280)

Fresh chervil sprigs for garnish (optional)

One day ahead

1. Soak the veal in enough milk to just cover the roast. Cover and refrigerate overnight. Discard the milk, rinse the veal, and pat it dry with paper towels.

Before roasting

2. Preheat the oven to 350°F.

3. To prepare the dry rub, combine the pepper, $1/2$ teaspoon chervil, sage, and salt. Rub the veal roast with this mixture.

4. Film the bottom of a heavy flameproof casserole with oil and sear the roast over high heat on all sides until it's golden brown. Transfer the roast to a plate and set aside.

5. Add the butter to the casserole and sauté the sliced mushrooms over high heat, stirring occasionally, until they squeak and their edges are brown, about 3 minutes. Add the salt and freshly ground black pepper. Remove the mushrooms from the casserole and set aside.

6. Cook the scallions, garlic, parsley, sage, and 1 teaspoon chervil in the same casserole over medium heat for 2 to 3 minutes, stirring occasionally, until the scallions are limp. Add the juniper berries and peppercorns. Return the roast and any juices that have escaped to the casserole. Add the wine and broth and bring to a boil.

7. Place the casserole in the oven and roast, uncovered, for approximately 1 hour, until a meat thermometer registers 140°F. Transfer the roast to a serving platter and let it rest for 20 minutes before carving.

8. Pour off any excess fat from the roasting pan. Strain the cooking liquid into a large saucepan. Cook over high heat until reduced to about 1 cup, about 10 minutes. Add the reserved mushrooms and their juices. Taste and correct the seasonings. Slice the veal and arrange on a platter. Ladle the sauce over the veal. If available, garnish with fresh chervil.

TOMATO-BRAISED VEAL ROAST

Begin one day in advance

Makes 8 to 10 servings

The slow-simmering union of tomato with garlic, onion, and basil is irresistible to any person in or near the kitchen. Even though this roast is expensive to buy, it's economical in the long run because there is no waste.

For a hot-weather cold supper, I roast this veal two days ahead and refrigerate it. I slice it while it's still cold and then serve it at room temperature. Arrange the veal on a parsley-lined platter, drizzle a sauce of tomato puree added to prepared mayonnaise, and then sprinkle snipped sun-dried tomatoes and chopped Italian parsley over the whole affair. It's a handsome as well as robust dish.

1 well-trimmed 3-pound boneless top round veal
    roast, tied

Milk for soaking veal, about 1 quart

3 cloves garlic, cut in slivers

¼ teaspoon salt

½ teaspoon freshly ground black pepper

Olive oil to film casserole, plus 1 tablespoon

2 medium onions, chopped

2 cloves garlic, chopped

2 stalks celery, chopped

2 carrots, peeled and chopped

1 small bunch fresh parsley, chopped

2 tablespoons chopped fresh basil or 2 teaspoons
    dried

3 to 4 tomatoes, seeded and chopped

½ bay leaf

1 cup Homemade Veal Stock (page 281),
    Homemade Beef Stock, (page 276), or Doctored
    Beef Broth (page 279)

One day ahead

1. Soak the veal in enough milk just to cover the roast. Cover and refrigerate overnight.

Before roasting

2. Preheat the oven to 350°F.

3. Rinse the veal and pat dry with paper towels. Using a knife with a sharp point, make 1- to 1½-inch-deep holes in the veal and insert the slivers of garlic. Rub the roast with salt and pepper.

4. Film the bottom of a heavy flameproof casserole with olive oil and sear the roast over high heat on all sides until it's golden brown. Set the veal aside.

5. Add the tablespoon of oil to the casserole and cook the onions and chopped garlic, stirring, over medium heat until the onions are soft and translucent, about 5 minutes. Add the celery, carrots, parsley, and basil and continue to cook, stirring, for another 4 or 5 minutes.

6. Stir in the tomatoes and bay leaf. Return the roast and any juices to the casserole. Add the broth and bring it to a boil.

7. Place the casserole in the oven and roast, uncovered, for approximately 1 hour, until a meat thermometer registers 140°F. Remove the roast and vegetables from the casserole. Let the roast rest for 20 minutes before carving.

8. Pour the cooking liquid into a saucepan and boil over high heat until it is reduced to about 1 cup, about 10 minutes. Taste and correct the seasonings. Slice the veal and arrange on the platter with the vegetables. Ladle the sauce over everything.

SPINACH-STUFFED ROAST VEAL

Makes 10 to 12 servings

For catering an elegant dinner party, this recipe is one of my standards because it is done in stages. There's no waste, as one large boneless roast feeds 10 to 12 people; it's easy to execute once we are on location; it looks beautiful on the plate and—most important—the flavor is unmatched.

The nutty taste and richness of nearly burned butter and nutmeg combines with the shallots and tarragon to make the spinach stuffing a staple I use as a bed for sautéed veal scallops, for stuffing chicken breasts, or with added toasted pine nuts as a vegetable. Yes, it's that good! An added bonus is that it can be done weeks in advance and kept in the freezer.

Stuffing

> One 10-ounce package frozen chopped spinach, thawed
>
> 1 tablespoon butter
>
> 2 teaspoons olive oil
>
> 1 large shallot, minced
>
> 1/2 teaspoon freshly ground black pepper
>
> 1/4 teaspoon freshly grated nutmeg
>
> 1 1/2 teaspoons minced fresh tarragon or 1/2 teaspoon dried
>
> 1 well-trimmed 4-pound boneless leg or loin of veal, untied
>
> Milk for soaking veal, about 1 quart

Seasoning Paste

> 1 tablespoon chopped fresh tarragon or 1 teaspoon dried
>
> 1 teaspoon chopped fresh parsley
>
> 1 clove garlic, minced
>
> 1/4 teaspoon salt

½ teaspoon freshly ground black pepper, or to taste

1 teaspoon oil, approximately

Vegetable oil to film casserole

8 medium carrots, peeled and halved lengthwise

1 leek, white only, cut in large chunks

1 onion, peeled and cut in eighths

½ cup white wine

½ cup Homemade Veal Stock (page 281), or low-sodium canned chicken broth

1. To prepare the stuffing, squeeze all the moisture out of the spinach until the spinach is as dry as you can get it.

2. Brown the butter and olive oil until the butter is dark brown, but not burned. Reduce the heat and add the shallot. Sauté briefly until the shallot is soft, about 2 minutes. Remove the pan from the heat and add the spinach. Mix thoroughly. Season with the pepper, nutmeg, and tarragon. Taste and correct the seasonings.

   The stuffing can be prepared up to 1 week ahead, covered, and refrigerated.

3. Soak the veal in enough milk to just cover. Cover with plastic wrap and refrigerate for 2 to 24 hours. Discard the milk, rinse the veal, and pat it dry with paper towels.

4. To prepare the seasoning paste, chop the tarragon with the parsley and garlic. Add salt and black pepper and only enough oil to make a paste.

5. Spread the spinach mixture over the veal roast. Roll up and tie with cotton kitchen string. Rub the roast with the seasoning paste and set aside for 1 to 2 hours. Or cover the seasoned roast with plastic wrap and refrigerate for up to 5 hours. Return the meat to room temperature before roasting.

6. Preheat the oven to 400°F.

7. Film a heavy casserole with oil. Brown the roast quickly on all sides, using the string to turn it. Strew carrots, leek, and onion around the veal. Cover and place the casserole in the oven. Bake for 15 to 20 minutes.

8. Add the wine and broth to the casserole. Reduce the heat to 325°F and continue to roast, covered, basting only if the top of the roast gets dry

for 1 to 1¼ hours more, until a meat thermometer registers 150°F. Transfer the meat and carrots to a platter and let the meat rest for 20 minutes.

9. Strain out the onion and leeks and puree them in a food processor. Skim any fat from the pan juices and reduce them by half. Stir the pureed vegetables back into the juices. Taste and correct the seasonings.

10. Remove the string from the roast. Slice the veal thickly and arrange the carrots attractively around the meat. Serve with the sauce on the side.

After removing the strings, hold the meat steady with a two-pronged fork. Cut the meat across the grain into thick slices.

It is important for the success of the stuffing to get all the moisture out of the spinach. I find that the best way to do this is to squeeze the defrosted chopped spinach in a linen tea towel until no more liquid comes out. The spinach will look like a ball no bigger than your fist.

ONION-DUSTED ROAST BEEF AND PORK

Makes 10 to 12 servings

Here's a perfect example of why roasts are so popular. This recipe is as easy as 1, 2, 3. The preparation time is only 5 minutes, and the oven does the work while you're free to do other things. Two hours later, dinner is ready.

The combination of pork and beef roasted together in the same pan is an idea from my sister Judy, a busy lady as well as fellow good cook, who often feeds a clan of hungry folks. She adds chunks of onions, potatoes, and carrots to the pan for a one-dish meal. Judy's instructions are "Dust the meat with onion soup and bake it covered."

3 pounds well-trimmed beef blade roast

3 pounds well-trimmed pork blade roast

1 cup water

1 package Lipton onion soup mix

4 medium onions, cut in chunks (optional)

10 medium boiling potatoes, peeled and cut in half (optional)

2 pounds carrots, peeled and cut in chunks (optional)

1. Preheat the oven to 350°F.

2. Place the meat in a large roasting pan. Pour the water into the bottom of the pan. Sprinkle the soup mix over both pieces of meat, cover tightly with aluminum foil, and roast for 2½ hours. Remove the foil, and if you wish, add the optional onions, potatoes, and carrots. Continue to bake until the meat is brown and fork-tender and the vegetables are cooked through, about 1 hour longer.

3. Remove the meat to a large platter. If you've cooked vegetables with the meat, spoon them around the roasts. Skim the fat from the juices (see page 79) and serve the juices in a gravy pitcher alongside.

Tasty Tip

If you have forgotten to defrost the roasts, don't fret. Simply place the frozen meat in the roasting pan, add the soup mix, cover with aluminum foil, and increase the cooking time to 3 hours.

THE STEW POT

Stews, ragouts, and fricassees: No one agrees on how they differ or if, in fact, they differ at all. And what about pot roast, a beef stew with its meat in one large piece. Having said this, I think of these as basically the same: slow-cooked meat, usually with vegetables, simmered until tender.

But what masterpieces of culinary architecture all these can be! The flavors in each succulent mouthful of a well-made stew reflect all the steps in its construction, rather like an elegant house that commands attention but which needs a hidden foundation and many invisible beams to support its beauty. A well-made stew, as opposed to one simply tossed together—which I do make when I'm in a hurry—has depth and heart and subtle nuances.

The Building Blocks for a Well-Made Stew

1. *First, sear the meat in a bit of oil over high heat until it's brown on all sides. Searing seals in the juices and gives the meat a rich, caramelized crust. If the meat has been dusted with flour or cornmeal, the stew will naturally thicken. Searing is the underpinning that gives a stew depth of flavor.*

2. *Set the meat aside while you sauté or cook the vegetables. As their starches turn to sugar, the carrots, onions, celery, garlic, and other vegetables take on a wonderfully sweet taste. Their natural juices season the oil, adding extra flavor and forming the stew's foundation.*

3. *Next come herbs and spices, which add sparkle, like the lights that illuminate a room.*

4. *Return the meat to the pot and, finally, add a full-bodied wine or a rich stock, which pulls the various parts into a compelling whole.*

Inexpensive, tough cuts of meat are best for stews. Tender, expensive cuts fall apart and become stringy when subjected to long cooking. Cook stews slowly and give the flavors time to develop. Once the meat and vegetables are cooked, taste and correct the seasonings.

Keep an eye on the liquid: you want it to cook down, but not boil out. The juices should be rich and flavorful, but not so reduced that the stew tastes dry and salty. Add liquid if needed; or if the stew is too soupy, uncover the pot and reduce the excess liquid.

Most of the time I cook stews in the oven. With the heat surrounding the pot, deeper, richer flavors develop than when the same stew is cooked on top of the stove. Still, cooking stews on the stove has its own advantages. It's a lot easier to keep an eye on the pot. Every now and then, you can give the stew a stir, and you can taste it frequently. Choose the method that most appeals to you.

I use heavy casseroles with heavy, tight-fitting lids, like Le Creuset, to keep in the flavors and bouquet. You know the incredible aroma in the blast of steam when you lift the lid of a fabulous stew? I don't want that fragrant steam to evaporate because of a thin pot or to escape into the oven due to an ill-fitting lid.

When I'm in a hurry, I put the ingredients in a stew pot, add the liquid, and cook everything together. Or I might toss everything into a crockpot and go off to work. When I come home, my crockpot has mysteriously transformed the raw ingredients into an instant, good-tasting dinner, a simple way to prepare a tasty stew that everyone from the ages of 2 to 92 enjoys. While these lack the layers of flavors of well-made stews, I've never had any complaints.

My stews taste good the day they're prepared, but I rarely serve them then. Since they taste even better after a day or two, when the flavors have had a chance to blend, I take advantage of this. What a pleasure to simply reheat the stew and watch the looks of delight and anticipation on my guests' faces as the lid is lifted and the aromas rush at them. A stew rarely needs much to go along with it: sometimes a potato or rice, a salad, and—*voilà!*

Getting the Fat Out

If you are going to serve the stew within an hour of cooking it, separate the solids and liquids. Let the liquid stand for a few minutes to allow the fat to rise, then skim it off.

I use a gravy strainer with a spout that pours from the bottom of the cup, leaving the fat on top. You can find one in any kitchen store, as well as in most supermarkets. Be sure to buy a gravy strainer that can go in the dishwasher. Pour in the gravy, let it sit a few minutes while the fat rises, and then pour out the gravy, leaving the fat in the cup.

If you have at least 30 minutes, put the liquid in the freezer. The fat will rise to the surface, and while it won't harden as completely as if you had chilled it for hours, it's still easier to spoon off than it would be at room temperature.

If you are going to serve the meat a day or two later, refrigerate the stew right in the casserole. When the sauce is chilled, the fat will harden on its surface and it can be skimmed off easily.

Three Ways to Thicken Sauce without Adding Fat

1. *Remove the meat and vegetables. Simmer the juices left in the pot to reduce them. If you want to thicken the sauce further, puree a few of the vegetables and stir the puree back into the liquid.*

2. *Leaving all the ingredients in the pot, remove the cover and raise the heat. Cook until the juices are rich and have begun to thicken. Sometimes I do this on top of the stove; other times I turn on my oven broiler and let the meat and vegetables brown and glaze while the juices are reducing.*

3. *Using a tiny wire whisk, mix 1 tablespoon of potato starch or cornstarch with 2 tablespoons of cold water. Gradually whisk this mixture into the simmering liquid, stirring continuously, until the sauce coats the back of a metal spoon. No matter how much thickener your stew or sauce needs, keep the proportion of 1 part starch to 2 parts water.*

Stews

MRS. B'S OLD-FASHIONED BRISKET

BALSAMIC BRISKET OF BEEF

AMERICAN BEEF MOLÉ

FIFTH AVENUE CHILI

ARIZONA BEEF STEW

COUNTRY CHOICE BEEF STEW

CORN BELT STEW

RAGOUT OF LAMB WITH ROASTED PEPPERS AND MUSHROOMS

BRAISED LAMB SHANKS

LAMB CURRY AMBROSIA

BEER-BRAISED COUNTRY PORK RIBS

DOWN-HOME COUNTRY BARBECUE SAUCE

VINTAGE SAUERKRAUT, POTATOES, AND PORK

FRICASSEE OF BONELESS BRAZILIAN PORK

CLASSY WILD MUSHROOM VEAL BUNDLES

VEAL RAGOUT

TRADITIONAL OSSO BUCCO

AMERICAN OSSO BUCCO

BLACK-TIE VEAL RAGOUT

NEW YORK CITY VENISON STEW

COUNTRY VENISON STEW

MRS. B'S OLD-FASHIONED BRISKET

Makes 8 servings with possible leftovers

Several years ago a friend of a client asked me to cater his family's Passover Seder. "What I want most is a fabulous brisket, just like my mother used to make!" I always love a challenge. I assured him I would do my best, but I reminded him that I wasn't his mother.

As soon as I got back to my kitchen-office, I called Mrs. B (which was what everyone who didn't call her Mom called her), a fabulous cook and a marvelous human being who came to cooking class every so often with her daughter, Susan Gellman.

She gave me the recipe she'd been using for her family for more than 50 years, emphasizing that the secret to any good brisket is slow, slow cooking.

If you have a problem finding Rokeach tomato sauce with mushrooms, substitute another brand of tomato sauce with mushrooms, undiluted.

P.S. My new client declared this brisket to be as good as his mom's.

Vegetable oil to film casserole, plus 1 tablespoon

One well-trimmed 3- to 4-pound first-cut brisket of beef

$1/2$ teaspoon salt

$1/2$ teaspoon freshly ground black pepper

$1 1/2$ teaspoons paprika

1 large onion, sliced

3 to 4 carrots, sliced

3 to 4 stalks celery with leaves, sliced

2 to 3 cloves garlic, minced

2 teaspoons dried oregano

One 16-ounce can Rokeach (or other brand) tomato sauce with mushrooms, undiluted

Pinch of sugar

$1/2$ cup full-bodied red wine

$1 1/2$ to 2 cups beef broth (canned is fine)

1. Film a large, heavy flameproof casserole with oil. Sear the brisket on both sides over high heat for 4 to 5 minutes on each side, or until it browns. Season with salt, pepper, and paprika. Remove the brisket from the casserole and set aside.

2. Add the tablespoon of oil to the casserole. Over medium-high heat, cook the onion, carrots, and celery, stirring, until the onion begins to soften, about 4 to 5 minutes. Add the garlic and oregano.

3. Return the brisket to the casserole and add the tomato sauce, sugar, red wine, and enough broth to barely cover the meat. Cover the casserole and bring to a boil. Reduce the heat and simmer slowly on top of the stove for 2 to 3 hours, until the meat is very tender. Check occasionally to make sure the stew isn't boiling and to make sure there's enough liquid. Add more broth as needed.

4. Remove the brisket and vegetables from the casserole. Either discard the vegetables or use them to thicken the sauce (see page 80). Skim the fat from the sauce before serving.

This brisket can also be baked in a covered casserole for 2 to 3 hours at 300° to 325°F, until the meat is tender.

BALSAMIC BRISKET OF BEEF

Begin three days in advance

Makes 8 servings, with leftovers

The recipe may sound crazy, but this brisket is one of the best I've ever eaten.

It happened by chance. I marinated the brisket with good intentions of cooking it the next day to test it for this book. In the meantime I had a big party to cater. In all the flutter the brisket was forgotten. Three days later I remembered the "test brisket" and decided to cook it anyway. The results are in—this one's a winner.

The rich balsamic flavor mingles with the juniper berries and renders the beef remarkably tender. Most of all, the aroma is irresistible. While the brisket simmered, my kitchen smelled like the caves in Modena where balsamic vinegar is aged.

Serve this brisket with fettuccine dressed with extra-virgin olive oil and a dusting of chopped parsley, then pray for leftovers.

Marinade

1 cup beef broth (canned is fine)

½ cup balsamic vinegar

1 large onion, chopped

1 teaspoon freshly ground black pepper

1 tablespoon juniper berries, crushed

1 well-trimmed 3- to 4-pound first-cut brisket of beef

Vegetable oil to film casserole

1 pound fresh mushrooms, cut in halves or quarters, depending on their size

Salt (optional)

1. Prepare the marinade by combining the broth, vinegar, onion, pepper, and juniper berries in a large nonreactive pan. Add the brisket, cover, and marinate in the refrigerator for 3 days (see head note), turning the meat each day to keep all the surfaces moist. Remove the brisket from the marinade and pat dry with paper towels. Reserve the marinade.

2. Preheat the oven to 300°F.

3. Film a large, heavy flameproof casserole with oil. Sear the brisket on both sides over high heat for 7 to 8 minutes on each side, or until it browns. Add the marinade and enough water just to cover the brisket.

4. Cover the casserole and place the brisket in the oven to bake for 2 hours. Add the mushrooms and bake for another hour. Remove the casserole from the oven, taste, and add salt if needed. The meat will be tender and the aroma irresistible.

AMERICAN BEEF MOLÉ

Makes 6 servings

Molé, a rich, dark Mexican sauce traditionally depends on a variety of hard-to-find chili peppers, seeds, and Mexican chocolate for its intense flavor.

In this easy-to-make version, which uses ingredients readily available in American supermarkets, the sauce is prepared first and then combined with browned meat and baked.

This recipe yields enough sauce for 2¹/₂ to 3 pounds of meat. Freeze the leftover sauce for another day to combine with a browned meat such as ground beef, chicken, or small cubes of pork for a no-work dinner.

Serve with saffron rice and a salad for family or informal company dinners. If you have any leftovers, try the Black Bean Chili (page 252).

Molé Sauce

1 tablespoon olive oil

4 shallots, minced

3 cloves garlic, minced

1 jalapeño pepper, seeded and minced

1 teaspoon ground coriander

2 teaspoons ground cumin

1 cup blanched slivered almonds, ground

One 14-ounce can whole tomatoes with puree

1 teaspoon dried oregano

1 square unsweetened chocolate, coarsely chopped

2 tablespoons unsweetened cocoa powder

2 tablespoons orange marmalade

1 cup beef broth (canned is fine)

¹/₂ teaspoon crushed red pepper flakes

Pinch of salt

¹/₂ teaspoon freshly ground black pepper

¹/₂ teaspoon chili powder

Vegetable oil to film skillet

1½ pounds well-trimmed lean beef, such as eye round, cut in 1-inch cubes

1. To prepare the molé sauce, heat the oil in a heavy skillet or flame-proof casserole over medium-high heat. Cook the shallots, stirring, until they begin to color, 3 to 4 minutes. Add the garlic, jalapeño pepper, coriander, cumin, and almonds and cook, stirring, for another 1 to 2 minutes.

2. Add the tomatoes with puree, oregano, chocolate, cocoa powder, marmalade, broth, red pepper flakes, salt, black pepper, and chili powder. Cook for 20 minutes over low heat, stirring occasionally to keep the sauce from burning and to break up the tomatoes. Taste and correct the seasonings.

   The molé sauce can be prepared ahead and refrigerated for up to 3 days or frozen for up to 1 month.

3. Preheat the oven to 350°F.

4. Lightly film a large nonstick skillet with oil and heat over high heat until very hot. Brown the beef in batches for 3 to 4 minutes, setting it aside as it browns.

5. Combine the beef and half of the sauce in a heavy casserole. (Freeze the remaining sauce for another time.) Cover and bake for 1 hour. The meat should be tender and the sauce dark and rich.

Tasty Tip

If you prefer a smoother molé sauce, process it in a blender until you achieve the smoothness you like.

Wear rubber gloves when handling hot peppers and keep your hands away from your eyes.

FIFTH AVENUE CHILI

Makes 12 servings

Two decades ago I established Cooking With Class, Inc., as a cooking school and catering business. Soon after, a marvelous writer and food professional, Irene Sax, wrote a story in the New York Post *about my giving private lessons to students who wanted one-on-one sessions.*

I created this recipe for a lovely lady who lived on Fifth Avenue with all the luxurious amenities you can imagine. Originally from Kansas, she yearned for a hearty chili without beans. Together we cooked this chili, steamed the rice, and prepared the garnishes.

Her butler served the chili in a huge heirloom silver bowl, while her waitress served the rice. Down the center of the mirror-polished dining room table stood silver glass-lined soup bowls, each filled with cool sour cream, tomato and avocado slices drizzled with lime juice, chopped green peppers, and onions for her guests to help themselves. Kansas had come to Fifth Avenue!

This chili tastes just as scrumptious straight from the pot. If you prefer, simmer it in the oven at 300°F for 2 to 3 hours. It's down home, and it's lip-smackin' good!

¹/₂ cup cornmeal

Pinch of salt

¹/₂ teaspoon freshly ground black pepper

Pinch of garlic powder

2 to 3 teaspoons ground cumin

4 pounds well–trimmed lean beef, such as eye round, cut in 1-inch cubes

¹/₄ cup olive oil

4 medium onions, chopped

4 cloves garlic, minced

2 to 3 teaspoons dried oregano

3 tablespoons chili powder, approximately

Pinch of sugar

One 28-ounce can whole tomatoes with puree

1 small can chopped green chilies

2 to 3 jalapeño peppers, seeded

1. Mix together the cornmeal, salt, black pepper, garlic powder, and a pinch of the cumin. Roll the beef in this seasoned cornmeal and shake off the excess.

2. Heat the oil in a heavy flameproof casserole over high heat. Brown the meat in batches for 3 to 4 minutes per batch, setting it aside as it browns.

3. Add the onions and garlic to the casserole. Cook, stirring, for 2 to 3 minutes over medium heat. Return the beef to the casserole and add the remaining cumin and the oregano, chili powder, sugar, and tomatoes with puree. Stir, cover, and bring to boil. Reduce the heat and simmer for 2 hours. Add the green chilies and jalapeño peppers and cook until the meat is tender and the sauce is thick, about 1 hour more. Taste and correct the seasonings.

When browning more than a small quantity of meat, I brown only several pieces at a time, setting them aside while I brown the next batch. You don't want to crowd the pan, as the meat will steam instead of brown.

ARIZONA BEEF STEW

Makes 6 servings

When I think of Arizona, I think of fresh air and lovely weather, casual clothing, and a free-and-easy lifestyle. The cooking, with its spicy flavors and fresh fruit and vegetables, reflects this.

After eating in several fine restaurants on a recent trip through the state, I created this dish combining opposite flavors. The celery root adds a sweet, slightly licorice flavor that is a counterpoint to the smoky chipotle and spicy-hot jalapeño peppers. Adding corn and chickpeas seemed the right thing to do.

Serve the stew on a bed of white rice. And if you like crunchy stuff, add a basket of blue corn chips.

1/2 cup cornmeal

1/2 teaspoon freshly ground black pepper

1/2 teaspoon salt

1/2 teaspoon dried thyme

1 3/4 pounds well–trimmed eye round, cut in 1 1/2-inch cubes

2 to 3 tablespoons oil

3 cloves garlic, minced

1 1/2 cups water, approximately

3 ears of corn, kernels removed (approximately 2 1/3 cups)

2 cups chopped onion

2 jalapeño peppers, seeded and chopped

One 16-ounce can chickpeas, drained

One 28-ounce can whole tomatoes with juice

2 cups 1 1/2-inch cubes celery root (optional) (see Tasty Tip, page 43)

1 chipotle pepper (optional) (see Tasty Tip, page 43)

1. Mix the cornmeal with the black pepper, salt, and thyme. Roll the beef lightly in this mixture, shaking off any excess.

2. Heat the oil in a heavy flameproof casserole over high heat. Add the beef and sauté, stirring occasionally, until brown, 4 to 5 minutes.

Reduce the heat to medium-high and add the garlic. Cook, stirring, for a few seconds. Add water to come halfway up the sides of the beef, cover, and bring to a boil. Reduce the heat and simmer for 20 to 30 minutes.

3. Add the corn, onion, jalapeño pepper, chickpeas, tomatoes with juice, and if desired, the celery root and chipotle. Cover the pot again and return the liquid to a boil. Reduce the heat and simmer 25 to 30 minutes longer, or until the vegetables and meat are tender. Taste and correct the seasonings.

If you prefer, cook this stew in the oven at 350°F for 1 1/2 hours.

COUNTRY CHOICE BEEF STEW

Makes 8 servings

When Mom made stew, which was often, the kitchen overflowed with the inviting smells of simmering vegetables and beef. She added rutabaga, white turnip, or cabbage, saying she liked their sharp tastes instead of the sweetness of onions, garlic, carrots, and parsnips. We kids complained, but she always responded, "It's my choice and I like them." I suspect the truth is that she had plenty on hand from the garden.

Choose any vegetables you like for this mouth-watering stew. The secret here is to add the peas (and cabbage, if that's your choice) near the end of the cooking time.

½ cup all-purpose flour

Salt

Freshly ground black pepper

One 2½-pound eye round, cut in 1½- to 2-inch cubes

2 tablespoons oil

1 clove garlic, minced

4 medium onions, cut in eighths

6 medium potatoes, cut in quarters

4 parsnips, cut in 2-inch pieces

6 medium carrots, cut in 2-inch pieces

6 whole cloves garlic, peeled

6 parsley stems

1½ cups beef broth, preferably Homemade Beef Stock (page 276) or Doctored Beef Broth (page 279), approximately

1½ cups water, approximately

Two 10-ounce packages frozen peas

1. Preheat the oven 350°F.

2. Combine the flour with a pinch of salt and a generous grinding of pepper. Roll the beef lightly in this mixture, shaking off any excess.

3. Heat the oil in a heavy flameproof casserole. Brown the meat over high heat, in batches if necessary, for 4 to 5 minutes. Reduce the heat to medium-high and add the minced garlic. Cook, stirring occasionally, for 2 minutes more. Add the onions, potatoes, parsnips, carrots, whole garlic, parsley stems, and cook, stirring occasionally, for 4 to 5 minutes longer.

4. Add equal amounts of broth and water to come to about an inch from the top of the meat and vegetables. Cover the casserole and bring to a boil on top of stove.

5. Place the casserole in the oven. After 1 hour, add the peas. Bake for another 30 minutes to 1 hour, or until the meat and vegetables are tender. Add salt and pepper to taste. Fish out the parsley stems before serving.

In New York City I can rarely find flavorful curly-leaf parsley like the kind we grew on the farm. So I use Italian flat-leaf parsley in all my cooking for its stronger, more pronounced taste.

CORN BELT STEW

Makes 8 to 10 servings

Liz Clark is a good friend, a fabulous cooking teacher, and an outstanding restaurateur. Her restaurant and school is located in a beautiful old Victorian house high on the banks of the Mississippi River, overlooking the locks in Keokuk, Iowa. Liz shared her mother's wonderful recipe for this Midwestern classic.

When I asked Liz, "Why black coffee?" she answered, "Any self-respecting farm woman always has the coffeepot on." I understood immediately. Like mine, her mother used what she had on hand.

The vegetables are sautéed with bay leaves and thyme, and the roux is prepared in the same pot, right in the center of the vegetables, eliminating another pot to wash.

Serve this marvelous stew with boiled potatoes.

> **1 cup plus 2 tablespoons all-purpose flour**
>
> **Salt**
>
> **Freshly ground black pepper**
>
> **3 pounds well-trimmed lean beef, such as eye round, cut in 2-inch cubes**
>
> **Olive oil to film skillet, plus 1 tablespoon**
>
> **3 large onions, diced**
>
> **6 carrots, peeled and cut in ¹/₂-inch rounds**
>
> **4 stalks celery, cut in ¹/₂-inch pieces**
>
> **¹/₄ pound mushrooms**
>
> **1 tablespoon butter**
>
> **1 cup strong black coffee**
>
> **3 bay leaves**
>
> **2 tablespoons fresh thyme leaves or 1 teaspoon dried**
>
> **4 cups beef broth, preferably Homemade Beef Stock (page 276) or Doctored Beef Broth (page 279)**

1. Combine 1 cup of the flour with a pinch of salt and a generous grinding of pepper. Roll the meat lightly in this mixture, shaking off any excess.

2. Film a large, heavy flameproof casserole with oil. Brown the beef in batches for 4 to 5 minutes over high heat. Remove the meat as it browns and set aside.

3. Reduce the heat to medium-high. Add the onions and cook, stirring, until soft and translucent, 2 to 3 minutes. Add the carrots, celery, and mushrooms and cook, stirring, for a couple of minutes more. Push the vegetables to the side of the casserole.

4. Add the butter, the remaining 1 tablespoon of oil, and the remaining 2 tablespoons of flour to the center of the casserole. Cook, stirring almost constantly, until the "roux" begins to brown, about 3 to 4 minutes.

5. Add the coffee and stir well. When the sauce has thickened, add the bay leaves, thyme, and broth. Return the meat to the pot, cover, and cook on the top of the stove until the meat is tender and the vegetables are cooked through, about 30 to 40 minutes. Add salt and pepper to taste.

RAGOUT OF LAMB WITH ROASTED PEPPERS AND MUSHROOMS

Begin one to two days in advance

Makes 10 to 12 servings

Ragout is a fancy name for stew, and this is a festive stew that isn't hard to make. Don't be put off by the steps; each one is uncomplicated. And remember, you're preparing this a day or two ahead, with nothing to do—to the stew, anyway—on the day of the party but pop it in the oven to heat.

Serve this ragout with brown rice, uncork a full-bodied red wine and— bon appétit!

Seasoning Mix

1 tablespoon dried rosemary

1 tablespoon *herbes de Provence*

1 tablespoon freshly ground black pepper

2 teaspoons coriander seed

4 pounds well-trimmed lamb cut from leg and cut in 2-inch cubes

5 large cloves garlic, minced

4 to 5 teaspoons olive oil, approximately

2 large onions, cut in large chunks

1 bottle (750 ml) full-bodied red wine (Burgundy is a good choice)

2¹⁄₃ cups beef broth, preferably Homemade Beef Stock (page 276) or Doctored Beef Broth (page 279), approximately

2 red bell peppers, cut in 1¹⁄₂-inch pieces

2 green bell peppers, cut in 1¹⁄₂-inch pieces

2 yellow bell peppers, cut in 1¹⁄₂-inch pieces

Pinch of salt

Generous grinding of black pepper

1 ½ pounds button mushrooms, cleaned (if large, cut in 1 ½-inch pieces)

3 tablespoons cornstarch

⅓ cup water

One to two days ahead

1. To prepare the seasoning mix, coarsely grind the rosemary, *herbes de Provence,* black pepper, and coriander seeds (see page 98). In a large bowl, toss the seasonings with the lamb and 3 cloves minced garlic. Cover, and refrigerate overnight or up to 2 days.

Before cooking

2. Preheat the oven to 350°F.

3. Film a large, heavy flameproof casserole with oil. Over high heat, brown the lamb cubes in batches for 4 to 5 minutes on all sides, removing them from the casserole as they brown.

4. Add 2 to 3 teaspoons of oil to the casserole and cook the onions, stirring, for 2 to 3 minutes, scraping up bits of meat and seasonings from the bottom of the pan as you stir. Add the remaining 2 cloves minced garlic and cook, stirring, for 1 to 2 minutes longer.

5. Add the lamb, red wine, and enough broth to come two-thirds of the way up the sides of the lamb cubes, about 2 cups. Cover the casserole and place it in the oven. Bake until the lamb is tender, about 45 minutes.

6. While the lamb is baking, place the red, green, and yellow peppers in a single layer on a foil-lined baking sheet. Sprinkle a bit of olive oil, salt, and black pepper over them. Roast along with the lamb, stirring the peppers occasionally, until they are lightly scorched at their edges and just tender, about 10 to 15 minutes. Remove the pepper pieces as they brown and set them aside in a bowl.

7. In a large, heavy skillet, heat 1 teaspoon of the olive oil. Add the mushrooms and sauté, stirring, over high heat until they "squeak," 3 to 4 minutes. Add the mushrooms and their juices to the bowl with the peppers.

8. Bring ⅓ cup beef broth to boil in the same skillet and stir occasionally to loosen any bits of mushroom stuck to the bottom of the pan. Add this to the mushrooms and peppers.

9. Strain the liquid from the cooked lamb into a saucepan and reduce by half over high heat to intensify the flavor. Taste and correct the seasonings. Stir the cornstarch and water together and add just enough to thicken the sauce so it coats the back of a spoon.

10. Combine the lamb, peppers, mushrooms and their juices, and thickened sauce in a large serving casserole.

The ragout can be prepared up to this point 1 to 2 days ahead.

11. Preheat the oven to 350°F.

12. Cover and bake until the ragout is heated through, about 1 hour. Taste and correct the seasonings.

Grinding Spices and Crushing Herbs

I grind my spices in a clean coffee grinder that I keep for that sole purpose. However, when I have only a small amount of spice to grind, I use a wooden mortar and pestle. I keep a small one next to my stove along with a ramekin of kosher salt and a pepper mill. Everything I need to quickly crush an herb or grind a spice is at my fingertips. There's no need to wash the mortar out every time, as the oils from one herb enhance the next.

A mini food processor works well too. Nor can you beat the old-fashioned method of crushing spices with a rolling pin or the bottom of a heavy skillet. Put the spices into a zipper-lock bag and crush them, and there's nothing to clean up.

I don't grind spices in my blender. When the oils are released, the spices sometimes stick to the bottom of the blender and create a pasty glob.

Before I add them to a dish, I crush dried herbs to release their oils and makes the flavors come alive. Try this: put a small amount of a dried herb in the palm of your hand and sniff; now rub your hands together and sniff again. You'll smell the difference.

Parsley helps dried herbs taste more like fresh. If a recipe calls for fresh herbs and all I have is dried, I add the dried herbs to the fresh parsley and chop them together.

BRAISED LAMB SHANKS

Makes 4 servings

In nearly every restaurant, especially in the fall and winter, the menu includes lamb shanks, and it's no wonder. They're economical, simple to make, and go well with any good red wine. That's a combination few restauranteurs can pass up!

Here is slow cooking at its best, giving the floral character of oregano enough time to do its magic by melding with the garlic, tomatoes, and vegetables to produce a deeply satisfying lamb dish.

4 small lamb shanks

Flour for dusting

Vegetable oil for filming casserole

1 large onion, coarsely chopped

2 stalks celery, cut in $^1/_3$-inch slices

2 medium carrots, cut in $^1/_3$-inch slices

2 medium potatoes, peeled and cut in 1-inch cubes

3 cloves garlic, minced

$^1/_2$ cup canned whole tomatoes with puree

$^1/_2$ cup full-bodied red wine

1 cup beef broth, preferably Homemade Beef Stock (page 276)

1 teaspoon dried oregano

$^1/_2$ teaspoon salt

$^1/_4$ teaspoon freshly ground black pepper

1. Preheat the oven to 400°F.

2. Dust the lamb shanks with flour. Film a large flameproof casserole with oil and brown the lamb over high heat. Set aside.

3. Reduce the heat to medium-high. Add the onion, celery, carrots, potatoes, and garlic. Cook, stirring, occasionally, for 3 to 4 minutes. Add the tomatoes with puree, wine, broth, oregano, salt, and pepper. Add the lamb shanks, burying them about halfway into the vegetables.

4. Cover the casserole and place it in the oven. Reduce the oven temperature to 350°F. Bake until the lamb is very tender, about 2 hours.

   The lamb can be cooked up to 3 days ahead, refrigerated, and reheated before serving.

LAMB CURRY AMBROSIA

Makes 12 servings

Surprisingly easy to make and with an astonishing explosion of fresh flavors, this dish will please even the most confirmed curry hater. A unique combination of seeds and spices flavors the lamb, which is simmered with chopped onion, apples, apricots, and raisins. Lemon slices are added as a counterpoint to the fruit's sweetness.

Serve with saffron rice, raita or plain yogurt, chopped scallions, pappadums, and assorted chutneys.

Curry Powder Ambrosia

¼ teaspoon cayenne pepper

1 teaspoon freshly ground black pepper

½ teaspoon cumin seed

1 teaspoon mustard seed

1 teaspoon poppy seed

1 teaspoon ground cardamom

½ teaspoon ground coriander

Pinch of ground cloves

¼ teaspoon ground cinnamon

1 bay leaf

3 large cloves garlic, minced

2 tablespoons minced fresh ginger

½ teaspoon salt

3 pounds well-trimmed boneless leg of lamb, cut in 1–inch cubes

1 tablespoon olive oil, approximately

3 large onions, chopped

2 large tart apples, peeled, cored, and chopped

1½ cups hot chicken broth, canned

1½ cups hot Homemade Beef Stock (page 276), Doctored Beef Broth (page 279), or canned beef broth

¹/₂ cup golden raisins

¹/₂ cup slivered dried apricots

1 lemon with its rind, thinly sliced and seeded

1. To make the curry powder, grind together the cayenne pepper, black pepper, cumin seeds, mustard seeds, poppy seeds, cardamom, coriander, cloves, cinnamon, and bay leaf.

2. Combine the curry powder with the garlic, ginger, and salt in a large bowl. Add the lamb and toss well. Cover and set aside at room temperature for 1 hour or refrigerate for 3 to 4 hours. Stir occasionally to make sure all surfaces of the lamb cubes are coated.

3. Film a large flameproof casserole with oil. Over high heat, brown the lamb and any loose seasonings for 4 to 5 minutes in batches, adding more oil as needed. Remove the meat and loose seasonings as they brown and set aside.

4. Add 1 teaspoon of oil to the casserole and heat over medium-high heat. Add the onions and apples and cook, stirring occasionally, until they begin to soften, 3 to 4 minutes. Add any spices that remain in the bowl in which the lamb was marinated, and cook for 4 to 5 minutes to bring out their flavors. Add the hot chicken and beef broths and bring to a boil, stirring occasionally.

5. Add the browned lamb, raisins, apricots, and half of the lemon slices and stir well. Cover and bring to a boil. Reduce the heat and simmer for 1 hour. Add the remaining lemon slices and cook until the lamb is tender and the sauce has thickened, about ¹/₂ to 1 hour more. Uncover for the last 20 minutes of cooking to reduce the sauce.

Tasty Tip

I usually make three to four times this amount of Curry Powder Ambrosia and use only 2 tablespoons for this recipe. I keep the rest on my spice shelf up to 1 month.

BEER-BRAISED COUNTRY PORK RIBS

Makes 8 sevings

Here's good news heading east from the Midwest. A new, lean cut of pork, called boneless country spareribs. It's for everyone who loves ribs but has stopped eating them for health reasons.

This streamlined recipe comes straight from my streamlined sister Judy, who makes these while she's out exercising. Sear the ribs, bake in beer, uncover, and slather with sauce.

In the summer I serve these with coleslaw, sliced tomatoes, and corn on the cob. In the winter I like them with roasted potatoes and steamed broccoli florets. You'll love 'em, too.

Vegetable oil to film skillet

3 pounds boneless country spare ribs, well trimmed

2 medium onions, sliced

One 12-ounce can beer

1 recipe Down-Home Country Barbecue Sauce (recipe follows) or your favorite brand

1. Preheat the oven to 325°F.

2. Film a heavy skillet with oil. Brown the ribs over high heat in batches on all sides for 7 minutes, removing the ribs to a baking pan as they brown.

3. Scatter the onions around the ribs. Pour the beer over the ribs and cover with aluminum foil, sealing tightly around the edges of the pan.

4. Bake until the pork is tender, 1½ to 2 hours. Remove and discard the onions and pour off the beer. Slather the pork with barbecue sauce and bake, uncovered, until the meat is brown and the sauce is thick, about 1 hour longer.

DOWN-HOME COUNTRY BARBECUE SAUCE

Makes approximately 2½ cups

You can't beat this quick and easy barbecue sauce for flavor or versatility. It takes only minutes to make. My mother and aunts used it on just about anything that came off the grill: ribs, chicken, steaks, London broil, and hamburgers.

During the summer I double or triple the recipe to have some on hand for last-minute cookouts.

1½ cups ketchup

3 tablespoons apple cider vinegar

1½ tablespoons brown sugar

1½ tablespoons Dijon mustard

1½ tablespoons dry mustard

3 tablespoons Worcestershire sauce

¾ teaspoon crushed red pepper flakes

¾ teaspoon freshly ground black pepper

¾ cup water

1½ teaspoons paprika

1½ teaspoons chili powder

Combine all the ingredients and bring to a boil. Reduce the heat and simmer for 15 minutes.

The sauce can be stored in a glass jar in the refrigerator for 3 to 4 weeks.

VINTAGE SAUERKRAUT, POTATOES, AND PORK

Makes 6 servings

This heirloom family recipe is one I ask Mom to make every time I visit. As a child, I loved to assist Grams as she shredded cabbage into a 30-gallon crock. I was the salt person, which meant every so often I sprinkled coarse salt on the cabbage. Then Grams set a handmade heavy wooden lid on top to weigh down the cabbage as it cured. Because this was "stinky business," the crock stayed outside under a big bush until the cabbage turned into sauerkraut, which took about 4 weeks.

Neither Mom nor I do this anymore. I buy a good-quality sauerkraut from Schaller & Weber, an old-time German butcher shop in New York City. You should be able to find good-quality sauerkraut in plastic bags near the deli section of your grocery store.

3 pounds shoulder pork roast with bones

1 teaspoon freshly ground black pepper

2 medium onions, chopped

1 to 1 1/2 quarts cold water, approximately

8 ounces good-quality sauerkraut

6 to 7 medium boiling potatoes, peeled and cut in quarters

Salt

Freshly ground black pepper

1. Place the pork in a large, heavy saucepan. Season with pepper. Add the onions and enough water to almost cover the pork. Cover and bring to a boil.

2. Reduce the heat and simmer until the meat falls off the bones, about 1 1/2 to 2 hours. Strain out the bones, fat, and meat. Cut the meat into small pieces and set aside. Discard the bones and fat.

3. Pour the cooking liquid through a strainer set over a large bowl. Let the liquid stand for 5 to 10 minutes to allow the fat to rise to the top. Skim off the fat.

4. Put the defatted liquid into a clean saucepan. Add the pork, sauerkraut, and potatoes. Cover and bring to a boil. Cook 20 to 30 minutes over moderate heat, until the potatoes are done. Season with salt and pepper to taste.

FRICASSEE OF BONELESS BRAZILIAN PORK

Makes 8 to 10 servings

Here cubed boneless pork is seasoned with pepper, sautéed, and then flavored with cumin, coriander, and garlic. The meat is simmered in white wine until it's tender. Lime slices and cilantro are added when the cooking's done for an original South American treat.

Serve on a cold winter night with black beans, saffron rice, and a leafy green salad. Or try this savory stewed pork over broad noodles with baked tomatoes on the side.

1 tablespoon oil

3 pounds well-trimmed boneless pork, cut in ³/₄-inch cubes

Freshly ground black pepper

1 cup dry white wine

2 teaspoons ground cumin

¹/₂ teaspoon ground coriander

1 large clove garlic, minced

1 teaspoon salt

8 thin slices of lime with rind

3 tablespoons chopped fresh cilantro

1. Heat the oil in a heavy flameproof casserole until very hot. Season the pork with pepper, and brown in batches for 2 to 3 minutes on all sides.

2. Drain off the excess oil, return the meat to the casserole, and add ³/₄ cup of the wine, the cumin, coriander, garlic, and salt. Bring to a boil. Reduce the heat, cover, and simmer for 20 to 25 minutes, until the meat is tender.

   The stew can be prepared to this point a day or two ahead. Cover and refrigerate.

3. Bring the stew to a boil. Uncover and add the remaining ¹/₄ cup wine and the lime slices. Simmer the stew over low heat, stirring frequently, until the juices reduce and begin to thicken, approximately 20 to 40 minutes, depending on how cold the stew is when you start. Add the cilantro and serve.

CLASSY WILD MUSHROOM VEAL BUNDLES

Makes 8 servings

Even though this recipe seems outrageously laborious, don't be put off. It's worth the effort for dinner guests who appreciate the finer things in life, such as woodsy wild mushrooms combined with the complex flavors of salty prosciutto, sweet shallots, anise-like tarragon, full-bodied, oaky chardonnay wine, a whisper of garlic, tender veal, and the time it takes to pack and roll each bundle.

Serve the bundles on a bed of fluffy rice pilaf, accompanied by a medley of garden-fresh baby vegetables.

Stuffing

- 1/2 ounce dried mushrooms (preferably porcini)
- 1/2 teaspoon unsalted butter
- 2 tablespoons olive oil
- 6 medium shallots, chopped (about 1/2 cup)
- 1 small clove garlic, minced
- 2 ounces prosciutto, julienned
- 1/2 cup chopped fresh parsley
- 1 teaspoon chopped fresh tarragon
- 1/2 teaspoon salt
- 1 to 1 1/2 teaspoons freshly ground black pepper
- 1 pound fresh mushrooms (portobello, cremini, chanterelle, oyster, shiitake, or a combination), coarsely chopped

- 16 veal scallops
- 2 to 3 cups milk to soak veal
- 1 tablespoon olive oil
- 2 carrots, peeled and chopped
- 2 stalks celery, chopped
- 1 medium onion, chopped
- 1 clove garlic, minced

1 cup white wine (I like Chardonnay), approximately

1 cup Homemade Veal Stock (page 281) or Homemade Beef Stock (page 276), approximately

1. To make the stuffing, soak the dried mushrooms in 1 cup of tepid water for 1 hour. Drain the mushrooms and chop. Discard the soaking water or reserve for another use.

2. In a large, heavy skillet, heat the butter and 1 tablespoon of the olive oil over medium heat. Add the shallots and garlic and cook, stirring, for 4 to 5 minutes, until the shallots are soft and translucent. Add the soaked dried mushrooms, prosciutto, parsley, tarragon, salt, and pepper and continue to cook for 1 to 2 minutes. Remove the mixture from the skillet and set aside.

3. Raise the heat to high and add the remaining tablespoon of olive oil to the same skillet. Add the fresh mushrooms and sauté, stirring occasionally, until the mushrooms have released their juices, about 5 minutes. Add the shallot mixture to the mushrooms and sauté for 1 to 2 minutes more. Taste and correct the seasonings.

    The stuffing can be refrigerated for several days or frozen for up to 1 month.

4. Pound the veal scallops between sheets of plastic wrap until thin. Cover with milk and soak for at least 2 hours or overnight in the refrigerator. Rinse off the milk and pat the veal dry with paper towels.

5. Spread 1 heaping tablespoon of the mushroom stuffing over each veal scallop. Tuck in the sides and roll into bundles. Secure with round wooden toothpicks or tie with cotton kitchen string.

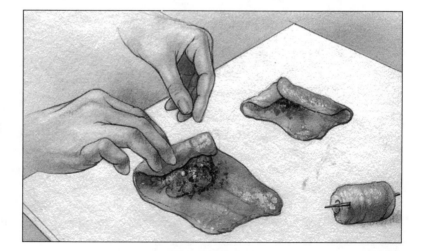

(1) Spread a tablespoon of stuffing on each scallop.
(2) Fold the top and both sides in toward the center and roll into a bundle.
(3) Secure with a wooden toothpick.

6. In a heavy flameproof casserole over high heat, brown the veal bundles on all sides in the oil. Remove as they brown and set aside. Add the carrots, celery, onion, and garlic to the casserole. Cook for 1 or 2 minutes, stirring occasionally.

7. Preheat the oven to 325°F.

8. Arrange the veal bundles on top of the vegetables. Add equal parts of the wine and stock until the liquid comes about one-third of the way up the sides of the veal bundles. Cover and heat on top of the stove just until bubbles break the surface.

9. Place the casserole in the oven. Bake, covered, until the veal is tender and the juices run clear when the veal is pierced with a fork, about 1 hour.

10. Transfer the veal bundles to a plate and remove the toothpicks or string. Strain the cooking liquid into a saucepan and discard the vegetables. Bring the cooking liquid to a boil over high heat and reduce to half its original amount. If desired, thicken until the sauce coats the back of a metal spoon (see page 80).

   Return the bundles to the sauce. The veal can be prepared up to this point and, if desired, covered and refrigerated for up to 2 days.

11. Gently reheat the veal bundles in the sauce. Arrange the bundles on a serving platter and nap each bundle with a bit of sauce. Serve any remaining sauce in a small pitcher.

 **Tasty Tip** Use only round toothpicks when skewering these veal bundles—or any meat. Flat toothpicks have an unpleasant tendency to break.

VEAL RAGOUT

Makes 8 servings

This simple recipe is wonderful for a dinner party, as the presentation gives it great panache. Your guests will think you've slaved for hours.

To the classic combination of veal with tarragon, shallots, and wine, I have added new potatoes and baby carrots, which not only impart extra flavor but make the dish a complete dinner-in-a-pot.

Steam fresh asparagus and arrange them around the edges of a large platter. Spoon the ragout into the center and nap the whole platter with the sauce.

½ cup all-purpose flour

1 teaspoon freshly ground black pepper

1½ teaspoons dried tarragon

Vegetable oil to film casserole

3 pounds lean veal, cut in large cubes

1 to 2 teaspoons butter or additional oil,
approximately

6 shallots, chopped

1 small bunch fresh parsley, chopped

½ cup white wine

1¾ cups Homemade Veal Stock (page 281),
Homemade Beef Stock (page 276), or Doctored
Beef Broth (page 279), approximately

1 bay leaf

1 pound baby carrots, peeled

16 new potatoes, unpeeled, cut in half

1. Preheat the oven to 350°F.

2. Combine the flour, pepper, and ½ teaspoon of the tarragon. Dredge the veal in the seasoned flour and shake off any excess.

3. Film a heavy flameproof casserole with oil. Brown the veal in batches over high heat for 4 to 5 minutes and set aside.

4. Add the butter or oil to the casserole and cook the shallots and parsley, stirring, over medium heat until the shallots are soft, 4 to 5 minutes. Add the wine and cook to reduce until syrupy, occasionally scraping up the bits of browned meat and flour from the bottom of the pan, 5 to 6 minutes.

5. Return the veal to the casserole. Add the broth, bay leaf, and remaining 1 teaspoon of tarragon. Cover and place the casserole in the oven. Bake until the veal is almost tender, about 30 minutes.

6. Add the carrots and potatoes, cover, and bake until the vegetables are cooked through and the veal is tender, about 30 minutes more. Thicken the sauce if desired (see page 80).

TRADITIONAL OSSO BUCCO

Makes 6 servings

In this classic Italian dish the rich flavor of the meaty veal shank comes from braising on a bed of sautéed carrots, celery, onion, and garlic and seasoning with lemon, tomatoes, basil, and thyme.

The gremolata—*chopped fresh garlic, parsley, and lemon zest—is like the frosting on a cake, not to be skipped. These flavors mingle to create a marvelous dish that can easily be prepared ahead of time and reheated. For a real treat, encourage your guests to scoop out the marrow from the center of each bone. Following tradition, I always serve risotto with osso bucco.*

Gremolata

Zest of 1 lemon (see Tasty Tip below)

3 tablespoons chopped fresh parsley

1 1/2 teaspoons minced garlic

1 teaspoon butter

3 to 4 teaspoons olive oil, approximately

1/2 cup chopped carrots

1/2 cup chopped celery

1 large leek (white part only), chopped, or 1 cup chopped onions

1 clove garlic, minced

6 meaty 2-inch-thick slices of veal shank

1/2 cup all-purpose flour, approximately

1/2 teaspoon salt

1 teaspoon freshly ground black pepper

1 cup white wine, approximately

1 teaspoon minced lemon zest (see Tasty Tip below)

One 14-ounce can chopped tomatoes or 4 peeled, seeded, and chopped fresh tomatoes

1/2 teaspoon dried basil

1/2 teaspoon dried thyme

1 cup beef broth, preferably Homemade Beef Stock (page 276), approximately

1 bay leaf

3 sprigs fresh parsley

1. Preheat the oven to 350°F.

2. Prepare the gremolata by combining the lemon zest, parsley, and garlic. Set aside.

3. Heat the butter and 1 teaspoon of the olive oil in a heavy flameproof casserole over medium-high heat and cook the carrots, celery, and leek or onions, stirring, until they are soft and translucent, 3 to 5 minutes. Add the garlic and cook, stirring, for a minute or two longer. Set aside.

4. Tie each slice of veal shank tightly around its circumference with cotton kitchen string. Combine the flour, salt, and pepper. Dredge the veal shanks in the flour mixture.

5. Film a nonstick skillet with olive oil and sauté the veal in batches over high heat until brown on both sides, about 3 minutes for each side. Remove the meat as it browns and transfer it to the casserole, burying the pieces halfway into the vegetables.

6. Deglaze the skillet by adding a splash of wine and stirring to release any bits of meat that may have stuck to the pan. Pour these juices over the veal. Add the lemon zest, tomatoes, basil, and thyme. Add equal amounts of wine and broth until the liquid comes almost to the top of the veal shanks. Add the bay leaf and parsley, cover and bring to a simmer on top of the stove.

7. Transfer the casserole to the oven and cook until the veal is very tender and beginning to come away from the bone, about 2 hours. Remove the bay leaf and parsley sprigs and discard.

   Place a dollop of gremolata atop each piece of veal just before serving.

I use a vegetable peeler to remove only the colored outer rind, called the zest, of lemons, oranges, grapefruits, and limes, leaving the bitter white pith on the fruit.

If the zest is to be blanched, drop it into boiling water for 1 or 2 minutes. Remove the peel from the water and pat it dry with paper towels. Then chop or cut the zest as called for in the recipe.

AMERICAN OSSO BUCCO

Makes 6 servings

I have Americanized a traditional jewel, the revered Italian classic osso bucco. I dust the sliced veal shanks with cornmeal, use parsnip in the vegetable mixture, and add orange zest, coriander, thyme, and cumin to create a delicious and unique new dish.

For the garnish I've added fresh cilantro and orange zest to chopped garlic and parsley.

Orange-Herb Garnish

1 tablespoon minced orange zest (see Tasty Tip, page 111)

1¹/₂ teaspoons minced garlic

1 tablespoon chopped fresh parsley

2 tablespoons chopped fresh cilantro

4 teaspoons olive oil, approximately

1 medium onion, chopped

1 carrot, chopped

1 parsnip, chopped

1 large stalk celery, chopped

4 cloves garlic, minced

6 meaty 2-inch-thick slices of veal shanks

¹/₂ cup cornmeal, approximately

Pinch of salt

¹/₂ teaspoon freshly ground black pepper

1 teaspoon minced orange zest (see Tasty Tip, page 111)

¹/₂ teaspoon ground coriander

¹/₂ teaspoon dried thyme

¹/₂ teaspoon ground cumin

1 bay leaf

1 ½ cups full-bodied red wine, approximately

1 ½ cups beef broth, preferably Homemade Beef Stock (page 276), approximately

Salt (optional)

1. Preheat the oven to 350°F.

2. Prepare the Orange-Herb Garnish by combining the orange zest, garlic, parsley, and cilantro. Set aside.

3. Heat 1 to 2 teaspoons of the olive oil in a heavy flameproof casserole over medium-high heat and cook the onion, carrot, parsnip, and celery, stirring, until they are soft and become translucent, 8 to 10 minutes. Add the garlic and cook, stirring, for a minute or two longer.

4. Tie each slice of veal shank tightly around its circumference with cotton kitchen string. Combine the cornmeal, salt, and pepper. Dredge the veal shanks in the cornmeal mixture.

5. Heat 1 to 2 teaspoons of the olive oil in a nonstick skillet. Sauté the veal in batches over high heat until brown on both sides, about 3 minutes for each side. Remove the meat as it browns and transfer it to the casserole, burying the pieces halfway into the vegetables.

6. Add the orange zest, coriander, thyme, cumin, and bay leaf. Add equal amounts of the wine and broth until the liquid reaches almost to the top of the veal. Cover and bring to a simmer.

7. Transfer the casserole to the oven and cook until the veal is very tender and beginning to come away from the bone, about 2 hours. Taste, add salt if needed, and correct the seasonings.

Place a dollop of Orange-Herb Garnish atop each piece of veal just before serving.

Tasty Tip

Whether or not you add salt to your stew depends on the kind of broth you are using, as well as on your taste. You'll likely want to add at least a pinch if you've used an unsalted homemade broth. However, if you've added canned broth to your stew, you may not need additional salt, as most canned broths are already quite salty.

BLACK-TIE VEAL RAGOUT

Makes 8 servings

After winning a case of fine red wine and a private screening for 55 at Warner Bros.' studio from my son's nursery school auction, my good friend and fellow party lover, Lorraine Zitone, and I decided to throw a black-tie dinner party after the screening.

We decorated in black and white—black candles, white tablecloths, black-and-white napkins, black plates, and all white flowers in black baskets.

We started with a green salad, then served this elegant ragout with a white- and wild-rice pilaf along with a red wine. For dessert I served espresso coffee and a chocolate torte filled with whipped cream and topped by fresh strawberries.

Prepare the ragout ahead, then finish the sauce just before serving.

2¹/₂ pounds lean veal, cut in 1¹/₂-inch cubes

1 teaspoon butter

2 teaspoons oil

1 medium onion, finely chopped

1 large clove garlic, minced

1 teaspoon salt

¹/₂ teaspoon freshly ground black pepper

¹/₂ teaspoon dried tarragon

1 pound mushrooms, sliced

Two 8–ounce cans water chestnuts, drained and cut in quarters

1 bay leaf

1¹/₂ to 2 cups Homemade Veal Stock (page 281) or Homemade Beef Stock (page 276)

1 teaspoon cornstarch

¹/₂ cup half-and-half

¹/₄ cup cognac

¹/₄ cup chopped fresh parsley

1. In a large pot, cover the veal with cold water. Bring to a boil over high heat, then reduce the heat and slow-simmer for 1 to 2 minutes. Drain the veal in a colander and rinse with cold water to remove the scum. Pat the meat dry with paper towels.

2. Preheat the oven to 325°F.

3. Heat the butter and oil over high heat in a large, heavy flameproof casserole. Brown the meat in batches for 2 to 3 minutes on all sides. Remove the meat as it browns and set aside.

4. In the same casserole, cook the onion and garlic, stirring occasionally, over medium heat until soft and translucent, 3 to 4 minutes. Return the veal to the casserole and season with salt, pepper, and tarragon. Add the mushrooms and water chestnuts and cook, stirring, for a minute or two longer. Add the bay leaf and enough broth to come about one-third of the way up the sides of the veal. Cover and bring to a simmer.

5. Place the casserole in the oven and cook until the veal is tender, about 40 minutes. Remove the casserole from the oven. Transfer the meat and vegetables to a bowl and set aside. Discard the bay leaf.

6. Bring the cooking liquid to a boil and reduce by half. Taste and correct the seasonings. Cool to room temperature, then pour the sauce over the veal, mushrooms, and water chestnuts.

   The stew can be prepared to this point 1 or 2 days ahead and refrigerated.

7. Reheat the stew in the casserole by slowly bringing it to a simmer. Using a small wire whisk, mix the cornstarch into the half-and-half and add this to the stew. Bring to a boil, then simmer for 3 to 4 minutes. Slowly whisk in the cognac and continue to cook over low heat until bubbles barely break the surface. Serve piping hot.

NEW YORK CITY VENISON STEW

Begin one to three days in advance

Makes 8 servings, with leftovers

No, we don't have herds of deer in the city, but venison is becoming so popular you can order it from most butchers. Because venison is low in fat, it's imperative to cook it fast and serve it rare, or cook it very slowly, as in this stew.

If you have doubts about the accuracy of your oven temperature, this is a good time to check it with an oven thermometer and adjust the setting. It's important that this stew simmer so slowly that the bubbles barely break the surface.

In case you wonder why I use bacon, the little fat it adds (most of the fat is discarded) keeps the meat tender, and the faint smoky flavor is just right for a game meat. Tenderizing and adding flavor to venison begins with a long period of marinating in orange zest, coriander, allspice, pepper, garlic, onion, and wine.

This fantastic-tasting stew is as diversified as New York City. After a salad for the first course, I serve it on a bed of brown rice that's been cooked in chicken broth.

3 to 3½ pounds venison, cut in 2-inch cubes

Zest of 1 large orange, blanched and minced (see Tasty Tip, page 111)

3 tablespoons coarsely ground coriander seed

1 teaspoon whole allspice, crushed

2 teaspoons freshly ground black pepper

3 large cloves garlic, minced

1 small onion, sliced

1 bottle (750 ml) full-bodied red wine, approximately

Olive oil to film skillet

4 ounces thickly sliced bacon, cut in ¼-inch strips

1 large leek, sliced

One 10½-ounce can Campbell's beef broth, undiluted

1 pound carrots, peeled, cut in 2-inch lengths

3 medium parsnips, peeled, cut in 2-inch lengths

Leaves of 1 bunch cilantro, minced

One to three days ahead

1. In a large nonreactive bowl, combine the venison, orange zest, corian-der, allspice, pepper, garlic, and onion. Toss well to coat all the surfaces of the venison. Add enough wine just to cover the meat. Cover the bowl tightly with plastic wrap and refrigerate at least 1 day, or even better, up to 3 days, stirring the meat occasionally.

Before braising

2. Drain the marinade and set aside. Pat the meat gently with paper towels, being careful not to remove the bits of orange peel and seasonings that cling to the meat.

3. Preheat the oven to 325°F.

4. Heat the oil in a heavy flameproof casserole until very hot. Film the skillet with oil. Sear the venison in batches for 2 to 3 minutes until brown on all sides. Set aside.

5. Reduce the heat to medium and sauté the bacon until cooked but not crisp. Drain the bacon and set aside along with the venison. Discard the excess grease but do not wash the casserole.

6. Add the leek, reserved marinade, venison, bacon, and broth to the casserole. Add enough red wine to barely cover the meat. Cover and bring to a simmer on top of the stove. Place the casserole in the oven and reduce the temperature to 300°F. Cook, covered, for 2 hours.

7. Remove the casserole from the oven. Add the carrots and parsnips. Stir. Return the casserole to the oven and cook until the carrots are tender, for about 1½ hours longer. Sprinkle with the cilantro and serve.

COUNTRY VENISON STEW

Makes 8 servings

Here's another of the wonderful recipes Liz Clark shared with me. Actually, it's a simplified adaptation of her recipe.

Liz makes puff pastry, cuts it to fit the baking dish that will hold the venison stew, places it over the stew, brushes it with an egg wash, and then bakes her "venison pie" until the top is puffed and brown. (I don't bother with a topping, but if you want one, frozen puff pastry is available at most supermarkets.)

In this simplified version the venison is quickly browned. Aromatic bay leaves and thyme flavor the onion, garlic, and celery base. Mushrooms, carrots, parsnips, and turnips complete the vegetables. Red wine and beef broth make the sauce, and the stew is thickened before baking.

2 pounds venison sirloin, cut in 1-inch cubes

2 tablespoons olive oil

4 bay leaves

1 tablespoon dried thyme

4 medium onions, diced

6 cloves garlic, minced

4 stalks celery, diced

$1/2$ pound mushrooms, quartered

4 medium carrots, cut in $1/2$-inch slices

4 parsnips, cut in $1/2$-inch slices

4 medium turnips, cut in $1/2$-inch dice

$1/2$ cup dry red wine

$3/4$ cup beef broth, preferably Homemade Beef Stock (page 276) or Doctored Beef Broth (page 279)

2 tablespoons cornstarch

$1/2$ cup cold water

Salt

Freshly ground black pepper

1. In a large, heavy flameproof casserole, sauté the venison in 2 teaspoons of the olive oil over high heat. As soon as the meat is browned, about 2 to 3 minutes, remove it with a slotted spoon and set aside.

2. Add the bay leaves and thyme to the casserole. Add 2 teaspoons of the remaining olive oil and cook the onions, garlic, and celery, stirring, until soft, about 3 to 4 minutes. Remove the onion mixture from the casserole and set aside.

3. Add 1 teaspoon of the remaining olive oil and cook the mushrooms, stirring, until soft, 4 to 5 minutes. Remove the mushrooms and set aside.

4. Add the remaining 1 teaspoon of oil and cook the carrots, parsnips, and turnips, stirring, until they begin to soften, about 3 to 4 minutes. Remove the vegetables from the casserole and add the red wine. Bring to a boil and scrape up any bits and pieces. Add the broth and heat. Stir in the venison and all the vegetables and bring to a boil.

5. Preheat the oven to 350°F.

6. Mix the cornstarch with the cold water. Stir into the hot venison stew and boil until the liquid thickens. Add salt and freshly ground pepper to taste.

7. Place the casserole in the oven and bake, covered, until the meat is tender and the vegetables are cooked through, about 30 minutes.

chapter 4

SAUTÉS: A FLASH IN THE PAN

I've often entertained the dream of owning a snazzy restaurant and being the sauté chef. Around me would be bowls filled with ingredients—stocks and broths, demi-glaces, seasoning pastes, herbs and spices—all prepared by assistant cooks.

Picture this—I'm to sauté veal chops for a party of four. The flames of my six-burner professional range leap high in the air. The chops take a short time to sear, and because they're thick—as they would be in a fine restaurant like mine—I flame them with a splash of cognac, transfer them onto a sizzle platter, and fire them in a 500°F oven to finish.

I quickly sauté herbs and exotic wild mushrooms. I ladle demi-glace over the mushrooms, taste it—ah, heaven! I place the perfect chops on hot plates and nap them with *marchand de vin*. They're rushed to the table by a waiter in a white jacket and black tie. I love this fantasy!

The reality ain't all that bad either. Sautéing—fast frying in a small amount of oil—really is quick and easy. It's the ideal technique for the modern-day home cook because more of us are eating on the run. Plus, it's a snap to make great sauces, even without your own staff, with excellent-quality mail-order demi-glace (see page 282)—unless you happen to keep *glace-de-viande* in your refrigerator or homemade stock in your freezer.

If you don't even have the time to cut up your own vegetables, supermarkets sell packaged and washed small portions of fresh lettuce, cauliflower florets, trimmed green beans, cut vegetables, and baby carrots. Be sure to use the best-quality ingredients you can afford. Tender chops and steaks, fresh vegetables, and the highest-quality condiments—you'll taste the difference.

One of my professional gigs is being a private dining-room chef. So my dream has come true, and it's better than owning a restaurant. My client likes steaks, chops, sautéed medallions of beef and pork, and veal scallops with intriguing sauces. I cook meals for him and his guests in my kitchen and carry them in containers to the kitchenette behind the executive dining room, where I reheat the dishes in a microwave oven.

You might think it requires substantial skill to create a "just-sautéed" chop when you've cooked it hours earlier. Truth is, it's easy.

Tricks for Reheating Food in a Microwave Oven

1. *Undercook the food so that when you reheat it, the food is correctly cooked.*

2. *Be sure the food is at room temperature before it goes into the microwave. It will take less time and cook more evenly.*

3. *Cover the container or plate with plastic wrap.*

4. *Heat the food for only a short period of time. Check to see how hot it's become (usually I do this by touching the bottom of the container), then continue to heat for another few seconds before checking again. For example, when warming thin slices of meat like veal scallops, heat them only 10 to 15 seconds. If the veal needs to be heated further, turn on the microwave for another few seconds and check again. I might heat a couple of chops for 30 seconds, check them, then heat them 10 or 15 seconds more before I check again.*

5. *To heat the food evenly, turn the dish or container on which you are heating the food frequently.*

6. *If there's a sauce to go over the meat, heat it in a separate container. I want the sauce to be very hot, but I don't want to overcook the meat.*

This approach also works for the hostess who wants everything done before her guests arrive. Dinner is prepared ahead of time; the kitchen is cleaned. After your guests are seated at the table, you pop the chops into the microwave oven. It looks easy—and it is.

Many of my students find the idea of putting an expensive veal chop or a filet mignon in a microwave oven an outrage. I tell them to try it—it works.

When I sauté, I rely on two kinds of skillets, my nonstick and my well-seasoned, old-fashioned cast-iron skillet. When I want to be sure the meat is well seared over high heat and has a nice crust, I turn to my cast-iron skillet. First I heat it; then I sprinkle a pinch of coarse salt over the bottom, which will produce a rich, brown crust. (If you're on a strict salt-restricted diet, you can sear meat without the salt. A very hot well-seasoned cast-iron skillet alone will sear the meat and form a crust—although that crust won't be quite as thick or rich as the one seared with salt.)

Having the cast-iron skillet well seasoned is the key to its effectiveness. I still use many of my grandmother's 100-year-old black skillets—and I still season them much as she did.

How to Season and Care For a Cast-Iron Skillet

1. *Preheat the oven to 350°F.*

2. *If the skillet is dirty, scour it to remove rust and caked-on dirt. To dry, heat the skillet on top of the stove.*

3. *Pour an inch or so of vegetable oil into the skillet, tilting the skillet to coat the sides. When the skillet is hot, place it in the oven for at least 1 hour. Remove the skillet from the oven, pour out the oil, and allow it to cool enough to handle safely.*

4. *Generously sprinkle the inside of the skillet (bottom and sides) with coarse salt. Using a couple of paper towels and plenty of elbow grease, scrub the inside of the skillet with the salt. Wipe out the salt, and the skillet is seasoned.*

5. *After cooking with your seasoned skillet, do not scour it. Instead, immediately after using it, wash it with soap and water, rinse it well, and heat it on top of the stove to dry it.*

6. *The skillet will need no other attention until food burns or sticks to it; that's when you season it again.*

Many sauté pans and skillets have handles that can't go into the oven. For these, clean them as described in step 2, pour in 1 inch of oil and heat over high heat until the surface of the oil begins to shimmer. Reduce the heat to low and continue to heat the skillet for 10 to 15 minutes, keeping the oil hot enough to continue shimmering. Follow steps 4, 5, and 6 above.

Both cast-iron and nonstick skillets can be used for any kind of sautéing. However, if I'm going to sauté a few vegetables such as garlic and onions to enrich a sauce, I use a nonstick skillet so that I can brown the vegetables with only a small amount of oil. Also, if I'm adding wine, I can prepare the sauce in the same skillet. (Wine and tomatoes shouldn't be cooked in cast iron because they can react chemically, changing their color and taste. Nonstick skillets are nonreactive.)

I rarely sauté when cooking for more than eight because I find juggling the timing and the number of skillets needed impractical, but any of the recipes in this chapter can be made for more or fewer people. Just scale them up or down. Use them to guide you, and as you gain confidence, let your taste buds and imagination take over.

FRENCH STUFFED SHELL STEAKS

BRANDY SNIFTER T-BONE STEAKS

HERB BEEF TOURNEDOS

MODERN STEAK AU POIVRE

MODERN PEPPERCORN MIX

JAPANESE-STYLE SIRLOIN STEAK

BIG-CITY SICHUAN BEEF

MODERN ORANGE BEEF

NEW MEXICAN FARM STAND BURRITOS

SUNFLOWER SEED–CRUSTED LAMB CHOPS

CORIANDER-SCENTED LAMB CHOPS

LAMB CHOP PARCELS

STUFFED LAMB CHOPS WITH SAUCE MADEIRA

SEARED PORK CHOPS BAKED WITH PEPPERS AND ONIONS

FRUIT-AND-NUT-STUFFED DOUBLE PORK CHOPS

MEXICAN STUFFED PORK CHOPS

PORK CHOPS FLAMBÉ

PORK MEDALLIONS WITH TOMATO CREAM

SWEET-AND-SOUR PORK

CRUSTY CORIANDER PAN-SEARED VEAL CHOPS

PORK RIBBONS WITH GARDEN TABBOULEH

JUNIPER BERRY VEAL CHOPS

TOMATO-KISSED VEAL CHOPS

VEAL CHOPS MARTINI

WILD MUSHROOM AND VEAL SCALLOP SAUTÉ

NEW BERLIN-STYLE VEAL SCALLOPS

LEMON TREE VEAL SCALLOPS

VEAL PUTTANESCA

ROSEMARY- AND GARLIC-INFUSED VENISON CHOPS

IMPROVISATIONAL CHOPS AND STEAKS

MARINATED VENISON CHOPS WITH HUNTER'S SAUCE

FRENCH STUFFED SHELL STEAKS

Makes 6 servings

Every now and then I invite friends and business associates to my cooking school for a dinner party. I plan the menu so that some dishes are done ahead of time. Usually a cold fish dish or interesting salad starts the meal, and vegetables and potatoes accompany the main course. However, I cook the entree in front of my guests as they eat their first course. They love it, and being a natural performer, I love it too.

The classic French combination of ham, shallots, and tarragon makes a savory stuffing for the tender, flavorful shell steaks. Make the stuffing ahead and freeze the leftovers. All that's left to do is fill the pockets and sear the steaks. These steaks can also be cooked on the grill.

I always garnish the plates with watercress and serve the steaks with roasted or au gratin potatoes, steamed broccoli florets or a seasonal green vegetable, and—yes, a chocolate cake with raspberry sauce for dessert.

Stuffing

1 teaspoon olive oil

1 teaspoon butter

3 shallots, minced

1/3 cup chopped ham

3 medium mushrooms, chopped

2 tablespoons chopped fresh parsley

1 teaspoon dried tarragon

Freshly ground black pepper

6 small well-trimmed 1- to 1 1/2-inch-thick shell steaks, with pockets cut for stuffing

Pinch of coarse salt

1. To prepare the stuffing, heat the oil and butter in a nonstick skillet. Cook the shallots over medium-high heat until soft, 3 to 4 minutes. Add the ham and mushrooms. Cook, stirring frequently, for 1 to 2 minutes. When the liquid has evaporated, add the parsley, tarragon, and pepper to taste. Allow the stuffing to cool.

2. Put a teaspoon or two of the stuffing into the pocket of each steak and press the edges together to seal. Season the steaks with additional pepper.

3. Heat a cast-iron skillet and sprinkle lightly with salt (or film a non-stick skillet with oil). Sauté the steaks over high heat for 4 to 5 minutes on each side for medium rare, or until done to your taste.

Holding one hand flat on top as a guide, insert the tip of the knife into the center of the steak and cut a deep slit, leaving the meat around three sides of the chop uncut. (See Tasty Tip below.)

To cut a pocket in a steak or a chop, place the trimmed meat flat on a cutting board. Place one hand flat on top to hold it in place. Holding a small sharp knife horizontally in your dominant hand, insert the tip of the knife halfway between the top and bottom of the meat (that is, if the steak is $1^{1}/_{2}$ inches thick, insert the knife $^{3}/_{4}$ inch from the bottom and the top). Carefully cut a deep slit into the center of the meat, leaving about $^{1}/_{3}$ inch of uncut meat around 3 sides.

BRANDY SNIFTER T-BONE STEAKS

Makes 6 servings

The light, lemony mint of thyme combines with brandy and fresh orange juice to make a fruity marinade for one of America's most often asked for steaks, the T-bone. These steaks cook quickly because the bone conducts the heat well.

6 small (or 3 large) well-trimmed T-bone steaks, edges scored

2 teaspoons dried thyme

Freshly ground black pepper

¼ cup brandy

Juice of ½ orange (approximately ¼ cup)

1 teaspoon olive oil

Pinch of coarse salt

1. Place the steaks in a nonreactive dish. Rub them with thyme and pepper and then drizzle with brandy, orange juice, and olive oil. Let stand at room temperature for at least 30 minutes.

2. Remove the steaks from the marinade, discard the marinade, and pat the steaks dry with paper towels. Heat a well-seasoned cast-iron skillet until very hot and sprinkle lightly with salt (or film a nonstick skillet with oil). Sear the steaks until browned, 3 to 4 minutes on each side, or until done to your taste.

To score the edges, slash the outside membrane of the steak or chop every inch or so.

If you want a sauce, remove the steaks from the pan, add the marinade, and bring it to a boil. Reduce it by half and spoon it on the meat. Garnish the plate with a sprig of fresh thyme from your herb garden.

I use a trick that I learned from my good friend Carolyn Buster, former owner and chef of The Cottage Restaurant in Calumet City, Illinois—sprinkle a hot, heavy skillet with a pinch of coarse salt before searing the meat. This not only eliminates the need for fat but keeps the crust on the chop, where it belongs.

HERB BEEF TOURNEDOS

Makes 8 servings

One of my students thought I was saying "tornadoes," as in big wind, rather than the French tournedos, the cut we Americans call filet mignon. I wondered if she'd arrived with Dorothy and Toto from Kansas. However, I liked that image for this dish, as it's elegant, dramatic, and takes only minutes to make.

Thaw a box of frozen baby peas and "cook" them under hot running water. Whip up wild rice from a mix—unless you've had the foresight to make a wild rice pilaf the day before, in which case simply reheat it. A whirlwind dinner!

2 teaspoons dried thyme

2 teaspoons dried basil

2 teaspoons dried marjoram

1 teaspoon freshly ground black pepper

Eight 1-inch-thick filet mignons, edges scored, tied

Pinch of coarse salt

1 to 2 teaspoons olive oil

3 to 4 shallots, chopped

¼ cup cognac (optional)

1 cup beef broth, preferably Homemade Beef Stock (page 276)

1. Crush the thyme, basil, marjoram, and pepper. Rub into both sides of the steaks.

2. Heat a nonstick skillet until very hot and sprinkle it lightly with salt. Sear the steaks for 3 to 4 minutes on each side, until browned but slightly undercooked. Remove the strings and set aside.

3. Heat the oil in same skillet over medium-high heat and cook the shallots until tender, about 2 minutes. Deglaze the skillet by adding the cognac and scraping up any bits of meat that are stuck to the bottom of the skillet. Add the broth and boil over high heat for about 5 minutes, until the sauce is reduced by half. Taste and correct the seasonings. Return the steaks to the sauce and heat for 2 to 3 minutes to complete the cooking.

Tie cotton kitchen string firmly around the center of each tournedo.

I often use a splatter shield, a fine-mesh screen lid, when pan-frying to eliminate splatters.

MODERN STEAK AU POIVRE

Makes 6 servings

One of the first recipes I taught at Cooking With Class was classic steak au poivre, seasoned with black and white cracked peppercorns and served with a sauce of shallots, brandy, and a stick or two of sweet butter to finish the sauce.

As my tastes changed, I eliminated the butter. Then I got rid of the shallots and brandy. Next I made the pepper mixture even more fiery. Finally I began to use a cast-iron skillet sprinkled with a pinch of coarse salt to pan-sear the steaks.

After it's cooked, the steak should be allowed to rest for at least 6 to 8 minutes before you slice it. While I occasionally embellish it with sauce, I usually prefer to serve it simply with the pan juices, a salad, and French fries or a baked potato.

1 1/2 tablespoons black peppercorns (see next recipe)

1/2 tablespoon white peppercorns

1/4 teaspoon juniper berries

1/4 teaspoon crushed red pepper flakes

One 2- to 2 1/2-pound 1-inch-thick boneless sirloin steak, edges scored (see illustration, page 127)

Pinch of coarse salt

2/3 cup beef broth, preferably Homemade Beef Stock (page 276)

1. Coarsely grind together the black peppercorns, white peppercorns, juniper berries, and red pepper flakes.

2. Using your fingers and the palms of your hands, press the peppercorns into both sides of the steak. Cover with plastic wrap and set aside for at least 30 minutes or refrigerate for 2 to 24 hours. Return the steak to room temperature before cooking.

3. Heat a well-seasoned cast-iron skillet over high heat until very hot and sprinkle lightly with salt (or film a nonstick skillet with oil). Sear the steak for about 4 minutes on each side, or until done to your taste. Remove the steak to a serving platter and allow to rest for at least 6 to 8 minutes.

4. Add the stock to the skillet, stirring occasionally, and cook for about 4 minutes, until the sauce is reduced by half.

5. Slice the steak and spoon the sauce over it.

MODERN PEPPERCORN MIX

I keep a tiny bowl of this pepper mixture next to the coarse salt so that I can use a pinch at a time.

Use it in any recipe that calls for freshly ground black pepper. Remember, however, that this peppercorn mix is more peppery than ordinary ground black pepper, so if you're not a pepper aficionado, start with less than your usual amount.

1 cup black peppercorns (I suggest a combination of Tellicherry and Lampong)

1/3 cup white peppercorns

1/3 cup freeze-dried green peppercorns

1/4 cup freeze-dried red peppercorns or 1 tablespoon red pepper flakes

1 tablespoon whole allspice

1 tablespoon juniper berries

Put all the ingredients in a bowl and mix well. Fill a pepper mill with part of the mixture. Store the rest at room temperature in a tightly covered jar.

If you plan to do a lot of cooking, measure about 1/3 cup of the mixture and grind it in an electric spice mill or coffee mill. I like a medium to small grind, but not too fine. Do not grind more pepper than you will use in the following 2 weeks.

JAPANESE-STYLE SIRLOIN STEAK

Makes 2 servings

Paper-thin sliced steak, onions, carrots, spinach, bamboo shoots, scallions, water chestnuts, shiitake mushrooms, and red peppers are quickly stir-fried, then seasoned with soy sauce, sherry, and a touch of sugar.

All the work is done ahead. I cut up the meat and vegetables in the morning, put them in individual bowls, cover them with plastic wrap, and refrigerate everything until I'm ready to cook.

This special dinner for two takes only minutes to cook. Perfect for a time when you don't want to spend a lot of time in the kitchen right before the meal—just light the candles, put on the music, and dine with your true love. I serve this with rice and a platter of fresh melon or pineapple for dessert.

Seasoning Sauce

$^1\!/_2$ cup beef broth (canned is fine)

$^1\!/_3$ cup soy sauce

2 tablespoons dry sherry

$^1\!/_2$ teaspoon sugar

1 tablespoon oil, preferably peanut

6 ounces well-trimmed boneless sirloin steak, sliced
    paper thin

1 medium onion, sliced

1 carrot, julienned

1 stalk celery, thinly sliced

$^1\!/_2$ red bell pepper, sliced

3 fresh shiitake mushrooms, sliced

1 bunch spinach (about $^1\!/_2$ pound), washed, spun
    dry, and stemmed

1 whole bamboo shoot (canned), sliced

1 bunch scallions (white part only), sliced into
    $^1\!/_2$-inch lengths

4 ounces water chestnuts, sliced

1. To make the seasoning sauce, mix together the broth, soy sauce, sherry, and sugar. Set aside.

2. In a wok or a large skillet, heat 1 teaspoon of the oil over high heat. Add the steak and stir-fry briefly, until it begins to brown. Remove the steak from the wok and set aside.

3. Heat the remaining 2 teaspoons of oil in the wok. Add the onion, carrot, celery, and red pepper and stir-fry for 1 to 2 minutes. Add the mushrooms, spinach, bamboo shoot, scallions, and water chestnuts and stir-fry for about 1 minute, or until the spinach begins to wilt.

4. Return the steak to the wok and toss all the ingredients together. Add the seasoning sauce and simmer for 1 to 2 minutes. Serve hot.

Freeze the steak for about 1 hour to make it easier to slice.

BIG-CITY SICHUAN BEEF

Makes 6 servings

A cooking technique that I use and stress in all my classes—especially when I teach private lessons to novice cooks—is mise en place. This French cooking term means having all the utensils and ingredients lined up and ready to use before you begin cooking. Knowing everything is at hand lowers the stress level of my students, especially when they solo at their first dinner parties. It's essential when stir-frying.

Some of these ingredients are usually found only in big cities, but with today's selection of Asian ingredients in supermarkets and gourmet food shops nationwide, they may be found in smaller communities. Otherwise, order them by mail (see page 282).

Even though this list of classic Sichuan ingredients may seem long, once the ingredients are assembled, this spicy dish is easy to prepare and fast to cook. Serve with bowls of sticky rice—and for fun, bring out the chopsticks!

6 small dried chili peppers

1 tablespoon minced ginger

1 tablespoon minced garlic

20 dried Chinese black mushrooms (also known as tree ears)

16 scallions (white and light green parts), halved lengthwise and cut in 2-inch pieces

6 tablespoons soy sauce, preferably dark

3 tablespoons dry sherry

2 teaspoons sugar

5 teaspoons Oriental sesame oil

Dash of chili oil for extra heat (optional)

1 to 2 tablespoons vegetable oil

2 pounds well-trimmed flank steak, julienned

2 tablespoons fermented black beans, rinsed (optional)

4 to 5 carrots, blanched 3 minutes and slivered

1. Soak the chili peppers in warm water for 15 minutes. Drain the peppers and discard the soaking water. Chop the peppers with the ginger and garlic and set aside.

2. Meanwhile, soak the mushrooms in a separate bowl of warm water for 15 minutes. Squeeze the excess moisture from the mushrooms. Cut the mushrooms into thin slices and set aside. Add the scallions to the mushrooms.

3. In a another bowl, mix together the soy sauce, sherry, sugar, sesame oil, and hot chili oil if desired, and set aside.

These preparations can be done several hours in advance

4. Heat 1 tablespoon of the vegetable oil in a wok or large nonstick skillet. Add the flank steak in small batches and stir-fry over high heat until the edges of the meat are crisp and browned, about 2 minutes. Add a bit more oil if needed with each batch of meat. Set the meat aside.

5. In the same wok or skillet, heat 1 teaspoon of the vegetable oil until very hot. Add the chili pepper mixture and stir-fry for a few seconds. Add the mushroom-scallion mixture and stir-fry for 1 to 2 minutes. Add the flank steak, black beans if desired, and carrots. Stir-fry for another minute or so, until all the ingredients are heated through.

6. Add the soy sauce mixture and toss again. Add more chili oil if you like your food very spicy. Serve immediately.

MODERN ORANGE BEEF

Makes 6 servings

This update of the classic Sichuan stir-fry uses fresh orange zest in place of the traditional dried orange peel for a more delicate flavor, and sun-dried tomatoes for their vibrant taste and smokiness. The tender filet of beef is cut into bite-sized strips, then marinated in brandy and soy sauce.

Serve this dish with steamed white rice. Any leftovers are great for lunch the next day served over a bed of baby salad greens.

3 tablespoons brandy

3 tablespoons soy sauce

2 pounds filet of beef, cut in thin strips

1 1/2 tablespoons cornstarch

3 tablespoons vegetable oil, approximately

4 cups boiling water

2 tablespoons sugar

Zest of 2 oranges, julienned (see Tasty Tip, page 111)

1/2 cup sun-dried tomatoes (dry, not oil-packed), cut in strips

1 bunch scallions (white and light green parts), chopped

6 medium white mushrooms, sliced

1 jalapeño pepper (with or without seeds), chopped, or more to taste

1 cup beef broth, preferably Homemade Beef Stock (page 276) or Doctored Beef Broth (page 279), approximately

Freshly ground black pepper

1. In a large bowl, mix the brandy and soy sauce. Add the beef and toss. Sprinkle the beef with the cornstarch and toss to coat each piece. Add 1 1/2 tablespoon of the oil and mix well. (I use chopsticks to separate the pieces of beef.) Set aside for 20 minutes or up to 1 hour.

2. Bring the water and sugar to a boil. Add the orange zest and simmer for 2 to 3 minutes. Remove the zest and discard the sugar-water. Drain the zest well and pat it dry with paper towels. Set aside.

3. Soak the sun-dried tomatoes in warm water for 5 minutes, or until softened; drain well. Set aside.

4. In large skillet or wok, heat 1 tablespoon of the oil until very hot. Add the beef and stir-fry for a minute or two, until all the pieces are browned. Remove the beef with a slotted spoon and set aside.

5. There should be some oil left in the wok; if not, add about 2 teaspoons of oil and heat. Add the orange zest, tomatoes, scallions, mushrooms and jalapeño pepper. Stir-fry over high heat until the mushrooms and scallions begin to brown, 1 to 2 minutes. Return the meat to the wok, add the broth, and cook, stirring constantly, until the liquid evaporates, 2 to 4 minutes. Season with freshly ground black pepper.

Salt and Pepper

Salt is one of the cook's most important ingredients. I use only coarse salt and recommend keeping a small bowl of it near the stove. (In these recipes, however, I've only specified coarse salt where it is absolutely necessary that you use it—to sprinkle a skillet in which the meat is to be seared.) Coarse salt is coarse grained and additive free. Table salt is a refined fine-grained salt with additives. Iodized salt is table salt with iodine.

As I cook, I add the salt with my fingertips. A pinch here, a pinch there is my way of controlling the amount—and I am quite stingy.

A word of encouragement for those on salt-restricted diets. I, too, watch my salt intake and cook gourmet meals for clients who eat only food with no added salt. If you do as I have, honing your skill with spices and herbs and cultivating your palate to appreciate the subtleties of various peppercorns, you'll adjust to cooking salt-free without much difficulty.

Preground and precracked pepper loses its flavor and becomes stale quickly. I prefer my own mixture. My peppercorn assortment packs quite a punch, so for those with timid palates, use it with caution. For me, freshly ground pepper is the spice that gives life and verve to many foods.

NEW MEXICAN FARM STAND BURRITOS

Makes 6 burritos

I devised this dish after visiting a farm stand in New Mexico that sold not only freshly picked corn, tomatoes, chili peppers, and greens, but also home-made burritos. They were in a large, old-fashioned electric roaster with the temperature set very low. Jalapeño peppers, onions, tomatoes, and diced beef were rolled inside a flour tortilla and wrapped in waxed paper for easy eating. Scrumptious!

I asked the young woman who ran the stand for the recipe. She asked her abuela, or grandmother, to come out from the back. Through hand gestures, the not-too-accurate translations of the granddaughter, and a lot of good-natured pointing and laughing, I came away with a pretty clear idea of how she'd made them. Here's my interpretation.

Serve with a side dish of sour cream and one of chopped onion. For a snack, serve as is.

> **2 tablespoons vegetable oil**
>
> **1 large onion, diced**
>
> **1 pound sirloin tip beef, cut in 1/2-inch cubes**
>
> **2 to 3 fresh jalapeño peppers, seeded and minced**
>
> **2 large fresh tomatoes, diced**
>
> **1 clove garlic, minced**
>
> **2 beef bouillon cubes**
>
> **3/4 cup hot water**
>
> **Freshly ground black pepper**
>
> **Salt**
>
> **6 large flour tortillas**

1. Heat a large nonstick skillet over medium heat and add the oil. Cook the onion until soft and translucent, 4 to 5 minutes. Add the beef, raise the heat, and sauté for 6 to 8 minutes, until browned. Add the jalapeño peppers, tomatoes, and garlic. Cook a few minutes longer.

2. Dissolve the bouillon cubes in the hot water and add to the skillet. Add a generous grinding of black pepper and a pinch of salt. Reduce the heat and simmer until the beef is very tender (nearly falling apart)

and the sauce thickens, about 20 to 30 minutes. Taste and correct the seasonings. Add more hot water as necessary to keep the meat moist.

3. Place $^{1}/_{3}$ to $^{1}/_{2}$ cup of the beef mixture in the center of each tortilla. Fold the bottom of the tortilla up to the center of the filling, fold in the sides, and roll up from the bottom to form a tight cylinder.

Tasty Tip

You can fill the tortillas an hour or two ahead. Place them in a rectangular baking/ serving dish. Spoon either red or green salsa over them, then top with shredded cheese. Bake for 20 minutes at 350°F.

SUNFLOWER SEED–CRUSTED LAMB CHOPS

Makes 4 servings

Like the sunflower, twisting to follow the sun, I, too, am an avid sun lover. I adore sunflower seeds and look for any opportunity to use them. I love them eaten as a quick snack, sprinkled over a green salad, scattered over granola as a topping on apple crumb pie, baked in brownies or chocolate chip cookies, or even added to a hamburger for crunch.

For this recipe I briefly grind salted sunflower seeds in a spice grinder or blender. I want them finely chopped but not turned into butter.

I spread the ground sunflower seeds on a plate and dip the mustard-coated chops on both sides to form a crunchy crust.

1 tablespoon fresh thyme leaves or 1 teaspoon dried

1 teaspoon freshly ground black pepper

2 large cloves garlic, minced

4 large or 8 small loin lamb chops, edges scored (see illustration, page 127)

¼ cup Dijon mustard

1 teaspoon port, approximately (optional)

2 tablespoons ground salted sunflower seeds

Vegetable oil to film skillet

1. Crush the thyme and mash together with the pepper and garlic. Rub both sides of lamb chops with this mixture.

2. Thin the mustard slightly with the port. Spread on both sides of chops. Spread the ground sunflower seeds on a plate. Press the chops into them to lightly coat.

3. Film a large nonstick skillet with oil and heat until very hot. Sauté the chops over high heat, about 3 minutes on each side, or until done to your taste.

Tasty Tip

Shelled sunflower seeds can be ground in a spice grinder or an old-fashioned nut grinder that looks like a mini threshing machine set into the lid of a jar. As a last resort, crush them with a mortar and pestle.

CORIANDER-SCENTED LAMB CHOPS

Makes 4 servings

Some people hate cilantro (fresh coriander). To them the taste is literally like soap. However, coriander seeds and dried coriander leaves are not pungent, but rather subtle with a slight lemon overtone, and do not taste soapy to anyone.

I serve parslied new potatoes and blanched green beans to complete this easy-to-make dinner.

4 large or 8 small well-trimmed rib lamb chops, edges scored (see illustration, page 127)

1 clove garlic, minced

2 teaspoons coriander seeds

2 teaspoons dried coriander leaves (not fresh) or parsley flakes

1 teaspoon freshly ground black pepper

Pinch of coarse salt

1. Rub the chops with the garlic. Mash together the coriander seeds, dried coriander leaves, and pepper. Rub this mixture into the chops. Cover the chops with plastic wrap and set aside for at least 30 minutes or, even better, refrigerate overnight.

2. Heat a nonstick skillet over high heat until very hot. Sprinkle lightly with salt. Sear the chops on each side, 2 to 3 minutes for rare chops, 4 minutes for medium, and 5 minutes for well done.

LAMB CHOP PARCELS

Makes 4 servings

Lean lamb chops, dipped in garlic- and rosemary-flavored water, are browned and set atop a bed of lightly sautéed carrots, onions, and mushrooms, then covered with a Savory Green Sauce of shallots, garlic, lemon juice, and parsley for a light, just-from-the-garden taste.

Serve asparagus vinaigrette as an appetizer and white rice on the side. Garnish the plate with a sprig of fresh rosemary.

Savory Green Sauce

2 tablespoons minced shallots

1 teaspoon minced garlic

Juice of 1 lemon

3 tablespoons chopped fresh parsley

1 teaspoon chopped fresh rosemary, plus 4 sprigs for garnish

¹/₂ teaspoon chopped fresh tarragon

¹/₃ cup water

1 clove garlic, smashed

¹/₂ bay leaf, crushed

2 teaspoons chopped fresh rosemary

4 well-trimmed 6-ounce lamb chops, edges scored (see illustration, page 127)

Freshly ground black pepper

2 medium carrots, julienned

2 medium onions, julienned

10 to 12 fresh white mushrooms, julienned

Pinch of salt

¹/₈ teaspoon cayenne pepper

1. To prepare the Savory Green Sauce, place the shallots, garlic, lemon juice, parsley, rosemary, and tarragon in the bowl of a food processor and process until finely chopped. Set aside.

2. Combine the water, garlic, bay leaf, and ½ teaspoon of the rosemary in a wide, shallow bowl. Dip each chop briefly in the mixture, turning to coat both sides.

3. Heat a nonstick skillet over high heat until very hot. Season the chops with black pepper and sear for 2 to 3 minutes on each side. Remove the chops from the skillet and set aside.

4. Add the carrots, onions, mushrooms, salt, cayenne pepper, a generous grinding of black pepper, and the remaining ½ teaspoon of rosemary to the juices in the skillet. Cook over medium heat for 1 to 2 minutes to absorb the juices.

5. Lay out 4 pieces of aluminum foil, each 12 by 18 inches. Divide the vegetables into 4 equal portions and place them in the center of each piece of foil. Set a seared chop on top of each bed of vegetables. Put 1 teaspoon of the Savory Green Sauce on each chop and seal the foil packets well. To keep the juices from leaking out of the packets, bring two opposite sides of the aluminum foil together over the middle of the packet. Fold them together 3 or 4 times, then fold the opposite two sides over 2 times as well and then fold back securely under the packet.

(1) Make a bed of vegetables in the center of each piece of foil and place a seared chop and a teaspoon of the Savory Green Sauce on top.
(2) Bring two opposite sides of the aluminum foil together over the middle of the packet and fold them together 3 or 4 times.

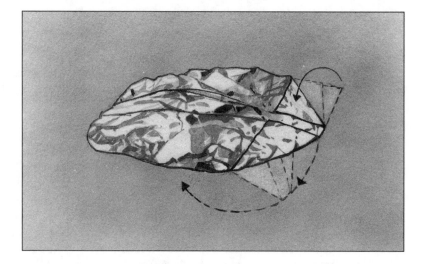

(3) Fold the opposite two sides over twice and then fold back securely under the packet.

The packets can be prepared up to 2 hours ahead and refrigerated. Remove from the refrigerator 1 hour before baking.

6. Preheat the oven to 400°F.

7. Place the foil packets on a baking sheet and bake 8 minutes for rare, 10 minutes for medium, and 12 minutes for well done. (Alternatively, grill the packets over hot coals.) Pass the extra sauce at the table.

STUFFED LAMB CHOPS WITH SAUCE MADEIRA

Makes 4 servings

As a youngster, my son, Scott, ate a peanut butter sandwich for lunch and a well-done hamburger with bacon on the side for dinner. For all too long, that was pretty much his diet. However, as he matured, so did his palate.

One evening while on a book tour, I invited Scott to join me for dinner at the Brown Palace in Denver. I was pleasantly surprised when he ordered a fillet-of-sole mousse with caviar to start and stuffed loin lamb chops, not unlike these, as his main course.

This is a dish Scott dreamed up and I executed for him. It's still one he adores and an excellent choice for a special small dinner party. If you serve these chops for the family, you can substitute chicken broth for the Madeira wine.

Stuffing

1 teaspoon butter

1 large onion, finely chopped

1 to 2 teaspoons rosemary

Freshly ground black pepper

8 well-trimmed 1- to 1¼-inch-thick loin lamb chops, with pockets cut for stuffing (see page 125)

½ cup all-purpose flour, approximately

Freshly ground black pepper

1 to 2 teaspoons olive oil

½ cup Madeira wine

1. To make the stuffing, heat the butter over high heat and cook the onion, stirring occasionally, until translucent, about 3 minutes. Put the onion into a small bowl and add the rosemary and pepper. Set the stuffing aside and allow it to cool.

2. Stuff each chop with 1 to 2 teaspoons of stuffing. Press the edges together to seal. Season the flour with pepper and dredge the chops in it.

3. Heat the oil in a nonstick skillet. Sauté the chops over high heat until browned on both sides, about 2 to 3 minutes on each side. Lower the heat to medium, add the wine, cover, and cook until the chops are tender and cooked through, 3 to 4 minutes. Remove to a heated platter.

4. Raise the heat, uncover the skillet, and cook the pan juices for 3 to 4 minutes to reduce, stirring to scrape up any bits of meat that have stuck to the pan. Pour the sauce over the chops and serve.

Tasty Tip

If you're in a hurry, omit the stuffing and poke a slit through the chop horizontally with the pointed tip of a sharp knife. Insert a length of scallion and a sprig of rosemary and proceed according to the recipe.

SEARED PORK CHOPS BAKED WITH PEPPERS AND ONIONS

Makes 8 servings

First I marinate the pork chops in thyme, onion, lemon juice, and vermouth overnight to absorb the piquant flavors and become more tender. Next I prepare a bed of sautéed onion and Italian frying peppers (the long, skinny, light green ones, also known as cubanelles). Then I bake the browned chops on top to create a rich, mouth-watering dish that needs only steamed brown rice or sliced potatoes baked in beef broth to make a simple family dinner. Add a lettuce and tomato salad and that's it.

Marinade

1/4 cup olive oil

1 small onion, sliced

1 tablespoon fresh thyme leaves or 1 teaspoon dried

1/2 teaspoon freshly ground black pepper

1 tablespoon fresh lemon juice

Splash of wine or vermouth

8 large well-trimmed 1-inch-thick pork chops, edges scored (see illustration, page 127)

1 teaspoon butter

1 teaspoon olive oil

1 large onion, sliced

1 clove garlic, minced

5 or 6 frying peppers, sliced

1 1/2 teaspoons fresh thyme leaves or 1/2 teaspoon dried

Pinch of salt

1/2 teaspoon freshly ground black pepper

1/2 cup beef broth (canned is fine)

1. Prepare the marinade by combining the oil, onion, thyme, black pepper, lemon juice, and wine or vermouth in a nonreactive dish. Add the pork chops, cover, and marinate for 3 to 24 hours in the refrigerator.

2. Preheat the oven to 325°F.

3. Heat the butter and oil over moderate heat in a large skillet. Cook the onion, garlic, and peppers, stirring every few minutes, until almost soft, about 5 minutes. Add the thyme, salt, and black pepper. Place the onions and peppers in a covered baking/serving dish large enough to hold the chops in 1 layer.

4. Remove the chops from the marinade and pat dry with paper towels. Reserve the marinade. Sauté the chops in the same skillet over high heat until they are browned, about 2 minutes on each side. Arrange the chops on top of the peppers and onions.

5. Pour the broth and remaining marinade around the chops. Cover and bake for 45 minutes. Uncover and continue to bake until the chops are tender and the juices run clear, about 15 minutes more.

FRUIT-AND-NUT-STUFFED DOUBLE PORK CHOPS

Makes 6 servings

These double pork chops are perfect when you have folks with hearty appetites over for dinner. While the chops look as if they're lots of trouble to make, they really aren't. For a more sophisticated dish, substitute bourbon for the orange juice.

All that needs to be done is to coat the chops with the fragrant dry rub of marjoram, summer savory, freshly ground black pepper, and orange zest; then let them stand while you prepare the stuffing. If you plan ahead, the stuffing can be done in advance.

An hour or so before the guests arrive, stuff and brown the chops, simmer them until tender, and finish the sauce. Reheat just before dinner. I like to serve nutty-flavored brown rice made with beef broth with this dish.

Dry rub

^{1}/$_2$ **teaspoon freshly ground black pepper**

1 clove garlic, minced

^{1}/$_2$ **teaspoon dried marjoram**

^{1}/$_2$ **teaspoon dried summer savory**

Zest of ^{1}/$_2$ **orange, grated (see Tasty Tip, page 111)**

6 well-trimmed double pork chops, with pockets cut for stuffing (see page 125)

Stuffing

6 to 8 dried apricots, diced

^{1}/$_4$ **cup orange juice, approximately**

1 tablespoon olive oil

^{1}/$_2$ **cup chopped onion**

^{1}/$_4$ **cup chopped fresh parsley**

^{1}/$_2$ **teaspoon dried marjoram**

^{1}/$_2$ **teaspoon dried summer savory**

Grated zest of ^{1}/$_2$ **orange**

2 tablespoons chopped toasted hazelnuts

³/₄ cup dry bread crumbs

Olive oil to film skillet

¹/₂ to ³/₄ cup beef broth (canned is fine)

¹/₄ to ¹/₂ cup orange juice

1. To prepare the dry rub, combine pepper, garlic, marjoram, summer savory, and orange zest. Rub this mixture into the pork chops and set the chops aside for 1 hour at room temperature or 6 to 24 hours in the refrigerator.

2. To prepare the stuffing, heat the apricots and 2 tablespoons of the orange juice. Cover and set aside for 5 minutes for the apricots to "plump."

3. Heat the oil in a large nonstick skillet. Cook the onion over medium-high heat until it's soft and translucent, 3 to 4 minutes. Add the apricots, parsley, marjoram, and summer savory and cook for 1 to 2 minutes. Stir in the zest, nuts, and bread crumbs. Remove from the heat and mix well. Taste and correct the seasonings. Add enough of the remaining orange juice for the stuffing to hold its shape in the spoon. Set aside and allow to cool.

4. Stuff each chop with about 1¹/₂ to 2 teaspoons of the stuffing. (Leftover stuffing can be refrigerated or frozen.) Press the edges of the chops together to seal.

5. Heat a large nonstick skillet and film it with oil. Sauté the chops over high heat for 3 to 4 minutes on each side. Remove the chops from the pan and deglaze the skillet by adding ¹/₄ cup of the broth and scraping up any bits of meat that are stuck to the bottom of the pan.

6. Return the chops to the skillet and add the orange juice and ¹/₄ cup of the remaining broth to pan. Cover and bring to a boil. Reduce the heat and simmer until the chops are tender, about 30 minutes. Add more broth if the liquid dries out.

7. Transfer the chops to a platter. Raise the heat and reduce the juices in the skillet until they thicken. Spoon the sauce over the chops.

Tasty Tip

An easy way to soften raisins and plump dried apricots—or any dried fruit—is to place them in a bowl with a tablespoon or two of liquid, cover, microwave for 1 minute, and set aside for a few minutes.

MEXICAN STUFFED PORK CHOPS

Makes 6 servings

Since I love to serve stuffed pork chops at informal dinner parties, I've invented quite a few stuffings.

This one invites you to be creative. Sometimes I make it very spicy, using 2 jalapeño peppers. Other times I vary the amount of green pepper and onion. Occasionally I add pimiento-stuffed olives.

If you have any stuffing left over, add chopped raw onion, tomatoes, and a bit of olive oil to make a quick salsa to serve on the side.

Marinade

1 tablespoon olive oil

1/2 teaspoon freshly ground black pepper

1 clove garlic, minced

2 teaspoons dried oregano

6 well-trimmed double pork chops, with pockets cut for stuffing (see page 125)

Stuffing

1/2 cup chopped onion

1 clove garlic, minced

1 tablespoon olive oil

2 tablespoons canned green chilies, chopped

1 jalapeño pepper, seeded and chopped, or more to taste

1/4 cup chopped fresh parsley

1/2 teaspoon dried oregano

1/2 teaspoon chili powder

One 14-ounce can whole tomatoes, drained, juice reserved

3/4 cup crushed corn chips

1 tablespoon olive oil

¼ to ½ cup beef broth (canned is fine)

1. To prepare the marinade, combine the oil, pepper, garlic, and oregano in a nonreactive dish. Add the pork chops, cover, and marinate for 1 hour at room temperature or 6 hours or more in the refrigerator.

2. To prepare the stuffing, cook the onion and garlic in the oil over medium-high heat until the onion is soft and translucent. Add the green chilies, jalapeño pepper, parsley, oregano, and chili powder and cook for a few minutes more. Stir in the drained tomatoes and corn chips and mix well. Taste and correct the seasonings. Add the juice from the tomatoes, a little at a time, until the mixture holds its shape in a spoon. (Reserve ¼ cup tomato juice for use later in the recipe.) Set the stuffing aside and allow it to cool.

3. Remove the chops from the marinade and pat dry with paper towels. Stuff each chop with about 1½ to 2 teaspoons of stuffing. (Leftover stuffing can be refrigerated or frozen.) Press the edges of the chops together to seal.

5. Heat a large nonstick skillet over high heat and film it with the olive oil. Sauté the chops for 3 to 4 minutes on each side. Remove the chops from the pan and deglaze the skillet by adding ¼ cup of the broth and scraping up any bits of meat that are stuck to the bottom of the pan. Add ¼ cup of juice from the tomatoes.

6. Return the chops to the skillet, cover, and bring to a boil. Reduce the heat and simmer until the chops are tender, about 30 minutes. Add more broth if the liquid dries out.

7. Transfer the chops to a platter. Raise the heat and reduce the juices in the skillet until they thicken. Spoon the sauce over the chops and serve.

Tasty Tip

An easy way to be sure pork is cooked through is to poke the meat with a two-prong meat fork. When the juices run clear, the meat is cooked through.

PORK CHOPS FLAMBÉ

Makes 6 servings

As usual, my guests follow me into the kitchen to visit and watch me cook. They stop talking as I warm the brandy over the burner. I extend my arms and tilt my head back (to keep my eyebrows and hair from singeing), pour the brandy over the chops, and light the fumes by tipping the brandy to the side of the skillet to catch the flame. Yellow, red, and blue, the flames dance around the chops. I turn off the gas and let the fumes burn off. As always, the audience is mesmerized.

The practical side of this show is that flaming the brandy burns off the alcohol and leaves only the sweet, rich flavor of the caramelized seal created by the brandy's sugar.

Serve with applesauce, sliced baked potatoes, honey-glazed baby carrots, and a green salad.

6 well-trimmed ¹/₂-inch-thick loin pork chops, edges scored (see illustration, page 127)

¹/₂ teaspoon salt

¹/₂ teaspoon freshly ground black pepper

1 tablespoon chopped fresh sage or 1¹/₂ teaspoons rubbed sage

1 tablespoon olive oil

1 large clove garlic, cut in half

2 to 3 tablespoons apple jack brandy

³/₄ cup Homemade Beef Stock (page 276) or Doctored Beef Broth (page 279)

1. Rub the chops with salt, pepper, and sage and set them aside.

2. Heat the oil over high heat in a large nonstick skillet. Add the garlic and cook, stirring, for 1 or 2 minutes, until it turns golden. Remove the garlic and discard. Add the chops and sear for 2 to 3 minutes on each side. Reduce the heat to low and cook slowly, turning once, until the meat is done, 15 to 20 minutes. Set the skillet aside.

3. Warm the brandy, pour it over the chops, and ignite. After the flames go out, transfer the chops to a serving platter.

4. Over high heat, reduce the juices in the skillet for 2 to 3 minutes. Add the broth and bring to a boil. Continue to boil, stirring occasionally, until the sauce is reduced by half. Pour the sauce over the chops and serve.

I find the easiest way to flame any meat is to heat the brandy in a small stainless-steel measuring cup—or a small saucepan will do—held over the stovetop flame carefully for about 45 seconds to 1 minute, until the vapors rise off the surface. Pour over the meat, strike a long match, stand back, and ignite. Be careful!

PORK MEDALLIONS WITH TOMATO CREAM

Makes 6 servings

One day when my co-author, Diane Porter, and I were working on this book, I said I'd like to include my recipe for pork medallions with a tomato-cream sauce. I showed her my 25-year-old recipe, which called for sautéing the pork in smoking fatback and thickening the sauce with 2 cups of heavy cream. She turned purple.

"Over my dead body," Diane swore.

"Nonsense," I said airily, "it just needs a couple of adjustments."

Okay, so it turned out to be many more than a couple. Now the intriguing flavors of allspice, thyme, and basil—instead of fatback and cream—enhance the original garlic, shallots, tomatoes, and mushrooms. A small amount of surprisingly low-in-fat half-and-half finishes the sauce. It's a lighter, cleaner, and more flavorful dish than my original.

Vegetable oil to film skillet

Six 1-inch-thick medallions of pork

¹/₂ teaspoon ground allspice

¹/₂ teaspoon dried thyme

¹/₂ teaspoon dried basil

Salt

Freshly ground black pepper

4 shallots, minced

1 clove garlic, minced

1 cup white wine

2 large tomatoes, peeled, seeded, and chopped

¹/₄ pound sliced mushrooms

2 tablespoons half-and-half

1. Film a large nonstick skillet with oil and heat over high heat until very hot. Sauté the pork medallions in batches for about 2 minutes on each side until browned. Remove the medallions from the skillet and season them with allspice, thyme, basil, salt, and pepper.

2. Add the shallots and garlic to the skillet. Reduce the heat to low, return the pork to the skillet, and cook slowly, covered, until the meat is cooked through, about 6 to 7 minutes. Remove the pork and set aside.

3. Raise the heat to high and deglaze the skillet with the wine, scraping up any bits of meat that are stuck to the bottom of the pan. Cook over high heat until the wine is reduced by half. Add the tomatoes and mushrooms and boil briefly to cook the vegetables a bit. Slowly add the half-and-half and reduce the sauce over moderate heat for 4 to 5 minutes. Return the meat to the skillet and cook until just heated through, basting the medallions of pork with the sauce as you heat them.

It's important not to crowd the meat when you sear or sauté it, or it will steam instead of brown. Cook the meat over high heat in small batches, removing the pieces as they brown.

SWEET-AND-SOUR PORK

Makes 6 servings

My taste testers and I found this version of sweet-and-sour pork lighter and more appetizing than the Chinese restaurant variety. Here the meat is neither breaded nor fried, but seared. Because I make this dish with tenderloin, it takes only a few minutes to cook.

I like the way the acidity of the apple cider vinegar balances the sweetness of brown sugar. Sort of like life: a blend of the sweet and the sour; part pain, part joy; yin and yang; always balancing the scales.

Vegetable oil to film skillet

1 ½ pounds pork tenderloin, cut in 1-inch cubes

One 20-ounce can pineapple chunks in juice

½ cup low-sodium canned chicken broth

¼ cup apple cider vinegar

2 tablespoons brown sugar

2 tablespoons soy sauce

½ teaspoon ground ginger

1 medium green or red bell pepper, cut in strips

1 medium onion, cut in thin wedges

2 tablespoons cornstarch

2 tablespoons dry sherry or Chinese rice wine

1. Film a large nonstick skillet with oil and heat until very hot. Over high heat, sauté the pork for 2 to 3 minutes in batches until browned on all sides.

2. Drain the pineapple chunks and set aside. Add the juice from the pineapple, broth, vinegar, sugar, soy sauce, and ginger to the pork. Bring to a boil. Reduce the heat, cover, and simmer for 15 to 20 minutes, or until the pork is tender. Add the pineapple chunks, green pepper, and onion. Simmer, covered, 5 minutes longer or until vegetables are "crunch tender."

3. Dissolve the cornstarch in the sherry. Add just enough of this mixture to thicken the sauce, stirring continuously, about 1 minute.

CRUSTY CORIANDER PAN-SEARED VEAL CHOPS

Begin one to two days in advance

Makes 4 servings

I serve these chops at special small dinner parties where I trust the guests to appreciate the nuances of veal subtly seasoned with celery, coriander seeds, and a hint of garlic, which have mingled in an overnight milk marinade. I crush coriander seeds and press them into the chops, sealing in the meat's flavor while forming a crust.

Garnish with a few sprigs of watercress and serve with saffron-scented risotto and young, tender steamed green vegetable.

> **4 well-trimmed 1-inch-thick veal loin chops, edges scored (see illustration, page 127)**
>
> **1 clove garlic, sliced**
>
> **5 teaspoons coriander seeds**
>
> **2 stalks celery, chopped**
>
> **1½ to 2 cups milk to soak veal**
>
> **Freshly ground black pepper**
>
> **Pinch of coarse salt**

One to two days ahead

1. Put the veal chops in a nonreactive pan with the garlic, 1 teaspoon of the coriander seed, and the celery. Add enough milk to barely cover the chops, cover with plastic wrap, and marinate in the refrigerator for 1 to 2 days, turning occasionally. Bring the chops to room temperature.

Before sautéing

2. Remove the chops from the marinade. Discard the marinade and pat the chops dry with paper towels. Dust with pepper. Crush the remaining 4 teaspoons of coriander seeds and press them into the chops.

3. Heat a nonstick skillet over high heat until very hot and sprinkle lightly with salt. Sear the chops until browned on one side, about 3 to 4 minutes. Turn the chops and cook until the other side is browned and the chops are done, about 6 to 8 minutes, or until done to your taste. The veal will be slightly pink inside and brown on the outside.

PORK RIBBONS WITH GARDEN TABBOULEH

Makes 12 to 14 servings

Imagine tender strips of stir-fried pork loin that have been marinated in soy sauce, sherry, chili oil, and garlic served atop a colorful salad of tabbouleh studded with red onion, tomato, scallions, and parsley and then dressed with lime juice and olive oil.

This is one of my most popular summertime buffet dishes, which I serve with sliced tomatoes and coleslaw, followed by mixed fresh berries with vanilla yogurt-cheese for dessert. I prepare the tabbouleh and marinate the pork a day ahead. On the day of the party it takes just a few minutes to finish the tabbouleh, cook the pork, and assemble.

Garden Tabbouleh

$1^3/_4$ cups fine-grained bulgur

7 cups boiling water

$^1/_4$ cup fresh lemon juice

$^1/_4$ cup fresh lime juice

1 medium red onion, chopped

6 to 8 plum tomatoes, seeded and chopped

1 bunch scallions (white and light green parts), minced

1 large bunch fresh parsley, chopped (approximately 1 cup)

Salt

Freshly ground black pepper

3 tablespoons extra-virgin olive oil, approximately

3 tablespoons light olive oil, approximately

Pork Ribbons

2 tablespoons soy sauce

2 tablespoons dry sherry

1 teaspoon chili oil

1 large clove garlic, minced

¹/₂ teaspoon sugar

2 pounds well-trimmed pork loin or tenderloin, julienned

Vegetable oil to film skillet

1 head romaine lettuce, washed and dried

1 large yellow bell pepper, seeded and finely chopped

1 large green bell pepper, seeded and finely chopped

1. To prepare the tabbouleh, place the bulgur in a large bowl and pour the boiling water over it. Let soak for 15 to 30 minutes at room temperature until the grains are tender and fluffy. Drain off any excess water and put the grains into a colander, shake vigorously, and allow the bulgur to drain for 1 to 2 hours, until dry.

2. Mix the bulgur with the lemon and lime juice, onion, tomatoes, scallions, and ¹/₂ cup of the parsley. Season to taste with salt and pepper. Combine the extra-virgin olive oil with light olive oil. Use only as much as you need to dress the tabbouleh.

   Refrigerate the Garden Tabbouleh for 6 to 24 hours. Remove from the refrigerator at least 1 hour before serving.

3. To prepare the Pork Ribbons, whisk the soy sauce, sherry, chili oil, garlic, and sugar together. Pour this mixture over the pork, cover, and marinate in a nonreactive pan for 6 to 24 hours in the refrigerator.

4. Coat a large nonstick skillet with the oil. Add the pork strips in batches and stir-fry quickly over high heat to sear them, 3 to 4 minutes. Transfer the meat to a bowl and set aside for up to 1 hour.

5. Arrange the lettuce leaves on a platter. Toss the tabbouleh with the yellow and green peppers and ¹/₄ cup of the parsley. Taste and correct the seasonings. Mound the tabbouleh in the center of the lettuce, scatter the pork on top, and garnish with the remaining ¹/₄ cup of parsley. Serve at room temperature.

Tasty Tip

While I like the taste of extra-virgin olive oil in this dish, I prefer to mix it with a light (essentially tasteless) olive oil to keep its strong taste from overwhelming the other flavors.

JUNIPER BERRY
VEAL CHOPS

Makes 4 servings

I crush the juniper berries by hand in a wooden mortar so I can inhale the intoxicating aroma of berry and pine before I mix them with the rosemary, black pepper, and sherry. Part of the seasoning paste remains in the pan after the chops are cooked, flavoring the sumptuous, aromatic sauce.

4 well-trimmed 1-inch-thick veal chops, edges scored (see illustation, page 127)

1 1/2 to 2 cups milk to soak veal

Seasoning Paste

1 tablespoon juniper berries, crushed

1 tablespoon freshly ground black pepper

2 sprigs fresh rosemary

2 tablespoons dry sherry

Vegetable oil to film skillet

2 tablespoons dry sherry

2 tablespoons Homemade Veal Stock (page 281) or canned low-sodium chicken broth

1. Soak the veal in milk to cover in a glass dish for 2 to 24 hours in the refrigerator. Discard the milk, rinse the chops, and pat them dry with paper towels.

2. To make the seasoning paste, crush the juniper berries and stir them together with the pepper, rosemary, and sherry. Spread on both sides of the veal chops and set aside for 1 hour.

3. Film a nonstick skillet with oil and heat until very hot over high heat. Brown the chops for about 3 to 4 minutes on each side. Remove from the skillet and set aside.

4. Deglaze the skillet by adding the sherry and scraping up any bits of meat and seasonings stuck to the bottom of the pan. Add the veal stock or chicken broth. Return the chops to the skillet, reduce the heat, and simmer for 4 to 5 minutes, turning once.

TOMATO-KISSED VEAL CHOPS

Makes 2 servings

Last Valentine's Day I invited a man I like over for dinner. Feeling particularly playful, I wanted to invent an entree to reflect the occasion. Mom always said, "The way to a man's heart is through his stomach."

I decided to stuff Sun-Dried Tomato Seasoning Paste (which I always have in the refrigerator) into the pockets of thick veal chops, rub the chops with garlic, and brown them. To finish the dish, I made a simple au jus sauce. To complete the menu I added sautéed exotic mushrooms, wild rice pilaf, and ended with a chocolate torte made in a heart-shaped pan. Voilà!— a perfect Valentine's Day dinner.

> **Two 1- to 1½-inch-thick veal chops, trimmed and scored, with pockets cut for stuffing (see illustration, page 125)**
>
> **1 cup milk, approximately, to soak veal**
>
> **3 to 4 teaspoons Sun-Dried Tomato Seasoning Paste (page 229)**
>
> **Freshly ground black pepper**
>
> **1 large clove garlic, minced**
>
> **Vegetable oil to film skillet**
>
> **½ to ⅔ cup Homemade Veal Stock (page 281) or canned low-sodium chicken broth**

1. Soak veal in milk to cover in a glass dish for 2 to 24 hours in the refrigerator. Discard the milk, rinse the chops, and pat them dry with paper towels.

2. Fill the pockets of the veal chops with 1 to 2 teaspoons of the seasoning paste. Press the edges of the chops together to seal.

3. Season the chops with pepper and rub the garlic into both sides of the chops. Set aside for 30 to 45 minutes.

4. Film a nonstick skillet with oil and heat over high heat. Sauté the chops about 3 to 4 minutes on each side, until browned. Add the broth, reduce the heat to low, and simmer until the chops are tender, about 5 to 6 minutes.

5. Remove the chops from the skillet, raise the heat to high, and reduce the sauce, scraping up any bits of the meat and seasonings stuck to the bottom of the pan, about 1 to 2 minutes. Spoon the sauce over the chops and serve.

VEAL CHOPS MARTINI

Makes 6 servings

The unusual combination of spicy green peppercorns and piquant capers mixed with gin, olive oil, and lemon juice creates a seasoning paste that inspires me to dream of sitting on the veranda of a large white hotel in Casablanca—preferably with Robert Redford—while sipping a martini.

6 well-trimmed 1-inch-thick veal chops, edges scored (see illustration, page 127)

2½ cups milk, approximately, to soak veal

1 teaspoon green peppercorns in brine, drained

2 tablespoons capers, drained

2 tablespoons gin

1 tablespoon olive oil, plus a bit more to film the skillet

Juice of 1 lemon

1 small onion, finely chopped

⅓ cup Homemade Veal Stock (page 281) or Homemade Beef Stock (page 276)

1. Soak the veal in milk to cover in a glass dish for 2 to 24 hours in the refrigerator. Discard the milk, rinse the chops, and pat them dry with paper towels.

2. Smash the green peppercorns and chop them together with the capers; rub into the veal chops.

3. In a small bowl, mix together 1 tablespoon of the gin, the olive oil, and 2 teaspoons of lemon juice. Drizzle over both sides of the chops. Set aside in a nonreactive dish for at least 30 minutes.

4. Film a nonstick skillet with oil and heat until very hot over high heat. Brown the chops about 4 minutes on each side.

5. Remove the chops to a serving platter. Reduce the heat to medium-high, add the onion, and cook until the onion softens, 2 to 3 minutes. Add the remaining tablespoon of gin, the remaining lemon juice, and the stock. Cook, stirring occasionally to scrape up bits from the bottom of the pan. Taste and correct the seasonings.

6. Return the chops to the skillet and simmer for 7 to 8 minutes, turning once, until the chops are tender and the juices run clear. Spoon the sauce over the chops and serve.

WILD MUSHROOM AND VEAL SCALLOP SAUTÉ

Makes 6 servings

Back in the mid-sixties—before I began cooking for a living—I worked in television. About two or three in the afternoon, while still at the office, I'd call a few good friends and invite them for dinner.

On the way home I'd stop at the local butcher shop to buy veal scallops, milk, and heavy cream. Now I've taken out the heavy cream and added wild mushrooms, fresh tomatoes, and white wine to the sauce. I still invite my friends at the last minute—they always show up.

6 large veal scallops, pounded thin

1 cup milk, approximately, to soak the veal

Salt

Freshly ground black pepper

1/2 cup all-purpose flour, approximately

1 tablespoon olive oil

3 shallots, chopped

6 to 8 mushrooms, sliced (preferably fresh shiitake; otherwise, portobello or cremini)

1/2 cup dry white wine

1 large tomato, peeled, seeded, and chopped

1/2 teaspoon dried tarragon or 2 teaspoons fresh

Chopped fresh parsley

1. Soak the veal in milk to cover in a glass dish for 2 to 24 hours in the refrigerator. Discard the milk, rinse the scallops, and pat them dry with paper towels.

2. Season the veal with salt and pepper, then dust lightly with flour.

3. Heat the oil in a nonstick skillet over high heat. Sauté the veal until golden brown, about 2 to 3 minutes on each side. Remove the veal from the skillet and set aside.

4. In the same skillet, cook the shallots, stirring, over high heat for 2 to 3 minutes, until they begin to color. Add the mushrooms and cook, stirring, for another 3 to 4 minutes, until they release their liquid. Add

the wine and cook until the liquid is reduced by half, 4 or 5 minutes. Add the tomato and cook 3 or 4 minutes more. Add the tarragon and salt and pepper to taste. Pour the sauce over the veal scallops and sprinkle parsley on top.

NEW BERLIN-STYLE SCALLOPS

Makes 4 servings

On a trip to Germany 20 years ago, we found a neighborhood brauhaus *in Berlin with the best* Wiener schnitzel *I'd ever tasted, served on a bed of braised sauerkraut thickened with heavy cream.*

Here I've made a stuffing with sautéed celery tops, shallots, parsley, sauerkraut, and raisins braised in beef broth and seasoned with freshly ground black pepper. Each veal package is rolled in seasoned flour, browned, and simmered in beer and beef broth until tender. It's fast and lusciously rich—without the cream!

Stuffing

2 to 3 teaspoons olive oil

2 large shallots, chopped

2 tablespoons chopped celery tops, with leaves

4 tablespoons chopped fresh parsley

1 cup good-quality sauerkraut

$1/2$ teaspoon sugar

4 tablespoons dark raisins

$1/2$ cup Homemade Beef Stock (page 276), Doctored Beef Broth (page 279), or canned beef broth

Freshly ground black pepper, to taste

4 large veal scallops, pounded thin

$1/2$ cup milk, approximately, to soak veal

$1/2$ cup all-purpose flour, approximately

$1/4$ teaspoon salt

½ teaspoon freshly ground black pepper

Olive oil to film the skillet

½ cup beer

½ cup Homemade Beef Stock (page 276), Doctored Beef Broth (page 279), or canned beef broth

1. To prepare the stuffing, heat the oil in a skillet over medium-high heat. Cook the shallots, celery tops, and parsley for 2 to 3 minutes. Add the sauerkraut, sugar, raisins, and broth and bring to a boil. Reduce the heat and simmer until the liquid has evaporated but the sauerkraut is still moist. Add pepper to taste. Set the stuffing aside and allow it to cool.

2. Soak the veal in milk to cover in a glass dish for 2 to 24 hours in the refrigerator. Discard the milk, rinse the scallops, and pat them dry with paper towels. Cut each scallop in half, making 8 small scallops.

3. Place about 1 tablespoon of the stuffing in the center of each scallop. Fold the ends over to meet at the edges and press to seal. Season the flour with salt and pepper and dredge the veal packages in it.

(1) Place the stuffing in the center of each scallop.
(2) Fold the ends over to meet at the edges and press to seal.

4. Film a nonstick skillet with oil. Sauté the veal packages over high heat for 2 to 3 minutes on each side, until golden brown. (The veal packages will open and some of the stuffing will fall out, but that's okay.)

5. Add the beer and broth. Cook over medium-high heat for 1 to 2 minutes, until the sauce begins to boil. Reduce the heat to medium-low and simmer until the sauce is reduced by half and the veal is tender, about 5 minutes. Spoon the sauce over the veal packages and serve.

LEMON TREE
VEAL SCALLOPS

Makes 6 servings

My lemony rendition of veal piccata always reminds me of my first visit to my sister Joan's home near Phoenix. I had seen pictures of the desert only in a magazine that Grams subscribed to, Arizona Highways. I loved the unfamiliar, alien-like cactus plants, the hot sun and cool evenings, and especially the lemon, grapefruit, and orange trees growing in the backyard.

If I make this dish before the guests arrive, I undercook the veal, finish making the sauce, and return the meat to the pan until just before I'm ready to serve it. I then reheat the sauce until it's bubbly, which finishes cooking the veal, and serve it with angel hair pasta that's been dressed with olive oil and fresh chopped herbs. Garnish the veal with rinsed capers and chopped fresh parsley.

12 small veal scallops, pounded thin

1 1/2 to 2 cups milk, approximately

1/2 cup all-purpose flour, approximately

1/2 teaspoon dried tarragon

Freshly ground black pepper

1 tablespoon olive oil, approximately

2 large lemons

1 teaspoon sugar, approximately

1/2 cup white wine

1 to 2 teaspoons butter

1. Soak the veal in milk to cover in a glass dish for 2 to 24 hours in the refrigerator. Discard the milk, rinse the scallops, and pat them dry with paper towels.

2. Season the flour with the tarragon and pepper. Dust the veal scallops lightly with the seasoned flour and shake off any excess.

3. Heat 1 to 2 teaspoons of the oil in a nonstick skillet. Sauté the veal scallops in batches over high heat until lightly browned, about 2 to 3 minutes on each side. If necessary, add a bit more oil. Remove the veal and set aside.

4. Slice 1 lemon into thin rounds. In the same skillet, cook the lemon slices for 1 to 2 minutes. Sprinkle with sugar, turn, and cook for 1 to

2 minutes on the second side. Remove the lemon slices from the skillet and arrange them attractively over the veal.

5. Leaving the heat on high, deglaze the skillet by adding the wine and the juice of the second lemon and scraping up any bits of meat that are stuck to the bottom of the pan. Reduce the liquid by half. Remove the pan from the heat and swirl in the butter. Whisk until the butter is incorporated. Pour the sauce over the veal and serve immediately.

Tasty Tip

With any meat that is thin and cooks quickly, it is important that the thickness of each piece be the same for even cooking. Every once in a while, I find that the veal scallops are too thick or that most of the scallop is thin but one section is thicker than the rest.

To remedy this, place the meat between 2 pieces of plastic wrap, and using a meat pounder, the side of a large knife or cleaver, or the smooth side of a wooden mallet, gently pound either the whole scallop, if it's too thick, or just the thicker section until the meat is even in thickness.

VEAL PUTTANESCA

Makes 6 servings

Marcheta Tate, a dear friend and an excellent cook, lives in North Manchester, Indiana. While we were classmates at Manchester College, we spent hours together studying and playing. I enjoyed cooking and eating many meals with her and her family, who became my family away from home.

Marcheta's husband, Roger, raises prime-quality milk-fed veal and Marcheta creates extraordinary veal dishes. She taught me that because veal is so tender and mild flavored, sauces for it can be either subtle or robust, as this veal recipe exemplifies.

Even the most avid anchovy haters will be amazed at the unique flavor anchovies give to veal. Chances are they won't have a clue that anchovies are the secret ingredient that makes this veal dish taste great. When you soak anchovies in a small amount of milk, they become less salty.

This dish is best when made a day or two ahead to give the seasonings a chance to blend. During the winter I make it with canned tomatoes and serve it hot with garlic-laced spaghetti. In the summer I make it with fresh tomatoes and serve it at room temperature with penne and sliced tomatoes topped with fresh basil leaves and drizzled with balsamic vinegar.

6 large veal scallops, pounded thin

1 cup milk, approximately, to soak veal

1/2 cup all-purpose flour, approximately

1/2 teaspoon dried basil

1/4 teaspoon freshly ground black pepper

1 tablespoon olive oil, approximately

1 large onion, chopped

2 cloves garlic, minced

4 anchovy fillets, rinsed, patted dry, and chopped

1/4 cup chopped fresh parsley, plus extra for garnishing

2 cups chopped fresh tomatoes or one 16-ounce can plum tomatoes

3 tablespoons tomato paste

1/4 cup white wine

¹/₄ cup water

Pinch of sugar

¹/₄ teaspoon crushed red pepper flakes, or more to taste

¹/₂ cup pitted oil-cured black olives, drained

Fresh flat-leaf parsley for garnish

1. Soak the veal in milk to cover in a glass dish for 2 to 24 hours in the refrigerator. Discard the milk, rinse the scallops, and pat them dry with paper towels.

2. Season the flour with the basil and black pepper. Lightly dust the veal with this mixture, shaking off any excess flour.

3. Heat the oil in a large nonstick skillet. Sauté the veal over high heat until lightly browned, about 1 to 2 minutes on each side. Remove from the skillet and set aside.

4. Add the onion and garlic to the skillet and cook until the onion begins to soften, about 2 to 3 minutes. Add the anchovies, parsley, tomatoes, tomato paste, wine, water, sugar, and red pepper flakes. Bring to a boil. Reduce the heat and simmer for 10 to 15 minutes, until the sauce begins to thicken. Taste and correct the seasonings. Stir in the olives. Return the veal scallops to the sauce and gently reheat. Garnish with parsley and serve.

You can prepare the entire dish a day ahead, but do not reheat the veal. Instead, arrange the veal in a single layer in a baking/serving dish. Pour cooled tomato sauce over the veal and add the olives. Cover and refrigerate. The next day, preheat the oven to 350°F and bake until the meat and sauce are just heated through, 10 to 15 minutes. Do not overcook. Garnish with the parsley and serve hot.

ROSEMARY- AND GARLIC-INFUSED VENISON CHOPS

Makes 4 servings

Contrary to the popular perception of game meat, venison is mild—similar to filet of beef.

For those unfamiliar with cooking venison, a warning is in order. Venison chops and steaks must be served rare to keep the meat tender. (If you eat only well-done meat, I suggest the venison stew on page 116).

If your venison comes from the butcher rather than a friendly hunter, I suggest buying Cervena venison, an excellent-quality venison currently the darling of fine chefs. Most butchers will be glad to order it for you (or call 800-877-1187).

Marinate the chops with bruised fresh rosemary, minced garlic, and olive oil. Use the flat side of a cleaver or chef's knife to bruise the fresh rosemary, then chop it to release its oil and flavor. Just before searing, dust the chops with coarse black pepper. That's it!

To complete the menu, serve roasted butternut squash and a savory grain pilaf.

1 teaspoon olive oil

1 tablespoon fresh rosemary, bruised and minced, plus sprigs for garnish

1 large clove garlic, minced

4 well-trimmed 1³/₄-inch-thick loin venison chops, with rib bone intact, edges scored (see illustration, page 127)

2 teaspoons coarsely ground black pepper

1. Mix together the olive oil, minced rosemary, and garlic. Spread the chops with this mixture and set aside for 1 hour at room temperature.

2. Heat a nonstick skillet over high heat until very hot. Dust the chops with pepper and sear for 3 to 4 minutes on each side. Remove to a heated plate and garnish with sprigs of fresh rosemary.

Tasty Tip

If you prefer, substitute lamb chops for venison.

IMPROVISATIONAL CHOPS AND STEAKS

Makes 4 servings

I learned to cook early on from Mom and Grams, wonderful cooks who believed in using what was on hand. While some dishes were the same each time, the majority changed depending on what had ripened in our garden, what was in the larder, and what meat Dad had butchered.

Every now and then after moving to New York, I'd remember a dish I'd eaten as a child and call Mom to ask for the recipe. More often than not she'd give me a rough idea and say, "Just use what you have in the house, Janeen."

The belief that you can always put together wonderful meals with what's available has led me to create innumerable new dishes for clients, students, and my weekly column. I urge you to do the same. Try a recipe; if you don't have all the ingredients, use what you do have. As long as you taste and correct the seasonings, you'll rarely go wrong. It's a matter of having confidence—and confidence comes with practice.

However, there's a drawback to improvising. My co-author, Diane Porter, likes to "wing" it. When she asked her husband, Donald, if he liked the new lamb stew—lamb stew being a particular favorite of his—he said, "I love it, but what's the difference? You'll never make it again." If you invent a great dish, jot down a few notes so you can duplicate it. You may think you'll never forget what you did, but chances are you will.

I might add mushrooms and garlic to beef, either apricots or fennel to pork, onions and apples to veal, or tomatoes to venison.

Olive oil to film skillet, plus approximately 1 teaspoon

Four 1-inch-thick chops or steaks

2 shallots

¼ cup wine (such as Madeira, Marsala, port, or sherry)

2 tablespoons demi-glace (page 273)

Salt (optional)

Freshly ground black pepper (optional)

1. Film a large nonstick skillet with oil and heat over high heat until very hot. Brown the chops or steaks about 4 to 5 minutes on each side for medium rare, or until done to your taste. Remove the chops or steaks to a serving platter.

2. Leaving the heat on high, add 1 teaspoon of oil to the skillet. Add the shallots and sauté for 1 to 2 minutes, until they begin to brown. Reduce the heat to medium and add the wine. Allow the wine to boil for 1 minute. Add the demi-glace and cook for about 2 minutes. Season to taste with salt and pepper. Spoon the sauce over the chops or steaks.

MARINATED VENISON CHOPS WITH HUNTER'S SAUCE

Makes 4 servings

One evening I made up this recipe for a well-traveled friend, just in from an exciting business trip to Hong Kong. I wanted to hear all about the exotic things he'd done rather than spend the evening cooking and then washing a sink full of pots and pans. These marinated venison chops are quickly cooked in the same skillet along with their sauce.

To the classic onion, capers, tomato, and bruised fresh rosemary, which remind me of the forest, I've added Pernod for its sweet licorice taste and marinated ginger root for its tang.

Marinade

3 tablespoons Pernod

One 3-inch sprig fresh rosemary

1 tablespoon dried minced onion

8 well-trimmed ³/₄-inch-thick loin venison chops, edges scored

Pinch of salt

1 large tomato, seeded and chopped

¹/₂ medium onion, thinly sliced

1 teaspoon marinated ginger, slivered (see Tasty Tip below; omit if unavailable)

1 tablespoon capers, including their brine

2 to 3 basil leaves, cut in slivers, for garnish

1. To prepare the marinade, combine the Pernod, rosemary, and dried onion in a nonreactive pan. Add the chops and marinate for 1 hour at room temperature or up to 6 hours in the refrigerator. Pat the chops dry with paper towels.

2. Heat a large nonstick skillet and add a pinch of salt. Sear the chops over high heat for 2 to 3 minutes on each side. Push them to the side of the skillet and add the tomato and onion in the center. Cook until the tomato and onion form a sauce, 2 to 3 minutes. Add the ginger and the capers with their brine.

3. Spoon the tomato sauce onto the dinner plates. Place the chops on top of the sauce and garnish with fresh basil.

Tasty Tip

To make marinated ginger, buy fresh ginger, peel it with a vegetable peeler or a small sharp knife, and cut it into slices about 1/8 inch thick. Put the slices in a glass jar, cover them with sherry or white wine, and store in the refrigerator, where they will stay fresh just about forever.

Marinated ginger is milder and doesn't have the same bite as raw ginger.

chapter 5

HOT OFF THE GRILL

Cavemen did it, as did the ancient Romans, Greeks, and Native Americans. Grilling over a fire is man's oldest form of cooking, yet most of us think of outdoor grilling as quintessentially American, our favorite summer-food pastime.

I love to grill. It's fast, easy, and everyone gets involved. While I still associate barbecues with balmy summer evenings on my deck, some cooks now grill straight through the winter, thanks to gas grills right outside the kitchen door. I have fond memories of my brother Joel donning boots, hat, gloves, and ski parka to grill steaks in the middle of a snowstorm.

Grilling is more an art than a science because the timing is even more imprecise than for other forms of cooking. You must adjust for the uneven heat of the coals, how far away from the heat the rack is, and for the thickness and texture of the meat.

Yet people who grill appear to have little difficulty with all this. Does some atavistic instinct tell us when a kebab is done? Is this a throwback to caveman times? In our backyards, wearing Williams Sonoma aprons, have we reverted to our prehistoric roots? Men who refuse to even boil water, grill. Hmmmm.

We Americans have a love affair with grilled food. Even a kid labeled as "the pickiest eater in the world" usually eats hamburgers. I confess that with all my fancy cooking, nothing beats a steak or chop grilled crusty on the outside, tender and juicy inside.

When I barbecue over charcoal, I use the more expensive natural charcoal rather than briquets treated with chemicals. However, I'd rather cook on a gas grill because the heat is more even and easier to regulate.

In today's health-conscious times, marinating and grilling have become quite fashionable. Dry rubs, seasoning pastes, and marinades with their spicy, exotic, or subtle flavors eliminate the need for fat-laden sauces. Any fat from the meat drips into the fire, and lean cuts like London broil that would otherwise be too tough for fast-cooking become tender enough to grill.

So be you male or female, don your apron, fire up your barbecue, and let's do what we've done for ten thousand years—grill our dinners.

Roasts on the Grill

SAVORY ROSEMARY LEG OF LAMB

ORANGE-SPICED LEG OF LAMB

POOLSIDE GRILLED EYE ROUND WITH SPICY PICKLED APPLESAUCE

LABOR DAY GRILLED LOIN OF PORK

SOUTHWESTERN GRILLED PORK TENDERLOIN

London Broil

LONDON BROIL À LA CLASS

PEPPERED LONDON BROIL

GRILLED CAJUN FLANK STEAK

TOP SIRLOIN MEXICANA

Steaks and Chops

MODERN GRILLED STEAK

ROSEMARY- AND COGNAC-SCENTED PORK CHOPS

RIB-EYE STEAK, MODENA STYLE

GRILLED SHELL STEAKS WITH TWO-TOMATO COGNAC SAUCE

Meat on Skewers

BEEF TERIYAKI

MILE-HIGH SKEWERED BEEF AND ONION

GRILLED RED ONION AND LAMB

OLD TESTAMENT SHISH KEBABS

MINT-MARINATED LAMB ON A STICK

GRILLED PORK TIDBITS WITH PORT-SCENTED LENTILS

Burgers, Plain and Fancy

BASIC BURGERS WITH VARIATIONS

CHUNKY VEGETABLE RELISH

GRILLED PESTO BURGERS

INDIAN LAMB BURGERS

AZTEC BURGERS

ST. GERMAIN VEAL PATTIES

ASIAN BURGERS

BASIL BEEF EN BROCHETTE

Roasts on the Grill

When cooking for a crowd—which is often the case on steamy summer days at my house in Bridgehampton—I grill a roast. Typically, I marinate it first. This tenderizes it, helps it cook faster, and eliminates the need for fancy sauces.

Roasts can't be beat for casual summer entertaining. They need so little attention, I can spend my time with my guests instead of standing at the grill.

I like to serve buffet-style during the summer, with the food at room temperature. I make the roast an hour or so ahead and give it a chance to cool. Then I set out some salads, relishes, maybe a homemade mustard sauce, so there's little last-minute work.

Although I've cooked roasts on covered charcoal grills, I much prefer a gas grill for its temperature control. While not as precise as an oven, it's far more precise than charcoal. Not having to work in a hot kitchen makes the less-than-precise timing of the grill worth it.

SAVORY ROSEMARY LEG OF LAMB

Makes 8 servings, with leftovers

A few steps from the kitchen door of my summer house, I am fortunate to have two huge herb boxes that my dad built for me over a Thanksgiving weekend visit. But even apartment dwellers can grow herbs on their windowsills.

In some years the rosemary is full and lush, while in others the sage and lavender take over. Feel free to substitute the most abundant herb that grows in your garden.

The peppery flavor of the delicate summer savory complements lamb. In Europe it's known as the "bean herb" because it blends well with beans, lentils, and peas.

If you don't have fresh rosemary for the marinade, rub dried rosemary in your hands. Chop it along with a bunch of fresh parsley and the garlic.

During the summer I like to serve this dish with a large bowl of blanched green beans, sliced fresh tomatoes drizzled with extra-virgin olive oil and chopped fresh rosemary, and garlic-roasted new red potatoes. In the winter I would serve garlic-scented lentils with a tossed mixed green salad dressed with a mustard vinaigrette.

Marinade

1 large onion, sliced

8 or 9 cloves garlic, crushed

5 or 6 sprigs fresh rosemary, bruised

5 or 6 sprigs fresh summer savory

2 tablespoons olive oil

½ cup full-bodied red wine

1 well-trimmed 6- to 7-pound leg of lamb, butterflied

Freshly ground black pepper

Salt

1. To prepare the marinade, place the onion in a large nonreactive pan. Scatter the garlic, rosemary, and savory over the onion. Add the oil and wine. Place the lamb in the marinade, cover, and marinate in the refrigerator for at least 4 hours or overnight, turning occasionally. Bring the lamb to room temperature before grilling.

2. Preheat the grill.

3. Remove the lamb from the marinade, discarding the marinade, and sprinkle generously with pepper and sparingly with salt. Grill over medium-high heat for 12 minutes on each side for rare, 15 minutes on each side for medium. Allow the lamb to rest for 10 to 15 minutes before slicing.

Tasty Tip

I often use zipper-lock bags for marinating meat. You don't have to turn the meat; you can just squish the bag or turn it over.

ORANGE-SPICED LEG OF LAMB

Begin one to two days in advance

Makes 8 servings, with leftovers

Made with orange marmalade, herbs, spices, and red wine, this marinade creates an exotic and elegant grilled leg of lamb that's perfect for a summer dinner party on the deck or on the northwest porch as the sun goes down.

However, if your grill is close to the back door, this lamb tastes just as good on New Year's Eve with an old Southern treasure, Hoppin' John, and a glass of champagne for good luck.

On warm nights I like to serve the lamb with couscous with toasted pine nuts and raisins, a tossed green salad, and a glass of slightly chilled pinot noir.

Marinade

1 cup dry red wine

³/₄ cup beef broth (canned is fine)

3 tablespoons orange marmalade

2 tablespoons red wine vinegar

1 medium onion, chopped

1¹/₂ tablespoons chopped fresh marjoram
   or 1¹/₂ teaspoons dried

3 tablespoon chopped fresh parsley

1 bay leaf, crumbled

¹/₄ teaspoon ground ginger

1 clove garlic, minced

1 well-trimmed 6- to 7-pound leg of lamb,
   butterflied

One to two days ahead

1. To prepare the marinade, combine the wine, broth, marmalade, vinegar, onion, marjoram, parsley, bay leaf, ginger, and garlic in a nonreactive saucepan. Bring to a boil and simmer, uncovered, for 20 minutes. Allow to cool.

2. Place the lamb in a shallow nonreactive pan with the marinade. Cover and allow to marinate for 24 to 48 hours in the refrigerator.

Before grilling

3. Bring the lamb to room temperature before grilling. Preheat the grill.

4. Remove the lamb from the marinade. Bring the marinade to a boil and cook for 5 minutes. Grill the lamb over medium-high heat, basting occasionally with the marinade, for 12 minutes on each side for rare, 15 minutes for medium. Allow the lamb to rest for 10 to 15 minutes before slicing.

Steady the meat with a two-pronged fork. Holding the carving knife at a moderate angle to the meat, cut into thin slices.

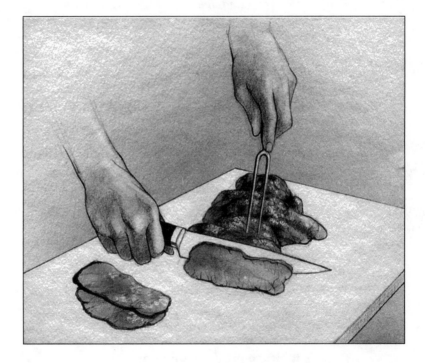

I allow at least 30 minutes to bring small pieces of meat to room temperature and from 1 to 1½ hours for large cuts and roasts.

POOLSIDE GRILLED EYE ROUND WITH SPICY PICKLED APPLESAUCE

Begin three to five days in advance

Makes 8 servings

I was musing with Margo, my good friend and a great cook, on the notion of grilling a beef eye round. She suggested I try it out on a few friends at her house because her gas grill is close to the pool. We planned to put the roast on the grill, take a swim, and check the meat occasionally while we basked in the sun.

The heat of the red chili peppers, married with the sweet spicy flavor of bay leaf, pickling spices, and garlic, plus the pungent oregano and hearty burgundy wine formed the perfect union to flavor the beef. The long marinating time, 3 to 5 days, is needed to tenderize the beef.

If you plan to make the Spicy Pickled Applesauce, I suggest simmering the marinade early in the day because it takes nearly an hour to reduce. The rest is as easy as a dip in the pool. Slice the roast thinly and pass the sauce.

We served barley and mushroom pilaf, sliced fresh tomatoes, and pan-roasted sweet corn off the cob seasoned with fresh cilantro and red chili peppers. The next morning the leftover roast was made into hash for breakfast.

Marinade

10 small dried chili peppers

1 bottle full-bodied red wine

1 bay leaf

2 tablespoons dried oregano

4 large cloves garlic, minced

1 tablespoon pickling spices

1 well-trimmed eye round roast (about 3 pounds)

Three to five days ahead

1. To prepare the marinade, combine the chili peppers, wine, bay leaf, oregano, garlic, and pickling spices in a nonreactive pan. Add the roast, cover, and marinate in the refrigerator for 3 to 5 days, turning daily.

Before grilling

2. Bring the roast to room temperature. Remove it from the marinade and reserve the marinade if you're going to make the Spicy Pickled Applesauce (recipe follows); otherwise, discard.

3. Preheat the grill.

4. Sear the roast, covered, turning once, over high heat for 10 to 15 minutes, or until it's blackened. If you have a gas grill, reduce the heat to low; otherwise, move the meat to a cool area of the grill. Continue to cook, covered, turning every 5 minutes, for an additional 20 to 30 minutes, or until an instant-read meat thermometer registers 125°F.

5. Transfer the roast to a platter and allow it to rest for 15 to 20 minutes before carving.

SPICY PICKLED APPLESAUCE

Marinade from Poolside Grilled Eye Round Roast (see previous recipe)

1 large tart apple, peeled, cored, and chopped

Juice of ½ lemon

¼ cup chopped onion

1 small sweet gherkin, chopped

1 tablespoon hot-pepper jelly or 1 tablespoon mint jelly plus 1 teaspoon red pepper flakes

2 teaspoons olive oil

1. Strain out the spices from the marinade and pour the marinade into a large nonreactive skillet. Bring to a boil over high heat and cook 20 to 40 minutes, until it is reduced by half. You'll end up with about 1½ cups of liquid.

2. Combine the apple, lemon juice, onion, gherkin, pepper jelly, and olive oil in a small bowl. Stir this into the reduced marinade. Cook over high heat until the sauce lightly coats the back of a metal spoon, about 10 minutes more.

LABOR DAY GRILLED LOIN OF PORK

Begin two to four days in advance

Makes 40 or more servings when part of a buffet,
or 18 to 20 servings as an entree

It started one August evening when I invited my cooking class of eight people to come for dinner on Labor Day weekend. Before I knew it, I had invited 55 friends to join us. It's true!

Making this roast turned out to be a laborless task, and the guests raved about the smoky, spicy flavor of the chipotle and dried ancho chili peppers, which mingled splendidly with the ripe tomatoes and chives in the marinade.

I grilled the pork loin late in the afternoon and let it rest at room temperature for about one hour. Then I cut the loin into thin slices and arranged them on a large platter lined with long chives. Just before serving, I spooned the Mustard and Wine Vinaigrette over the entire dish.

1 well-trimmed 7-pound boneless loin of pork, tied

6 cloves garlic, cut in slivers

Salt

Freshly ground black pepper

5 or 6 sprigs fresh oregano or 2 teaspoons dried

2 ancho peppers or other large dried, mild chili peppers, cut in chunks

1 chipotle pepper, cut in chunks (see Tasty Tip, page 43)

4 very ripe large tomatoes, sliced

1 cup snipped chives or chopped scallion greens

2½ cups dry white wine

Mustard and Wine Vinaigrette (recipe follows)

Two to four days ahead

1. With the point of a small sharp knife, poke 1- to 1½-inch-deep holes in the roast and insert the slivers of garlic. Rub the pork with salt and pepper.

2. Place the pork in a large nonreactive roasting pan or dish. Sprinkle with the oregano and surround the roast with the ancho and chipotle peppers, tomatoes, and chives or scallions. Pour the wine over the pork, cover, and refrigerate for at least 2 days or up to 4 days, turning the roast every 8 to 12 hours.

Before grilling

3. Bring the pork to room temperature before grilling. Preheat the grill.

4. Remove the pork from the marinade. Bring the marinade to a boil in a small saucepan to kill any bacteria, and set it aside for basting.

5. Grill the pork loin, covered, 5 to 6 minutes on each side, or until browned and seared. If you have a gas grill, reduce the heat to medium; otherwise, move the pork to a medium-hot area of the grill and continue to cook, covered, basting occasionally, for approximately 35 minutes more, or until the temperature registers 155°F on an instant-read meat thermometer. Let the roast rest for at least 20 minutes before slicing. To serve, pour Mustard and Wine Vinaigrette over the sliced roast.

Cut the roast in half if it's too big to store in your refrigerator or cook on your grill.

MUSTARD AND WINE VINAIGRETTE

Makes approximately 1½ cups

This vinaigrette makes a good, pungent salad dressing too.

½ cup red wine vinegar

½ cup Dijon mustard

1½ cups olive oil

1 tablespoon freshly ground black pepper

Mix the vinegar and mustard together in a bowl. Gradually whisk in the olive oil and pepper. This vinaigrette can be prepared several days ahead and refrigerated. Return to room temperature before serving.

SOUTHWESTERN GRILLED PORK TENDERLOIN

Makes 8 servings

While waiting to witness my son's rocket launch—he's an astrophysicist—in White Sands, New Mexico, last December, my sister Joan and I went to the open-air farmers market. We found handmade chili pepper wreaths of every size and shape. She bought dozens of tiny chili pepper Christmas trees, and I purchased several bags of large chili peppers from mild to very hot, plus wreaths for both the front door and my kitchen window.

That Christmas in Arizona I marinated pork tenderloins with a handful of tiny red-hot chili peppers that I snitched from one of her decorative Christmas trees out on the patio. I crushed them with the side of a knife and added a little chili powder—just in case they weren't hot enough—salt, freshly ground black pepper, minced garlic, olive oil, and fresh lime juice from limes off a neighbor's tree.

We served the pork with blue corn chips and, to cool our palates, sliced avocado, mango, red onion, and fresh spinach salad dressed with a creamy cilantro-scented mayonnaise.

If you are not accustomed to so much heat, limit the chili peppers to one or two in the marinade. If you like, serve Tropical Salsa (page 25) with the tenderloin.

Marinade

1 teaspoon chili powder

1 teaspoon ground coriander

1 teaspoon salt

1 teaspoon freshly ground black pepper

¼ cup dried chili peppers, crushed (or less to taste)

3 cloves garlic, minced

Juice of 3 limes (about ½ cup)

⅓ cup olive oil

4 boneless tenderloins of pork (approximately ¾ pound each)

1. To prepare the marinade, combine the chili powder, coriander, salt, black pepper, chili peppers, garlic, lime juice, and olive oil.

2. Pour the marinade over the pork, cover, and marinate in a nonreactive dish in the refrigerator for several hours, preferably overnight. Bring the pork to room temperature before grilling.

3. Preheat the grill.

4. Remove the pork from the marinade and discard the marinade. Grill over high heat, turning often, for 5 to 10 minutes to sear the meat. If you have a gas grill, reduce the heat; otherwise, move the pork to a cooler area of the grill. Cook for approximately 12 minutes longer, continuing to turn frequently, or until an instant-read meat thermometer registers 155° F. The pork is done when there is still a hint of pink in the center. Let the pork rest for 10 to 15 minutes.

5. Slice on a cutting board set over a pan to catch the juices. Arrange the slices on a platter and drizzle with the spicy juices.

Any kind of meat thermometer is fine for an oven-baked roast, but only an instant-read meat thermometer is good for grilled roasts that are turned frequently. These thermometers are wonderfully easy to use. Insert into a meaty part of the roast—never near the bone—and within seconds the temperature will register. I test the temperature in several places so I can tell exactly how well done each part of the roast is.

London Broil

The large, thick steaks called London broil that you find at the supermarket are usually cut from the shoulder or round section of the beef carcass. I always choose the first cut from the round for London broil. (You can recognize it in the package by its unusual shape; the sides of the meat angle down, making it look like a slice taken from the middle of an upside-down pyramid.) This cut is juicy and more tender than the larger, straight-sided round steaks in your supermarket's meat case.

I prefer one or two pieces about 2 inches thick because they are easy to handle on and off the grill, marinate overnight, and cook in a reasonable amount of time, about 30 minutes—any thicker takes forever!

If you have a big crowd to feed and your budget is small, this cut is the answer.

LONDON BROIL À LA CLASS

Makes 6 to 8 servings

In 1975 when I established my catering business and cooking school, Cooking With Class, Inc., my children were small and we had just bought a house in the Hamptons across the street from the ocean.

I didn't want to stay in Manhattan for their summer vacation, but I was concerned about my fledgling business. Luckily, most of my students that first year also planned to be at the beach.

I packed up the equipment, took my show on the road, and held cooking classes by the sea. Ever since that first summer, I've held a series of summer classes during the month of August.

This classic recipe is my updated version of one of the first recipes I taught that summer. What tasted good then still tastes good some 20 years later. I served vichyssoise, fluffy rice with celery, tomato and cucumbers with fresh basil, and for dessert, peaches Cardinal. Today I'd keep the rest of the menu, but cut out the vichyssoise.

Marinade

1 cup soy sauce

6 cloves garlic, minced

¼ cup olive oil

1 cup Madeira wine

½ teaspoon dried basil

½ teaspoon dried thyme

¼ teaspoon freshly ground black pepper

1 well-trimmed 2- to 3-pound 2-inch-thick London broil (round steak)

1. To prepare the marinade, combine the soy sauce, garlic, olive oil, wine, basil, thyme, and pepper in a nonreactive pan. Add the London broil, cover, and refrigerate for at least 6 hours or overnight, turning occasionally. Bring the meat to room temperature before grilling.

2. Preheat the grill.

3. Remove the meat from the marinade and discard the marinade. Grill over high heat for 1 to 2 minutes on each side to sear the meat. If you have a gas grill, reduce the heat to medium; otherwise, move the meat to a slightly cooler area of the grill. Cook for 8 minutes on the first side and 18 minutes on the second side for rare, 20 minutes on the second side for medium, or until done to your taste.

4. Place the meat on a serving platter and allow it to rest for 10 to 15 minutes. Cut the London broil against the grain into thin slices.

Holding the carving knife at a slight angle, cut the London broil across the grain into thin slices.

PEPPERED LONDON BROIL

Begin one day in advance

Makes 6 to 8 servings

Pepper lovers—like me—will adore this recipe! The triple-pepper dry rub adds heat to the beef while the beef rests in the refrigerator overnight.

If the deck is not icy nor your grill too far from the kitchen door, why not serve this for a crowd of football fans? If there's a snowstorm, preheat the broiler and cook it the same way right in the cozy comfort of your warm kitchen.

Serve with brown rice and grilled red, green, and yellow peppers for a mélange of pepper flavors.

Dry Rub

**1 tablespoon chopped fresh marjoram or
   1 teaspoon dried**

1 jalapeño pepper, stemmed, seeded, and minced

¼ teaspoon whole allspice

¼ teaspoon crushed red pepper flakes

¼ teaspoon freshly ground black pepper

**1 well-trimmed 2- to 3-pound 2-inch-thick London
   broil (round steak)**

One day ahead

1. To prepare the dry rub, crush together the marjoram, jalapeño pepper, allspice, red pepper flakes, and black pepper. Rub this mixture into both sides of the London broil, cover, and refrigerate for at least 6 hours or overnight.

Before grilling

2. Bring the London broil to room temperature. Preheat the grill.

3. Grill the London broil over high heat for 1 to 2 minutes on each side to sear the meat. If you have a gas grill, reduce the heat to medium; otherwise, move the meat to a slightly cooler area of the grill. Cook for 8 minutes on the first side and 18 minutes on the second side for rare, 20 minutes on the second side for medium, or until done to your taste.

4. Place the London broil on a serving platter and allow it to rest for 10 to 15 minutes. Cut against the grain into thin slices.

If it's a buggy evening, I lightly cover the cooked meat with aluminum foil while it rests. If the weather's cold or rainy, I bring it inside.

GRILLED CAJUN FLANK STEAK

Begin one day in advance

Makes 5 servings

Generally, flank steaks are no thicker than ¹/₂ inch, and they normally tip the scale at only 1¹/₂ pounds, so I usually plan on one steak for five people—unless I've invited the local teenage track team for dinner.

The first rule for flank steak is to cook it quickly over hot heat and only just until it's rare. Equally important is to slice it thinly on an angle immediately after taking it off the grill, as this cut toughens as it cools. I set a cutting board inside a jelly roll pan to catch the juices, which I drizzle back over the sliced steak.

This marinade contains all the flavors of Cajun cooking: rosemary, pepper, garlic, Worcestershire sauce, Tabasco, lemon, and bourbon. I can almost hear zydeco music in the background. This is not a marinade for the faint-hearted.

Serve with "dirty" mashed potatoes (made with red-skinned spuds, unpeeled) and some chèvre-stuffed tomatoes.

Marinade

2 teaspoons minced fresh rosemary

1 tablespoon freshly ground black pepper

2 cloves garlic, crushed

1 tablespoon Worcestershire sauce

¹/₂ teaspoon Tabasco sauce

Juice of 1 lemon

¹/₄ cup bourbon

One 1¹/₂-pound flank steak, scored on both sides

2 teaspoons olive oil, approximately

One day ahead

1. To make the marinade, crush the rosemary and pepper together. Add the garlic, Worcestershire sauce, Tabasco sauce, lemon juice, and bourbon and stir well.

2. Place the steak in a nonreactive pan and pour the marinade over it. Marinate in the refrigerator, covered, overnight, turning several times.

Before grilling

3. Bring the steak to room temperature. Preheat the grill.

4. Remove the steak from the marinade, discard the marinade, and rub both sides with olive oil. Grill for 3 to 5 minutes on each side. Carve immediately, cutting across the grain into slices about ¼ inch thick.

Steady the just-grilled steak with a two-pronged fork. Holding the carving knife parallel to the meat, cut across the grain into thin slices.

TOP SIRLOIN MEXICANA

Begin at least one day in advance

Makes 6 servings

Most folks think of oregano as Greek or Italian, an herb to sprinkle on pizza, but it's also found in many Latin cuisines. Mexican oregano has a stronger flavor than the Greek variety. Oregano belongs to the mint family and is a south-of-the-border relative of thyme and marjoram.

If you don't have fresh oregano, substitute fresh thyme or marjoram. Remember to marinate this steak for at least 24 hours. If you can plan that far ahead, 48 hours is even better.

Marinade

Juice of 1 lime

1 teaspoon salt

¹/₂ teaspoon sugar

1 teaspoon freshly ground black pepper

2 tablespoons olive oil

2 teaspoons chopped fresh oregano, thyme, or marjoram or ¹/₂ teaspoon dried

2 tablespoons sherry vinegar

1 shallot, chopped (about 1 heaping tablespoon)

1 well-trimmed 2-pound 1-inch-thick lean top sirloin steak

At least one day ahead

1. To prepare the marinade, combine the lime juice, salt, sugar, pepper, oil, oregano, vinegar, and shallot in a nonreactive pan. Add the steak, cover, and marinate for at least 24 or up to 48 hours in the refrigerator, turning occasionally.

Before grilling

2. Bring the steak to room temperature. Preheat the grill.

3. Remove the steak from the marinade and discard the marinade. Grill over high heat for 3 to 4 minutes on each side, or until done to your taste. Let the steak rest for 10 to 15 minutes. Cut on a sharp angle into thin slices. Serve with a good quality store-bought tomato salsa.

Steaks and Chops

"Let's throw a steak on the grill for dinner!"

Grilling steak is an all-American phenomenon. Generally speaking, the most often asked-for steaks at the meat counter are shell steak, rib steak, and T-bone. They are tender as is, and like my good friend Phillip Stephen Schulz, author of the grill book of the century, *Cooking with Fire and Smoke,* I suggest marinating these steaks for only a short time.

I use an unscientific approach to see if a tender steak is done: "the finger test." I press each steak in the center, and if the meat stays depressed for a few seconds, it's very rare, hardly cooked at all. If the meat springs back, it's cooked to my taste, rare to medium rare. If there's little or no give to it, the meat is overdone and it's time to think about how to mask the mistake.

Try this method yourself. The next time you grill, press the steak with your finger and notice how it feels. Then cut into it to see exactly how well it's done. You'll get the hang of it quickly and you, too, will be an expert at the finger test.

You can get three portions from a pound of boneless steak and two portions if the steak has a bone—unless you're serving serious meat eaters and are skimpy on the side dishes.

MODERN GRILLED STEAK

A grilled steak can be served with anything and everything. The beauty here is in the meat itself. These steaks are tender, fast-cooking, and will absorb herb rubs, pastes, marinades, and barbecue sauces in less than 10 minutes— about how long it takes the grill to heat.

Well-trimmed steaks (T-bone, shell, sirloin, New York strip, your choice), edges scored (see illustration, page 127)

Cloves of garlic, cut in slivers

Crushed or coarsely ground black peppercorns

1. Using a sharp-pointed knife, poke deep holes over the surface of the steak and insert slivers of garlic. Spread both sides of the steak generously with pepper. Wrap the steaks in plastic wrap and set aside while you heat the grill.

2. Preheat the grill.

3. Grill the steaks over high heat for 3 to 5 minutes on each side, or until done to each person's taste. Let the steaks rest for 4 to 5 minutes before serving.

ROSEMARY- AND COGNAC- SCENTED PORK CHOPS

Makes 6 servings

The trick in cooking pork chops on the grill is not to overcook them. Once they're seared on both sides, move them to a cooler section of the grill. If you have a gas grill, lower the heat to moderate to finish cooking them.

Throw the woody rosemary stems directly on the hot coals. They smell so wonderful the neighbors are likely to join you for dinner. Rubbing the chops with fresh rosemary and freshly ground black pepper imparts a deep forest-herb undertone. A splash of cognac adds a rich, delicate flavor and makes the chops mouth-watering.

With these pork chops I serve brown rice made with shiitake mushrooms and sweet baby carrots.

6 well-trimmed ¹/₂-inch-thick pork chops

2 large sprigs fresh rosemary

1 teaspoon freshly ground black pepper, or more to taste

2 tablespoons cognac

1. Rub the chops with the rosemary and pepper. Sprinkle with cognac and set aside for 30 minutes to 1 hour.

2. Preheat the grill.

3. Sear the chops over high heat for 2 to 3 minutes on each side. Continue to grill over moderate heat for 10 to 12 minutes, turning occasionally. The chops should still be juicy and slightly pink inside. Let the chops rest 4 to 5 minutes before serving.

RIB-EYE STEAK, MODENA STYLE

Makes 4 servings

The rib-eye steak comes from the short loin section of the beef. It's so tender you can grill it straight from the butcher's package. Marinate it for only a short time: you want to add the flavor of the marinade, not soften the meat.

Here the great tastes of garlic and basil blend with balsamic vinegar and oil to glaze the beef with the flavors reminiscent of Modena, Italy. If you have a "fine-quality" balsamic vinegar, sprinkle a few drops on each piece just before serving. Or bring the marinade to a boil and spoon a bit on each grilled steak.

Serve freshly cooked pasta dressed with olive oil and lots of chopped fresh basil, along with ripe beefsteak tomatoes and sweet onion slices.

Marinade

2 teaspoons olive oil

1/3 cup chopped fresh basil or 2 1/2 tablespoons dried

6 tablespoons balsamic vinegar

1 large clove garlic, minced

Freshly ground black pepper

4 well-trimmed 1- to 1 1/4-inch-thick small rib-eye steaks

1. To prepare the marinade, combine the oil, basil, vinegar, garlic, and pepper in a nonreactive pan. Add the steaks, cover, and marinate for 10 to 20 minutes.

2. Preheat the grill.

3. Remove the steaks from the marinade. Grill over high heat for 3 to 4 minutes on each side for rare. Cook a minute or two longer on each side for medium. Let the steak rest for 5 to 6 minutes before serving.

GRILLED SHELL STEAKS WITH TWO-TOMATO COGNAC SAUCE

Makes 2 servings

If you've invited a special dinner guest, serve these steaks. This dish is an 11 on a scale of 1 to 10. (Your guest should be too.) Coming from the short loin section of the beef, this steak is already as tender as can be. It's also long on flavor and taste.

Make the Two-Tomato Cognac Sauce in the morning or the day before. You can double or triple the recipe to serve this dish for more than two.

Two-Tomato Cognac Sauce

1 cup Homemade Beef Stock (page 276) or 2 tablespoons demi-glace (page 273)

1 tablespoon olive oil

1 small onion, minced

2 plum tomatoes, peeled, seeded, and chopped

4 oil-packed sun-dried tomatoes, well drained and sliced

¼ cup cognac

Salt

Freshly ground black pepper

2 well-trimmed 1-inch-thick shell steaks, edges scored (see illustration, page 127)

½ teaspoon freshly ground black pepper, or more to taste

1. Unless you are using demi-glace, boil the broth until it is reduced to 2 to 3 tablespoons, about 10 minutes. Set aside.

2. Heat the olive oil in a nonreactive skillet and cook the onion, fresh tomatoes, and sun-dried tomatoes, stirring, over moderate heat until the onion is soft and translucent, 8 to 10 minutes. Add the cognac and ignite. (The flames will go out on their own in less than a minute.)

When the flames go out, add the reduced broth or demi-glace. Cook the sauce until reduced to about ¼ cup, 3 to 4 minutes. Taste and add salt and pepper if needed.

The sauce can be prepared up to 2 days ahead.

3. Preheat the grill.

4. Sear the steaks over high heat for about 1 minute on each side until they are browned. If you have a gas grill, reduce the heat to medium-high; otherwise, move the meat to a moderately hot area of the grill. Grill for 3 to 4 minutes on each side for rare, or until done to your preference. Let the steaks rest for 4 to 5 minutes.

5. Gently reheat the sauce and spoon it over the steaks to serve.

Meat on Skewers

Meat cooked on skewers can be traced back to cavemen. As ancient stone carvings depict, the cooking of meat began with men throwing meat directly into the fire. Doubtless an early genius invented meat-on-a-twig or on-a-branch for hunks of venison and boar.

One of my fondest childhood memories is of a cheery bonfire that was lit after we'd cleared the woods west of the farmhouse. Grams came out to help Mom and, more important to me, to bring a package of wieners from our trusted meat man, Lyle Austin, in Preston, Minnesota.

From a supple willow branch whittled to a fine point, we've "advanced" to using water-soaked 2-inch-long bamboo toothpicks for one-bite hors d'oeuvres; 12- to 18-inch metal skewers for one-portion servings; and an 8-foot stainless-steel spit custom-made for roasting a whole baby lamb, pig, or side of beef.

BEEF TERIYAKI

Makes 8 servings

Here's a hot item at a cocktail party. Using the ingredients called for in this recipe, cut the beef and peppers into pieces no bigger than ¼ to ⅓ inch square and marinate them for up to 30 minutes. Alternate the tiny tender tidbits of marinated beef with colorful, crisp peppers on soaked round toothpicks, and grill for 2 to 3 minutes.

A note here on using long bamboo skewers. I don't recommend them for serving hors d'oeuvres, even though they look dramatic on the tray. When guests mill around at a crowded cocktail party, long skewers are a hazard to both the diners and those near them.

On the other hand, long bamboo skewers are fine for a main course, as in this recipe, especially at an informal outdoor dinner. For more formal dinners I slide the beef and vegetables off the skewer onto the platter or plate for the guests.

Teriyaki Sauce

½ cup soy sauce

½ cup oil

¼ cup dry sherry

2 cloves garlic, minced

2 tablespoons grated or minced fresh ginger

Zest of ¹/₂ lemon, grated (see Tasty Tip, page 111)

1¹/₂ teaspoons rice wine vinegar

¹/₄ teaspoon freshly ground black pepper

3 to 3¹/₂ pounds lean top sirloin, cut in 1-inch cubes

1 large red bell pepper, cut in 1-inch pieces

1 large yellow bell pepper, cut in 1-inch pieces

1 large green bell pepper, cut in 1-inch pieces

1 large onion, cut in 1-inch pieces

1. Soak bamboo skewers in hot water for 2 to 3 hours or use metal skewers.

2. Prepare the teriyaki sauce by combining the soy sauce, oil, sherry, garlic, ginger, lemon zest, vinegar, and black pepper.

3. Thread beef cubes alternately with red, yellow, and green peppers and onion on a skewer. Start and end with a cube of beef. Place the skewers in a flat nonreactive dish and pour teriyaki sauce over them. Marinate for up to 1 hour at room temperature.

4. Preheat the grill.

5. Remove the skewers from the marinade and discard the marinade. Grill 3 to 4 minutes, turning often to brown all sides, or cook to personal preference.

I double or triple the teriyaki sauce and keep it in the refrigerator (but never save what you've already used for marinating). Use it for brushing on pork chops or chicken breasts just before grilling. I don't recommend marinating small pieces of meat and vegetables in teriyaki sauce for more than a couple of hours; the meat absorbs the flavors quickly, and vegetables will discolor if left in it too long.

MILE-HIGH SKEWERED BEEF AND ONION

Makes 4 servings

The juxtaposition of fresh jalapeño peppers, red onion, lemon juice, cilantro, and red wine with the hot-and-sweet pepper jelly elevates cubed beef to a high and spicy level. If you like it fiery, add yet more jalapeño.

Slide the skewered beef and onion onto a bed of chiffonade of romaine lettuce, surround with cherry tomatoes, and serve with a medley of corn off the cob and black beans accented with fresh cilantro.

Marinade

¹/₂ jalapeño pepper, seeded and chopped

¹/₂ red onion, thinly sliced

1 teaspoon freshly ground black pepper

1 tablespoon grape jelly

3 tablespoons hot-pepper jelly or 3 tablespoons grape jelly plus 1 teaspoon red pepper flakes

3 tablespoons red or white wine

3 tablespoons chopped fresh cilantro

1 tablespoon freshly squeezed lemon juice

1 pound well-trimmed beef round, cut in 1¹/₂-inch cubes

1 large onion, cut in eighths and each eighth cut in half

1. To prepare marinade, mix together the jalapeño pepper, onion, black pepper, grape jelly, pepper jelly, wine, cilantro, and lemon juice in a large bowl. Add the beef and toss well. Marinate for at least 3 hours in the refrigerator or, even better, for 1 to 2 days. Bring the beef to room temperature before grilling.

2. Preheat the grill.

3. Thread the beef and onion alternately on metal skewers. Grill over high heat for 10 to 12 minutes, turning a quarter turn every 2 to 3 minutes, until the meat is browned. Let rest for 5 minutes before serving.

GRILLED RED ONION AND LAMB

Makes 6 servings

Fragrant coriander has a taste reminiscent of caraway, lemon, and sage combined in one small seed. When it's added to fresh ginger, garlic, and jalapeño peppers, there's a taste explosion in your mouth. Red wine transports these exotic flavors to the lamb, and the sweet and colorful red onions add their pungent taste.

Fresh sage makes an aromatic bed for couscous made with chicken broth, dusted with chopped parsley, and then topped with the onions and lamb.

2 pounds well-trimmed boneless leg of lamb, cut in 1 1/2-inch cubes

3 tablespoons olive oil

2 teaspoons coriander seeds, crushed

2 tablespoons grated fresh ginger

4 cloves of garlic, minced

1 tablespoon freshly ground black pepper

2 jalapeño peppers, seeded and coarsely chopped

1 cup full-bodied red wine

4 medium-size red onions, peeled and cut in eighths

1. Place the lamb in a nonreactive bowl. Add the oil and toss with the coriander, ginger, garlic, black pepper, and jalapeño peppers. Add the wine and toss again. Cover and refrigerate for at least 4 hours or up to 24 hours. Toss the lamb occasionally to keep the surfaces moist. Remove the lamb from the refrigerator and bring to room temperature. Add the onions to the marinade 10 minutes before grilling.

2. Preheat the grill.

3. Remove the meat and onions from the marinade. Pour the marinade into a saucepan and bring it to a boil. Set aside.

4. Alternate the meat and onions on long metal skewers. Grill 3 inches from the heat, turning frequently and brushing occasionally with the marinade, for 6 to 10 minutes, or until done to your taste.

OLD TESTAMENT SHISH KEBABS

Makes 8 to 10 servings

Cumin and turmeric are aromatic spices that date back to Biblical times. At one time turmeric was part of the formula for perfume. I don't suggest you spritz this marinade behind your ears, but your mouth will welcome its fragrance.

The distinct taste and color of turmeric marries well with the nutty, almost peppery cumin. A word of caution, however: do not marinate the vegetables, only the lamb.

The secret of this recipe is the separate skewers for the lamb and the vegetables, as each takes a different time to cook.

To serve, I arrange alternating skewers on a platter and serve aromatic basmati rice alongside.

3 pounds well-trimmed boneless leg of lamb, cut in 1¹/₂-inch cubes

3 tablespoons olive oil, plus oil to brush vegetables

1 medium onion, chopped

1 teaspoon cumin

¹/₂ teaspoon turmeric

2 tablespoons chopped fresh cilantro

1 medium eggplant, unpeeled, cut in 1¹/₂-inch cubes

Salt

2 medium green bell peppers, cut in large triangles

8 to 10 medium onions, quartered

36 small mushroom caps

1 teaspoon lemon juice, approximately

1. Put the lamb and oil in a large nonreactive bowl and toss. Add the chopped onion, cumin, turmeric, and cilantro and toss again. Marinate at room temperature for at least 1 hour or overnight in the refrigerator. Bring the lamb to room temperature before grilling.

2. Salt the eggplant and set it aside for approximately ¹/₂ hour. Drain off the liquid. Wash the eggplant to remove the salt, pat dry with paper towels, and brush with olive oil.

3. Brush the green peppers and quartered onions with olive oil. Brush the mushroom caps first with lemon juice and then with olive oil to prevent discoloration.

4. Preheat the grill.

5. Remove the lamb from the marinade, reserving the marinade. Bring the marinade to a boil and cook for 5 minutes. Set aside. Thread the lamb on long metal skewers. On separate skewers, assemble the vegetables, alternating green peppers, onions, eggplant, and mushrooms.

6. Grill the lamb about 3 inches from the heat, turning frequently and brushing occasionally with the marinade, for 6 to 10 minutes, or until done to your taste. Grill the vegetables alongside the meat for 5 to 8 minutes, turning and brushing them occasionally with the marinade.

Tasty Tip

If you're lucky enough to grow your own eggplant or can find slender Japanese eggplants at your local market, eliminate step 2.

Onions to be skewered are less likely to fall apart if you first cut them in half horizontally and then cut each half into quarters. You should end up with 8 chunks from each onion, each about the size of a 1- to 1 1/2-inch lamb cube.

MINT-MARINATED LAMB ON A STICK

Makes 4 servings

The combination of yogurt and lamb has been a staple in Middle Eastern cuisine for centuries. Yogurt's lactic acid tenderizes the lamb, while the mint and its distant cousin, thyme, the fiery chili pepper, and the tart lime juice add their exuberant flavors.

I make a saffron-scented long-grain rice to serve with the lamb, accompanied by Minted Yogurt Sauce (recipe follows).

Marinade

1 cup plain nonfat yogurt

1 tablespoon minced fresh peppermint or spearmint leaves

2 small dried chili peppers

¹/₂ tablespoon freshly ground black pepper

¹/₂ teaspoon dried thyme

Juice of ¹/₂ lime

1¹/₄ to 1¹/₂ pounds well-trimmed lamb, cut in 1¹/₂-inch cubes

4 small onions, peeled and quartered

1. To prepare the marinade, combine the yogurt, mint, chili peppers, black pepper, thyme, and lime juice in a large nonreactive bowl. Add the lamb and marinate for 1 hour at room temperature or for up to 2 days in the refrigerator. Bring the meat to room temperature before grilling.

2. Place 8 bamboo skewers in hot water and soak for 2 to 3 hours.

3. Preheat the grill.

4. Remove the lamb from the marinade and discard the marinade. Alternate cubes of lamb and onion on bamboo skewers. Grill over high heat for 6 to 10 minutes, turning frequently, or until the lamb is done to your preference. (I like the lamb still rosy inside.)

MINTED YOGURT SAUCE

Makes about 1¼ cups

By adding saffron rice, an assortment of chutneys, and this sauce, you can turn any plain grilled meat, chicken, or fish into a festive Indian entree.

This sauce tastes best when made at least 30 minutes ahead.

1 small cucumber, peeled and finely chopped

1 to 2 tablespoons minced fresh mint

1 cup plain nonfat yogurt

¼ teaspoon salt

¼ teaspoon freshly ground black pepper

1 teaspoon white wine vinegar

Stir the cucumber and mint into the yogurt. Add the salt, pepper, and vinegar. Taste and correct the seasonings.

GRILLED PORK TIDBITS WITH PORT-SCENTED LENTILS

Makes 6 servings

The addition of port to both the pork and the lentils lends a rich, slightly sweet flavor that tricks the palate. The combination tastes fattening, but it's not— it's just super scrumptious.

Port-Scented Lentils

$1\frac{1}{2}$ **cups dried lentils, picked over and rinsed**

2 stalks celery, chopped

2 carrots, peeled and chopped

1 medium onion, chopped

One $10\frac{1}{2}$-ounce can Campbell's beef broth

2 cups water, approximately

Salt

Freshly ground black pepper

$\frac{1}{3}$ **to** $\frac{1}{2}$ **cup port**

$1\frac{1}{2}$ **pounds pork tenderloin, cut in 1-inch cubes**

1 tablespoon fresh thyme leaves or 1 teaspoon dried

Pinch of salt

1 teaspoon freshly ground black pepper

2 tablespoons port

1. To prepare the Port-Scented Lentils, place the lentils, celery, carrots, and onion in large saucepan. Add the beef broth plus enough water to cover by at least 2 inches. Cover and bring the lentils to a boil. Reduce the heat and gently simmer over low heat, with the lid ajar, until the lentils are tender and the liquid is nearly absorbed, about 30 to 40 minutes. Add salt and pepper to taste.

2. Add the port, increase the heat to high, and boil for 1 to 2 minutes. Reduce the heat to low and simmer about 5 minutes. Taste and correct the seasonings.

   The lentils can be prepared up to 2 days ahead and refrigerated.

3. Toss the pork cubes with the thyme, salt, pepper, and port. Let stand for at least 30 minutes at room temperature, or cover and refrigerate overnight. Bring the pork to room temperature before grilling.

4. Preheat the grill.

5. Thread the seasoned pork onto metal skewers. Grill for about 8 to 10 minutes, turning occasionally to brown evenly.

6. Spoon the hot lentils onto a heated platter. Using a fork, push the pork tidbits off the skewers and onto the bed of lentils.

Burgers, Plain and Fancy

Traditionally, home and restaurant cooks make hamburgers with chuck, a less-expensive and higher-fat cut of beef. It's the fat that gives burgers their moist and juicy taste.

I prefer lean ground sirloin for its superb flavor and lower fat content. To compensate for the lack of fat and to keep these burgers moist and delicious, I add finely chopped onion.

I'm tired of people saying in a ho-hum manner, "I guess we'll make burgers for dinner." Reading these recipes should give you a clue as to how I feel about them. Live dangerously, try them all, and invent a few of your own.

Sometimes when I don't feel like serving burgers on buns, I top them with Chunky Vegetable Relish (page 209) and serve them on a bed of spaghetti or with baked potatoes on the side. Definitely not ordinary!

BASIC BURGERS WITH VARIATIONS

Makes 4 servings

1 pound lean ground sirloin

1/2 teaspoon salt

1/2 teaspoon freshly ground black pepper

1/2 cup finely chopped onion

1. Brush or spray the grill with oil and preheat.

2. Lightly mix all the ingredients together and shape into 4 patties.

3. Grill for 3 to 4 minutes on each side for rare, or until cooked to your preference.

HERB AND TOMATO BURGERS

Ingredients for 1 recipe Basic Burgers (page 207)

¼ cup chopped fresh parsley

1 teaspoon dried basil

¼ cup extra chopped onion

4 oil-packed sun-dried tomatoes, well drained

Follow the directions for Basic Burgers, sticking 1 sun-dried tomato into the center of each burger.

RUSSIAN BURGERS

Ingredients for 1 recipe Basic Burgers (page 207)

¼ cup extra chopped onion

¼ cup chopped fresh parsley

4 teaspoons drained horseradish

Follow the directions for Basic Burgers.

ITALIAN BURGERS

Ingredients for 1 recipe Basic Burgers (page 207)

4 teaspoons capers

¼ cup extra chopped onion

1 teaspoon chopped fresh parsley

Follow the directions for Basic Burgers.

CHEESEBURGER SURPRISE

Ingredients for 1 recipe Basic Burgers (page 207)

¼ cup chopped fresh parsley

2 ounces Cheddar cheese, cut in 4 pieces

Follow the directions for Basic Burgers, sticking 1 piece of cheese into the center of each burger.

CHUNKY VEGETABLE RELISH

Makes about 2 quarts

This coarse-style vegetable relish tastes great not only while it's still hot from the skillet and all the garden-fresh tastes are separate and distinct, but also 5 days later, when the flavors have mingled.

The relish is great with burgers, swordfish steaks, grilled chicken breasts, and ham sandwiches. Add a tablespoon or more of extra-virgin olive oil if you plan to use it as a warm pasta sauce.

2 to 3 tablespoons olive oil

1 large or 2 medium sweet onions, sliced

1 clove garlic, minced

2 red bell peppers, seeded and cut in 1-inch chunks

6 small zucchini, scrubbed and cut in 1-inch chunks

1 pound mushrooms, cleaned and sliced

2 large ripe tomatoes, peeled, seeded, and chopped

1/4 cup chopped fresh basil

Salt

Freshly ground black pepper

1. Heat 1 tablespoon of the olive oil in a large nonreactive skillet. Cook the onion and garlic, stirring, over medium heat until the onion is soft and translucent, about 3 minutes. Add the red peppers and zucchini, raise the heat to medium-high, and cook, stirring, for 5 to 8 minutes, until the peppers and zucchini are lightly browned. Add a bit more of the olive oil if needed to keep the vegetables lightly coated.

2. Meanwhile, in separate skillet, heat 1 tablespoon of the olive oil over high heat. Add the mushrooms and sauté, stirring, until they are tender and their liquid has evaporated, about 5 minutes.

3. Add the mushrooms, chopped tomatoes, and basil to the zucchini mixture and cook over low heat just until the tomatoes are soft. Add salt and pepper to taste. Serve warm or cover and refrigerate for up to 1 week.

GRILLED PESTO BURGERS

Makes 4 servings

Pepper-packed Watercress Pesto (page 27) is combined with lean ground round to keep these burgers moist when they're grilled—besides it adds a great taste!

Serve this burger with a sprinkle of Parmesan cheese and a thick slice of ripe tomato.

1 pound extra-lean ground round

2 tablespoons Watercress Pesto (page 27) or store-bought pesto

1/2 teaspoon freshly ground black pepper

1. Brush or spray the grill with oil and preheat.

2. Combine the meat, pesto, and pepper and shape into 4 patties.

3. Grill over high heat until medium rare, about 3 minutes on each side, or cook until done to your taste.

Tasty Tip

I keep Watercress Pesto in my freezer so I can quickly thaw it for a last-minute meal. If you use store-bought pesto, you can improve its flavor by adding a bit of fresh parsley and some freshly ground black pepper.

INDIAN LAMB BURGERS

Makes 4 servings

Lean ground lamb is not generally available packaged in the supermarket. When I order a butterflied leg of lamb, I ask the butcher to trim off the small pieces of meat that might otherwise be tossed away and grind this lean lamb for me.

Serve these tasty burgers with Minted Yogurt Sauce (page 205) and basmati rice, or stuff into a pita pocket with chopped fresh tomato seasoned with fresh mint or mango chutney.

1 pound lean ground lamb

1/4 teaspoon salt

1/2 teaspoon freshly ground black pepper

1/4 teaspoon ground cumin

1/4 teaspoon curry powder

Pinch of turmeric

1/3 cup finely chopped onion

1 tablespoon chopped fresh mint

1 egg white, beaten

1. Brush or spray the grill with oil and preheat.

2. Lightly mix all the ingredients together and shape into 4 patties.

3. Grill for 3 to 4 minutes on each side for rare, or until done to your taste.

AZTEC BURGERS

The smoky flavor of the chipotle pepper is the secret to this savory burger. Serve with grilled corn on the cob or as an open-faced sandwich on corn bread.

1 pound lean ground pork

1/2 teaspoon salt

1/2 teaspoon freshly ground black pepper

1/2 cup finely chopped onion

4 teaspoons chopped fresh cilantro

1/2 teaspoon chopped chipotle pepper (see Tasty Tip, page 43)

1. Brush or spray the grill with oil and preheat.

2. Lightly mix all the ingredients together and shape into 4 patties.

3. Grill for 4 to 5 minutes on each side, or until done to your taste.

St. Germain Veal Patties

Makes 4 servings

Mild and tender veal combined with lean sirloin and fresh mushrooms, sea-soned with French tarragon, reminds me of sitting in a French bistro on the Boulevard St. Germain.

Serve on a crusty baguette with its center scooped out, pommes frites *(a.k.a. French fries), and a glass of French wine.*

½ pound lean ground veal

½ pound lean ground sirloin

½ cup finely chopped onion

¼ cup finely chopped mushrooms

2 teaspoons finely chopped chives

1 tablespoon chopped fresh tarragon or 1 teaspoon dried

½ teaspoon salt

½ teaspoon freshly ground black pepper

1. Brush or spray the grill with oil and preheat.

2. Lightly mix all the ingredients together and shape into 4 patties.

3. Grill for 3 to 4 minutes on each side, or until done to your taste.

ASIAN BURGERS

Makes 4 servings

Hot sesame oil imparts an exotic flavor to these slightly sweet, yet peppery and ginger-spicy burgers. You can also put the mixture in a loaf pan, drizzle a tablespoon of soy sauce mixed with mirin (sweet Japanese rice wine) over the top, and bake it as you would a meat loaf.

1 pound mixture of ground pork, veal, and beef (available in meat section of most supermarkets, often labeled as meat loaf mixture). (See Tasty Tip below.)

³/₄ cup finely chopped onion

1 teaspoon minced garlic

2 teaspoons minced fresh ginger

1 teaspoon chili oil

¹/₂ teaspoon soy sauce

¹/₄ teaspoon freshly ground black pepper

Pinch of salt

1. Brush or spray the grill with oil and preheat.

2. Lightly mix all the ingredients together and shape into 4 patties.

3. Grill for 4 to 5 minutes on each side, or until cooked to your taste.

Unfortunately, the meat loaf mixtures sold at many supermarkets are high in fat. If they look too fatty, ask the butcher to grind lean meat for you.

BASIL BEEF EN BROCHETTE

Makes 6 servings for hors d'oeuvres
(6 small meatballs per person)

Wrapping each miniature meatball in a large basil leaf takes extra time, but it's worth the trouble. A long time ago I made these for a summer cocktail party, and ever since they've been a staple in my catering repertoire.

There are never enough to go around, so don't hesitate to double or triple the recipe. I suggest you fry a small patty of the meat mixture to check the seasonings before you go through the bother of wrapping them.

Thread about 6 meatballs on a metal skewer. (This can be done early in the day.) Grill 3 to 4 minutes on each side, then remove the meatballs from the skewers with a fork directly onto a bed of shredded Chinese cabbage. I put the two sauces into small rice bowls and nestle them in the cabbage along with a shot glass filled with wooden toothpicks, which the guests use to help themselves.

³/4 pound lean ground beef

¹/4 cup finely chopped onion

1 large scallion (white and light green parts), finely minced

1 tablespoon finely minced fresh basil

Freshly ground black pepper

1¹/2 tablespoons soy sauce

Pinch of sugar

34 to 36 large fresh basil leaves, washed and dried

Mustard Sauce

¹/2 cup Dijon mustard

1 teaspoon chopped fresh parsley

¹/2 teaspoon soy sauce

1 clove garlic, minced

Ginger Dipping Sauce

¹/2 cup light soy sauce

¹/4 cup red wine vinegar

1 tablespoon oil

1 tablespoon honey

1 to 2 teaspoons grated fresh ginger

2 scallions (white and light green parts), minced

1. Combine the beef, onion, scallion, minced basil, pepper, soy sauce, and sugar. Form into 1-inch balls, about the size of cherry tomatoes. Wrap a basil leaf around each ball and refrigerate for 30 minutes to 4 hours.

(1) Place a meatball at the stem end of the basil leaf. Tuck the sides of the leaf over the meatball and roll.
(2) Secure with a toothpick.

2. Prepare the Mustard Sauce by mixing together the mustard, parsley, soy sauce, and garlic. Set aside.

3. Prepare the Ginger Dipping Sauce by combining the soy sauce, vinegar, oil, honey, ginger, and scallions. Refrigerate until serving time.

4. Brush or spray the grill with oil and preheat.

5. Place 6 meatballs on each skewer. Grill 4 to 5 minutes, turning frequently. Serve with the Mustard Sauce and Ginger Dipping Sauce.

chapter 6

COUNTRY MODERN
CHOPPED MEAT

P art country and part city; sometimes modern, other times old-
fashioned; now and then homey, occasionally sophisticated. Just
like me!

These chopped-meat recipes reflect decades of cooking and a wide range
of tastes. They also reveal how significantly my cooking has changed over the
years. Now even my old tried-and-true recipes are made with meat ground
from low-fat cuts, little added fat, and more imaginative seasonings.

Kids love ground-meat casseroles and meat loaves—but then so do
adults. Here are Just-for-Kids Sloppy Joes; 1950s Beef and Cabbage Supreme,
an old family treat; and for adults only, Mediterranean Twin Meat Loaves with
their unusual combination of anchovies and cilantro.

Those swanky pâtés you buy at specialty shops and fine delis are nothing more than chopped meat, spicy seasonings, and lots of fat. They once
were among my favorite hors d'oeuvres. However, as I became aware of the
importance of eating less fat, I shied away from eating them and preparing
them for clients.

I now make several lean pâtés that clients and guests adore. I'd like a
new name for them because when I pass them around at parties without
announcing what they are, I receive enthusiastic compliments. However, if I
say, "Won't you try some lean pâté?" I get only lukewarm reactions. People
expect the mouth-filling sensation of fat when they think of pâté; no low-fat
meat mixture, no matter how tasty and moist, can provide that.

It's a bonus that these lean pâtés are much easier to make than the high-
fat varieties, which have to be pressed with a heavy object to compact them
and remove some of their fat. My thrifty country heart is delighted by another
bonus: how little it costs to make these fancy pâtés or any dish based on
ground meat unless, like some elite chefs, you add truffles.

What is meat loaf but lean pâté with less spice, usually served hot? I had great fun creating Fantasy Meat Pie, with its sweet and spicy combination of dried fruit and crystallized ginger, which is rich and savory.

I make these in a standard metal loaf pan (8$^1/_2$ x 4$^1/_2$ x 2$^5/_8$ inches). I often line the pan with parchment paper sprayed with vegetable oil. While the parchment paper isn't necessary, it offers some advantages. It keeps the loaves moist—a plus when you're preparing low-fat meat loaves—and provides an extra layer of wrapping for storage.

If you use a glass loaf pan, you may need to increase the cooking time, as glass doesn't conduct heat as well as metal.

I use an instant-read meat thermometer to tell me when the meat loaf or pâté is done. I like the outside of the loaf crusty and the inside cooked through but still moist. Years ago, as a teaching assistant at the Culinary Arts Shoppe, I learned from John Claude Szurdak, formerly one of General de Gaulle's chefs, to stick a small paring knife into the center of the pâté, then hold it to my lower lip. If the knife was too hot to touch to my lip, the pâté was done; if it wasn't hot, the pâté needed to cook longer. This method of testing the temperature reminds me of Grams—she put her hand in the oven, and the length of time she could tolerate the heat told her how hot the oven was. I'm more scientific now!

No matter how often I make a meatball, meat loaf, or pâté recipe, I form a small test patty of the seasoned meat and brown it in a nonstick skillet so I can taste it and modify the seasonings before I cook the rest. Natural, unprocessed food does not taste the same each time. One day an herb is stronger; another day the meat a bit more fatty; one day you make the recipe with an unsalted homemade stock; the next you use a salty canned broth. Test and taste. I stress this over and over in my classes.

I hesitated to include my sausage recipes in this book, but when I serve them, friends and clients love them. While sausages aren't all that good for you, the way I make them minimizes the fat and maximizes the taste.

These days the lean content of ground beef is often shown on the package label. At my local supermarket, ground round steak is 85% lean (that is, 15% fat) and sirloin is 90% lean. The fat in preground pork and lamb is not marked and appears higher than I like, so I recommend asking the butcher to grind lean cuts of these meats.

chopped Meats

OLD SAN JUAN TORTILLA

1950s BEEF AND CABBAGE SUPREME

CHEESE-TOPPED BAR-B-Q CUPS

CLASSY SIRLOIN SKILLET SUPPER

JUST-FOR-KIDS SLOPPY JOES

GARDEN VEGETABLE AND BEEF SAUTÉ

AUTUMN DELIGHT

SAVORY MEATBALLS IN LEMON-DILL SAUCE

CALIFORNIA CRISPY MEATBALLS

OVEN-BAKED MEATBALLS WITH ONION-APPLE STEW

CONFETTI LAMB PATTIES

MEDITERRANEAN TWIN MEAT LOAVES

HIGH-FLYING MEAT LOAF

BODY BUILDER'S LAMB AND SPINACH LOAF

FANTASY MEAT PIE

GRAM'S MEAT AND HAM LOAF

GUILT-FREE COUNTRY PÂTÉ

THE NEW MEAT LOVER'S PÂTÉ

OVEN-BAKED TOMATO SAUCE WITH SAUSAGE

CINDY'S BEST BAKED ITALIAN SAUSAGE

OLD SAN JUAN TORTILLA

Makes 4 servings

Here a tortilla replaces the rich pastry crust traditionally used to make the meat appetizer known as an empanada. The tart capers and sweet raisins, tender ground beef and salty ham, and crunchy green pepper are accented by garlic and roasted pepper. The dish comes on strong, like a street band marching through the heart of Old San Juan.

If you like this filling as much as I do, it can be spooned onto corn chips, sprinkled with shredded Cheddar cheese, and baked for a few minutes in a hot oven to create a zesty after-school snack, flavorful hors d'oeuvres for an informal party, or festive dish for a family supper.

Vegetable oil to film skillet and pie plate

1 pound lean ground round

1 green bell pepper, diced

1 clove garlic, minced

4 ounces boiled ham, finely chopped

4 ounces canned tomato sauce

2 tablespoons capers, drained

1 tablespoon dark or golden raisins

1 bay leaf

1 roasted pepper

Freshly ground black pepper

Salt

2 large flour tortillas

1. Heat a large nonstick skillet over high heat and film with oil. Add the beef and brown, stirring occasionally, for about 5 minutes. Add the green pepper and cook until the pepper softens, 4 to 5 minutes. Add the garlic and cook for a minute or two. Add the ham, tomato sauce, capers, raisins, bay leaf, and roasted pepper. Cook for 15 minutes, or until the sauce has thickened. Taste and correct the seasonings.

2. Preheat the oven to 375°F.

3. Film an 8-inch pie plate with oil. Line with the tortillas slightly overlapping in the middle of the pie plate. Cover with the meat mixture and bake until the shell is crisp on the edges and the meat is heated through, about 20 to 25 minutes.

1950s Beef and Cabbage Supreme

Makes 6 to 8 servings

Remember all those recipes from the fifties with the same formula? Brown the meat, add a vegetable or two, pull it together with a can of cream soup, and top the whole business with crushed potato chips. Although we don't cook that way anymore, once in a blue moon there's a recipe from that period worth saving.

In the fall Mom would put this casserole in the oven in the late afternoon to bake while she raked leaves. By the time I had biked home from grade school, the robust aroma of beef, onion, cabbage, and tomato greeted me. I couldn't wait for supper!

Just like Mom, I serve potatoes baked alongside the casserole, kosher-style garlic dill pickles, and sliced tomatoes.

Vegetable oil to film skillet and casserole

2 pounds lean ground beef

1 large onion, chopped

1 1/2 teaspoons dill seed

Salt

Freshly ground black pepper

6 cups coarsely shredded cabbage

1 to 2 cans Campbell's tomato soup, undiluted

1. Heat a large nonstick skillet and film with oil. Add the beef and brown over high heat, stirring occasionally, for about 5 minutes. Add the onion and cook until soft, about 3 to 4 minutes. Add the dill seed and salt and pepper to taste.

2. Film a large casserole with oil. Place half the shredded cabbage in the casserole. Spread the browned meat over the cabbage and top with the remaining cabbage. Pour in enough tomato soup just to cover the top layer of cabbage.

   The recipe can be prepared up until this point early in the day. Cover and refrigerate until ready to bake.

3. Preheat the oven to 350°F.

4. Cover the casserole and place it in the oven. Bake for 45 minutes. Uncover and bake for an additional 15 minutes.

CHEESE-TOPPED BAR-B-Q CUPS

Makes 12 cupcake-size servings

For more than 10 years I taught children's Christmas Cookie Classes with one of the best assistants I've ever had, my daughter, Paige, now an accomplished cook in her own right. I enforced only one rule—No Mothers Allowed—except me, of course.

After each class the kitchen was a holy mess. It took hours to wipe sprinkles from the open shelves and scrape frosting off the floor, but the kids and I loved every minute.

Along with the frosting and the sprinkles, we always made lunch to tide us over. The kids never tired of these tasty meat cupcakes. It's easy enough for kids to make—with a little help from a grown-up. Moms and dads like these barbecued-beef cups too!

For a children's birthday party, serve with crunchy vegetables and apple slices.

Vegetable oil to film skillet

1 pound lean ground beef

1 small onion, finely chopped

2 tablespoons brown sugar

¹/₃ cup Down-Home Country Barbecue Sauce (page 103) or your favorite brand

Salt

Freshly ground black pepper

1 package crescent rolls (found in dairy case)

¹/₂ cup shredded Cheddar cheese

1. Preheat the oven to 375°F.

2. Heat a large nonstick skillet over high heat and film with oil. Add the beef and brown, stirring occasionally, for about 5 minutes. Add the chopped onion and cook for 5 minutes longer. Stir in the brown sugar and barbecue sauce and cook for another 5 minutes. Add salt and pepper to taste.

3. Line a muffin tin with the crescent rolls. Put ¹/₄ cup of the meat mixture into each cup. Bake for 15 minutes. Sprinkle Cheddar cheese on top and bake until the cheese melts, about 5 minutes.

CLASSY SIRLOIN SKILLET SUPPER

Makes 2 servings

Combine a rich and robust portobello mushroom, smoky sun-dried tomatoes, elegant fresh asparagus, enticing seasonings, ground beef, and rice to create a classy but easy-to-whip-up supper-in-a-skillet. It's great for two and can be doubled or tripled for a last-minute dinner party.

On your way home from work, pick up a fresh fruit tart for dessert. Serve a green salad sprinkled with shaved Parmesan for the first course, and pour a glass of pinot noir to go with the steak.

Olive oil to film skillet, plus 1 to 2 teaspoons

½ pound lean ground sirloin

4 cloves garlic, coarsely chopped

1 portobello mushroom, cut in 1-inch pieces

8 asparagus stalks, cut in 1-inch pieces

1 cup cooked rice

¼ teaspoon grated lemon zest, or more to taste

¼ teaspoon minced fresh ginger, or more to taste

¼ cup well-drained oil-packed sun-dried tomatoes

1 to 2 tablespoons soy sauce

¼ cup canned low-sodium chicken broth

¼ teaspoon freshly ground black pepper

Salt

1. Heat a large nonstick skillet over high heat and film with oil. Add the beef and brown, stirring occasionally, for about 5 minutes. Remove the meat from the skillet and set aside.

2. Add the remaining olive oil to the skillet and sauté the garlic and mushroom, stirring, over high heat until the garlic begins to brown and the mushrooms "squeak," 1 to 2 minutes. Add the asparagus and sauté for another minute.

3. Return the meat to the skillet. Add the rice, toss well, and cook for 1 minute. Add the lemon zest, ginger, tomatoes, soy sauce, broth, and pepper. Stir, cover, and cook for 2 to 3 minutes, until the asparagus are tender and the liquid has been absorbed. Add salt to taste.

JUST-FOR-KIDS SLOPPY JOES

Makes enough for 2 teenage boys,
4 elementary-school kids, or 6 toddlers

We lived next door to my daughter's school, which meant most days after school one or two extra hungry kids were in my home playing the piano or working on homework. I never suspected any of them were picky eaters, but often their mothers asked me how I got their kids to eat. My answer was this quick and easy Sloppy Joe recipe.

I served it on hamburger rolls, along with dill pickles, mashed potatoes, and a green salad, followed by a baked apple or brownies for dessert.

Vegetable oil to film skillet

1 pound lean ground beef

½ teaspoon onion powder

¼ teaspoon garlic powder

1 medium onion, chopped

½ cup ketchup

¼ cup water

Salt

Freshly ground black pepper

1. Heat a large nonstick skillet over high heat and film with oil. Add the beef, onion powder, and garlic powder, and sauté, stirring occasionally, for about 5 minutes. Add the onion and continue to sauté for 3 to 4 minutes more.

2. Stir in the ketchup and water. Simmer slowly for 15 minutes. Add salt and pepper to taste.

GARDEN VEGETABLE AND BEEF SAUTÉ

Makes 4 servings

Having lived in the city since they were born, my children found it exciting to plant a garden during their first spring at our weekend house.

We planted nearly every vegetable imaginable. We ate the sugar snap peas that appeared in the late spring straight from the vine. The tiny haricots verts never saw a pot of boiling water, as all three of us ate them raw. However, the zucchini, onions, peppers, and tomatoes were more plentiful and made it to the table.

Use this recipe as a rough guide, substituting the vegetables that grow in your own garden—or those from generous neighbors.

Vegetable oil to film skillet

1 pound lean ground round steak

1 large onion, chopped

1 large green bell pepper, chopped

1 clove garlic, minced

Salt

Freshly ground black pepper

1 teaspoon chili powder, approximately

1 tablespoon chopped fresh basil

4 medium zucchini, sliced

2 large tomatoes, peeled, seeded, and chopped

1/2 red bell pepper, chopped

3 or 4 ears of corn, kernels removed

1/2 small bunch fresh parsley, chopped

1. Heat a large nonstick skillet over high heat and film with oil. Add the beef and sauté, stirring occasionally, for about 5 minutes. Add the onion, green pepper, and garlic and continue to sauté, stirring, until the vegetables begin to brown, another 4 to 5 minutes.

2. Add a pinch of salt, a generous grinding of black pepper, chili powder, and basil, and mix well. Add the zucchini, tomatoes, red pepper, and corn, and stir. Cover and simmer for 15 to 20 minutes, until the vegetables are cooked. Taste and correct the seasonings. Sprinkle the parsley on top and serve hot.

AUTUMN DELIGHT

Makes 4 servings

I have never been able to resist acorn squash. Each year their naturally sweet autumn-gold flesh seduces anew my insatiable sweet tooth.

Here I've stuffed them with beef, onion, red and green bell peppers, minty floral marjoram, rich port, and pecans. This simple and hearty down-to-earth supper is great to come home to after a brisk walk in the autumn woods when the leaves are at their peak.

2 large acorn squash, cut in half, seeds removed

1 teaspoon olive oil

1 pound lean ground beef

1 medium onion, chopped (about 1 cup)

¹/₂ green bell pepper, chopped

¹/₂ red bell pepper, chopped

1 teaspoon dried marjoram

¹/₂ cup chopped fresh parsley

¹/₂ teaspoon salt

¹/₂ teaspoon freshly ground black pepper

¹/₄ to ¹/₃ cup port, Madeira wine, or beef broth (canned is fine)

¹/₄ cup toasted pecans (optional) (see Tasty Tip, page 262)

1. Preheat the oven to 350°F.

2. Place the squash halves, cut side down, in a shallow baking pan and bake for 30 minutes.

3. Meanwhile, heat the oil in a nonstick skillet. Add the beef and brown over high heat, stirring occasionally, for about 5 minutes. Add the onion, green pepper, red pepper, marjoram, and parsley and continue to cook for 5 to 6 minutes more. Season with salt and pepper. Add the port or broth and cook for 4 to 5 minutes, until most of the liquid has been absorbed. (The meat should remain moist.) If pecans are desired, stir them in now.

4. Remove the squash from the oven and turn cut side up. Spoon the meat filling into the squash. Return the squash to the oven and bake until they can be pierced easily with a fork and the top of the filling is crusty, about 30 minutes.

SAVORY MEATBALLS IN LEMON-DILL SAUCE

Makes 4 servings

When I think of meatballs, beef comes to mind. But in this recipe pork is mixed with onion, chervil, and nutmeg to create savory morsels. As they poach, the meatballs impart their delicate seasonings to the lemon- and dill-flavored chicken broth. Then the broth is thickened with cornstarch, turning it into a subtle yet tart sauce that's great over fluffy white rice.

1 pound lean pork, finely ground

1 small onion, finely chopped

2 teaspoons chopped fresh chervil

Pinch of freshly grated nutmeg

1 egg, beaten

$\frac{1}{2}$ teaspoon salt, or more to taste

$\frac{1}{2}$ teaspoon freshly ground black pepper

Flour for dusting hands

3 cups canned low-sodium chicken broth

6 parsley stems

2 tablespoons cornstarch

2 tablespoons cold water

Juice of 1 lemon

2 to 3 tablespoons chopped fresh dill

Fresh chervil sprigs for garnish (optional)

1. Combine the pork with the onion, chervil, and nutmeg. Add the egg and mix well. Season with salt and pepper.

2. Dust your hands with flour and form the meat mixture into small (about 1-inch) meatballs. Place them on a baking sheet lined with waxed paper and chill until firm, about 30 minutes.

   The meatballs can be prepared to this point up to 4 hours ahead.

3. In a large saucepan, bring the broth to a boil over high heat. Add the parsley stems. Reduce the heat and, keeping the broth at a simmer, drop the meatballs in a few at a time. Poach the meatballs until

cooked through, about 5 to 7 minutes. Using a slotted spoon, remove the meatballs from the broth and place them in a baking/serving dish.

4. Strain the parsley stems out of the broth and discard. Return the broth to a boil.

5. Mix together the cornstarch and cold water and, whisking continuously, slowly pour it into the broth. Simmer, stirring continuously, until the broth lightly coats the back of a spoon, about 3 minutes.

6. Stir in the lemon juice and dill. Taste and correct the seasonings. Pour the broth over the meatballs and, if you choose, garnish with sprigs of chervil.

I suggest using clean rubber gloves for mixing meat. Make sure the gloves are large enough so you can slip them off when the phone rings—which it always does.

CALIFORNIA CRISPY MEATBALLS

Makes 10 to 12 servings as an hors d'oeuvre and 5 to 6 as a main course (makes 30 to 36 meatballs)

No ironclad law dictates that meatballs need to be made with a filler of bread crumbs and milk, fried, and then doused with a rich or spicy sauce.

Sun-Dried Tomato Seasoning Paste (recipe follows), pine nuts, Parmesan cheese, and fresh parsley are mixed with pork and lamb, molded into meatballs, and then baked into moist-on-the-inside and crispy-on-the-outside morsels that are so outrageously delicious they need no sauce. Better make a double batch; they disappear quickly.

Serve them on top of pasta dressed with olive oil and parsley as a main course. Or make bite-sized meatballs and serve them as hors d'oeuvres.

Vegetable oil spray

1 pound lean ground pork

³/₄ pound lean ground lamb

¹/₃ cup Sun-Dried Tomato Seasoning Paste (recipe follows)

¹/₃ cup pine nuts

¹/₃ cup freshly grated Parmesan cheese

¹/₃ cup chopped fresh parsley

¹/₄ teaspoon freshly ground black pepper

1 whole egg, beaten

1 egg white, beaten

1. Preheat the oven to 425°F. Line a baking sheet with aluminum foil, and spray with vegetable oil.

2. Combine all the ingredients and mix well. Dip your hands into cold water and roll the meat mixture into 1¹/₂-inch balls.

3. Place the meatballs in a single layer on the foil-lined baking sheet. Bake for about 30 minutes, or until done to your taste.

SUN-DRIED TOMATO SEASONING PASTE

Makes about ³/₄ cup

I use this simple, intensely flavored seasoning paste in many ways. For hors d'oeuvres I make small tarts of pie crust, spread the seasoning paste over them, sprinkle with cheese, and bake. I slather it on steaks before I grill them. I also stuff a spoonful or two of this paste under the skin of chicken breasts before baking them. I stuff chops with it, such as Tomato-Kissed Veal Chops (page 161), and I use it to jazz up tomato sauce. Make up a batch and taste it—I'll bet you'll come up with a dozen more uses.

2 tablespoons olive oil

1 large onion, chopped

2 large cloves garlic, minced

¹/₂ cup chopped oil-packed sun-dried tomatoes

2 tablespoons dried basil

1 teaspoon freshly ground black pepper, or more to taste

Pinch of crushed red pepper flakes

1. Heat the oil in a large nonstick skillet over medium heat. Add the onion and cook until it begins to soften, about 4 to 5 minutes. Add the garlic and continue to cook until the onion is soft and translucent, about 5 minutes longer.

2. Add chopped sun-dried tomatoes, basil, black pepper, and red pepper flakes and mix well. Cook for 5 to 6 minutes. Taste and correct the seasonings. Set aside to cool.

   This seasoning paste can be prepared ahead. Refrigerate for up to 1 week or freeze for up to 1 month.

OVEN-BAKED MEATBALLS WITH ONION-APPLE STEW

Makes 6 servings

One cold, blustery afternoon, happy to be inside writing, I noticed my appetite increasing from the heavenly aroma of these crispy meatballs browning in the oven. Sweet apples, onions, and cinnamon simmered on the stove. I stopped writing and dreamily inhaled the smells drifting in from the kitchen. Impulsively, I reached for the phone and invited a few friends over for dinner, who were as happy as I for a diversion.

Crusty French bread, a green salad with mustard vinaigrette, and fresh pears topped with chocolate sauce, plus lots of good talk, completed the meal—a delicious end to a delicious day.

Meatballs

1 thick slice white bread, crusts removed

1/3 cup skim milk

1 1/2 pounds lean ground beef

1/2 pound lean ground pork

1 egg white, beaten

1 teaspoon salt

1/2 teaspoon freshly ground black pepper

1/4 teaspoon freshly grated nutmeg

1/4 cup chopped fresh parsley or 1 tablespoon dried parsley flakes

Vegetable oil spray

Onion-Apple Stew

1 tablespoon olive oil

1 tablespoon butter

1 pound onions, sliced

Pinch of sugar

3 pounds red apples, unpeeled, cored and sliced

One 3-inch stick cinnamon

¹/₂ teaspoon freshly ground black pepper

¹/₄ cup full-bodied red wine

**¹/₂ to ²/₃ cup Doctored Beef Broth (page 279)
or canned broth**

1. Preheat the oven to 375°F.

2. To prepare the meatballs, soak the bread in the milk for a few minutes; squeeze out the excess liquid. Mix the ground beef and pork with the egg white, soaked bread, salt, pepper, nutmeg, and parsley. Dip your hands in cold water and roll the mixture into small meatballs.

3. Spray a jelly roll pan with vegetable oil spray (or line the pan with oiled aluminum foil). Place the meatballs on the pan and bake them until they're browned and crispy on one side, about 10 minutes; then turn to brown the other side, about 10 minutes more. Take the meatballs out of the oven and set aside. The meatballs can be prepared 1 or 2 days ahead and reheated in the oven or on top of the stove.

4. While the meatballs are baking, heat the oil and butter in a heavy flameproof casserole. Add the onions and slowly cook until soft, about 5 minutes. Add the sugar and cook a bit longer to slightly caramelize. Add the apples, cinnamon stick, pepper, wine, and ¹/₂ cup of the beef broth. Slowly simmer, uncovered, until the apples are soft but not mushy, about 10 to 15 minutes. Add more broth as necessary to keep the apple stew from drying out. Taste and correct the seasoning. Gently stir the meatballs into the stew and cook together for several minutes.

CONFETTI LAMB PATTIES

Makes 10 patties—enough to serve
5 lamb lovers or 10 light eaters

These colorful patties are perfect for parties. Sweet tiny green peas and tart red cranberries combine surprisingly well with ground lamb seasoned with lemon zest, onion, garlic, and parsley. Work carefully; these patties crumble if not handled gently.

For a great dinner in a hurry, omit the oatmeal and yogurt, film a large nonstick skillet with olive oil, and sauté the mixture until the meat is browned and the vegetables are cooked through, about 20 minutes. Serve over a bed of rice and top with a dollop of yogurt and chopped parsley.

1 1/2 pounds lean ground lamb

2/3 cup frozen baby peas, thawed

2/3 cup raw cranberries, thawed if frozen

1 tablespoon grated lemon zest (see Tasty Tip, page 111)

3/4 cup chopped onion

1 small clove garlic, minced

1/4 cup chopped fresh parsley

1/4 teaspoon freshly ground black pepper

3/4 teaspoon salt

1/3 cup quick-cooking oatmeal

2/3 cup plain nonfat yogurt

Vegetable oil to film skillet

Parsley sprigs for garnish

1. Combine all the ingredients except the oil and parsley in a large mixing bowl. Form into 10 patties, pushing any protruding cranberries back into the meat. Flatten the patties for even cooking.

2. Heat a large nonstick skillet and film with oil. Brown the patties for 5 minutes on the first side, then 4 to 5 minutes on the second, or until cooked to your taste. Carefully remove the patties from the skillet and pour any pan juices over them. Garnish with parsley and serve.

MEDITERRANEAN TWIN MEAT LOAVES

Makes 6 to 8 servings

Odd bedfellows certainly, but salty anchovies mix with cilantro and oregano to create a singular taste that will baffle even the most discerning palate.

Serve with garlic mashed potatoes or crispy French fries. Any leftover meat loaf can be sliced and made into a sandwich with sliced tomato and lettuce on Tuscan bread, or placed in a romaine lettuce leaf for a quick appetizer.

Vegetable oil spray

1 cup firmly packed crumbled Italian bread, with crusts

³/₄ cup skim milk

¹/₂ cup chopped fresh cilantro

¹/₂ teaspoon dried oregano

1 pound lean ground pork

1 pound lean ground round

2 ounces canned anchovies, drained and chopped

1¹/₂ cups chopped onion

1 large clove garlic, minced

¹/₂ teaspoon freshly ground black pepper, or more to taste

1. Preheat the oven to 350°F. Spray a 12-inch-long loaf pan or regular loaf pan (see step 4) with vegetable oil spray.

2. In a small bowl, thoroughly mix together the bread and milk and set aside until the milk is absorbed.

3. Chop the cilantro and oregano together and combine them with the pork, beef, anchovies, onion, garlic, and bread and milk mixture. Season with pepper and mix well.

4. Form into 2 equal-sized oval loaves. Place them, end to end, in a 12-inch-long loaf pan so that each loaf is about 6 inches long. (If you don't have a long loaf pan, you can bake this as a single loaf in a standard loaf pan, but it will take about 20 minutes longer to cook through.) Bake until the temperature on an instant-read meat thermometer registers 155°F, about 1 hour. Allow the loaves to rest for 5 to 10 minutes before slicing.

HIGH-FLYING MEAT LOAF

Makes 12 or more servings

This recipe comes from Gayle Martz, a good friend and one of my first students 21 years ago. Gayle's gone from being a TWA flight attendant to owning her own company, which manufactures—guess what?—carry-on luggage and pet carriers.

Gayle's love of cooking shows in the imaginative dishes she creates. She often whips up what she calls "pâté hamburg." Shredded carrots and potatoes stirred into the meat give this loaf a wonderful coarse texture, and raisins add a touch of sweetness. A meal in a loaf!

Cut the meat loaf into thick slices and serve with sliced tomatoes and Dijon mustard on the side. Or slice thinly, arrange on a bed of lettuce, garnish with fresh parsley, and serve with cornichons and black bread or crackers.

2 pounds lean ground sirloin

³/₄ pound lean ground veal

³/₄ pound lean ground pork

2 eggs, lightly beaten

1 large onion, coarsely chopped

3 large carrots, shredded

2 large potatoes, peeled and shredded

1 clove garlic, minced

¹/₂ cup golden raisins

2 teaspoons salt, or more to taste

2 teaspoons freshly ground black pepper

¹/₂ to ²/₃ cup seasoned bread crumbs

Vegetable oil spray

¹/₃ cup Dijon mustard

¹/₃ cup ketchup

1. Preheat the oven to 350°F.

2. In a large bowl, combine the beef, veal, pork, eggs, onion, carrots, potatoes, garlic, raisins, salt, and pepper. Mix well. Add enough bread crumbs to hold the mixture together.

3. Spray a large baking pan with vegetable oil spray. Divide the meat mixture in half and make 2 loaves. Place them next to each other in the pan.

4. In a small bowl, mix the mustard and ketchup together. Spread over the top of the meat and bake for 1 to 1½ hours, until crusty on the outside and cooked through on the inside, or until an instant-read meat thermometer registers 155°F. Allow the meat loaves to rest for 10 to 15 minutes before slicing.

When cooled, remove the meat loaves from the pan and wrap one or both in a double thickness of plastic wrap, then in a double thickness of aluminum wrap, making sure to seal the packet well. Refrigerate for up to 1 week or freeze for up to 1 month.

BODY BUILDER'S LAMB AND SPINACH LOAF

Makes 4 to 5 servings

I exercise three or four times a week with a group of women friends. Guess what is the most often discussed topic of conversation? Food, of course. My friends were curious about this book, so I brought them samples of this lean meat loaf. They loved it! Energized by the snack, when we went back to our workouts, we each added another pound to the free weights. I can't promise this meat loaf will make your biceps bulge like Popeye's, but I'm quite sure it won't make your waistline expand.

The lively combination of carrots, raisins, and parsley, along with the savory spinach stuffing, mixes well with the heartiness of lean ground lamb. Wholesome cooked oatmeal (prepared according to the directions on the box) binds the ingredients and keeps them moist. The taste is rich and slightly sweet.

**2 tablespoons plus ¹/₂ cup beef broth
   (canned is fine)**

¹/₃ cup golden raisins

1¹/₂ pounds lean ground lamb

1 carrot, peeled and shredded

¹/₂ cup Spinach Stuffing (page 74)

¹/₄ cup chopped fresh parsley

¹/₂ teaspoon salt

¹/₄ teaspoon freshly ground black pepper

¹/₂ cup cold cooked oatmeal

Vegetable oil spray

1. Preheat the oven to 375°F.

2. Warm the 2 tablespoons of beef broth. Soak the raisins in it until they soften, about 10 to 15 minutes.

3. In a large bowl, combine the lamb, carrot, Spinach Stuffing, parsley, salt, pepper, oatmeal, soaked raisins with the broth, and remaining ¹/₂ cup of broth. Mix well.

4. Spray a loaf pan with vegetable oil spray. Place the meat mixture in the pan and bake until the temperature on an instant-read meat thermometer reaches 155°F, about 60 to 70 minutes.

Although you can make this recipe by cooking thawed frozen spinach with onion, nutmeg, and freshly ground black pepper in a bit of oil, I prefer the easy-to-make spinach stuffing I use for my roast veal.

FANTASY MEAT PIE

Makes 4 servings

One Christmas I received a sampling of dried fruits as a gift from a fellow foodie. While nibbling away, I fantasized about how they would taste in a pie. Tart dried cherries, spicy crystallized ginger, and sweet dried apricots added to ground pork, chopped onion, parsley, rubbed sage, salt, and pepper. Hmmm, a tasty dish to set before a king! Here it is, even better in reality.

¼ cup Campbell's beef broth, undiluted

½ cup dried cherries

¼ cup chopped dried apricots

1 pound lean ground pork

1 teaspoon chopped crystallized ginger

½ cup chopped onion

¼ cup chopped fresh parsley

½ teaspoon rubbed sage

½ teaspoon salt

¼ teaspoon freshly ground black pepper

1 egg, beaten

Vegetable oil spray

1. Preheat the oven to 375°F.

2. Warm the beef broth. Soak the cherries and apricots in it for 10 to 15 minutes, until they plump up.

3. Mix the pork, ginger, onion, parsley, sage, salt, pepper, and egg together in a large bowl. Add the cherries and apricots with the broth and mix well.

4. Spray an 8- or 9-inch pie plate with vegetable oil spray. Press the meat mixture into it and smooth the top of the meat. Bake for approximately 35 to 45 minutes, or until an instant-read meat thermometer registers 155°F. Allow the pie to rest for 10 minutes.

Gram's Meat and Ham Loaf

Makes 4 servings, with leftovers

That's what our family always called this loaf, so I was startled when a student said it was a silly name because ham was meat too.

When I was a little girl, I often accompanied my grandmother when she cooked for a crowd at church. She made this recipe in single-serving size loaves because it was easier for a church supper and "everyone likes the glaze." (Most of the time I make one loaf, but you can do it either way.)

I think a sweet tooth runs in my family. Grams learned to make this flavorful ham loaf coated with rich sweet sauce from her mother. When my son, Scott, was a graduate student in Colorado, he called me for the recipe so he could make it for his friends.

This recipe serves four with maybe a leftover sliver for a late-night snack. It can be scaled up easily and it freezes well. Wrap the loaf first in plastic wrap and then in zipper-lock bags.

Grams always served this meat loaf hot with scalloped potatoes and peas. It can also be served cold with coleslaw and potato salad.

Glaze

1 cup brown sugar

1¼ teaspoon dry mustard

¼ cup apple cider vinegar

¼ pound lean ground veal

¼ pound lean ground pork

¼ pound lean ground beef

¾ pound ham, coarsely ground

1 egg, beaten

¾ cup low-fat milk

1 cup fresh white bread crumbs

1 small onion, grated (¼ cup)

¼ cup chopped fresh parsley

Pinch of salt

½ teaspoon freshly ground black pepper

Vegetable oil spray

1. Preheat the oven to 375°F.

2. To prepare the glaze, stir together the brown sugar, mustard, and vinegar in a small saucepan. Boil for 5 minutes. Set aside.

3. In a large bowl, combine the veal, pork, beef, and ham. Add the egg, milk, bread crumbs, onion, parsley, salt, and pepper, and mix well.

4. Spray a loaf pan with vegetable oil spray and place the meat mixture in it. Pour the glaze over the meat and bake until the top is dark brown and the juices run clear, about 30 to 35 minutes.

GUILT-FREE COUNTRY PÂTÉ

Begin one day in advance

*Makes a 1- to 1½-pound pâté;
12 servings as an hors d'oeuvre*

This pâté has all the flavor of my original high-fat country pâté. Its texture is fairly coarse, so don't expect the rich smoothness of the high-fat version.

The best results are obtained when the meat is finely ground. Ask your butcher to grind the meat twice. If you buy your meat already ground, grind it again in your food processor or meat grinder.

Added to the ground meat are sautéed mushrooms, onions, garlic, and parsley, along with herbes de Provence, *brandy, and demi-glace. Baking the loaf in a pan of hot water keeps the pâté moist and flavorful.*

Arrange thin slices of pâté on a bed of shredded lettuce, garnish with cornichons, and serve with thinly sliced black bread. You may want to double the recipe—whenever I serve it, there are never leftovers.

1 cup Homemade Beef Stock (page 276)
   or 2 tablespoons demi-glace (page 273)

1 slice white bread

½ cup milk

1 tablespoon olive oil, approximately

1 medium onion, finely chopped

3 cloves garlic, minced

1 small bunch fresh parsley, minced

½ pound mushrooms, chopped

½ pound lean pork, finely ground

½ pound lean veal, finely ground

½ pound lean sirloin beef, finely ground

2 to 3 teaspoons salt

½ teaspoon freshly ground black pepper, or more
   to taste

1 heaping tablespoon freeze-dried chives

1 teaspoon *herbes de Provence* (see Tasty Tip below)

2 eggs, lightly beaten

2 tablespoons brandy

Vegetable oil spray

1. Preheat the oven to 350°F.

2. If using demi-glace, skip to the next step. Otherwise, simmer the beef stock over high heat until reduced to 2 tablespoons, about 20 minutes. Set aside to cool.

3. Pour hot water into a 9- x 12-inch cake pan until the water reaches halfway up the sides of the pan. Place in the oven to heat while preparing the pâté.

4. Tear up the bread and soak the pieces in the milk. Set aside.

5. Heat 1 to 2 teaspoons of the oil in a nonstick skillet. Cook the onion and garlic until the onion is soft and translucent, 3 to 4 minutes. Stir in the minced parsley and set aside to cool to room temperature.

6. Film the bottom of the same skillet with oil and heat. Cook the mushrooms over high heat until soft, about 8 to 10 minutes. Remove the mushrooms and their liquid to small bowl and set aside to cool to room temperature.

7. In a large bowl, combine the pork, veal, and beef with the onion mixture, the mushrooms and their liquid, salt, pepper, chives, herbes de Provence, eggs, brandy, and reduced beef stock or demi-glace. Mix well. (Be sure to test a patty for seasonings; see page 217.)

8. Spray a loaf pan with vegetable oil spray. Pat the meat mixture evenly into the pan and tap the pan firmly on a countertop to remove any air pockets. Using a double thickness of aluminum foil, cover the top of the pan and seal the edges tightly.

9. Place the loaf pan in the large pan of hot water that's been heating in the oven. Bake until an instant-read meat thermometer registers 155°F, about 1 hour 10 minutes. Remove the pâté from the oven and allow it to come to room temperature. Refrigerate at least overnight.

Herbes de Provence is a dried herb mixture available in most supermarkets, at specialty food stores, and through mail-order companies. If you want to make your own, combine equal amounts of thyme, sage, lavender, marjoram, basil, oregano, summer savory, and rosemary. I usually make up a batch with 1 tablespoon of each herb and keep it in a covered jar. I rub it on meat roasts and roasted chicken, use it to season vegetables, and add it to eggs.

THE NEW MEAT LOVER'S PÂTÉ

Begin one day in advance

Makes 12 servings as an hors d'oeuvre

There are two secrets to this veal, pork, and beef pâté: for flavor, the balsamic vinegar sweetened with brown sugar, and for moistness, the yogurt.

While not absolutely necessary, I usually line the pan with parchment paper to keep this pâté as moist as possible.

This is best served cold, sliced thin for hors d'oeuvres, with a strong, coarse-grained mustard alongside. I also like it as the center of a salad with a glass of red wine.

¹/₂ **pound lean ground veal**

¹/₂ **pound lean ground pork**

¹/₂ **pound lean ground beef**

1 cup minced onion

¹/₃ **cup chopped fresh parsley**

1 tablespoon freshly ground black pepper

1¹/₂ teaspoons salt

1 teaspoon paprika

2 cloves garlic, minced

¹/₄ **cup balsamic vinegar**

1 tablespoon brown sugar

¹/₃ **cup plain low-fat yogurt**

¹/₃ **cup uncooked rolled oats**

Vegetable oil spray

One day ahead

1. Using a food processor, grind together the veal, pork, beef, onion, parsley, pepper, salt, paprika, and garlic.

2. In a medium nonreactive bowl, stir together the vinegar and brown sugar. Add the meat and mix well. Cover and refrigerate overnight to allow the flavors to blend and develop.

Before baking

3. Preheat the oven to 350°F.

4. Add the yogurt and oats to the meat mixture and mix well.

5. Spray a loaf pan with vegetable oil. (Line with parchment paper if desired.) Add the meat mixture and bake for 1 to 1½ hours, or until an instant-read meat thermometer registers 155°F.

Tasty Tip

I again urge you to always test a small patty before making pâté, meat loaf, or meatballs. The test patties for pâtés should taste slightly salty if eaten hot; when cold, the pâté won't taste salty.

OVEN-BAKED TOMATO SAUCE WITH SAUSAGES

Makes enough for 12 servings over pasta or rice;
20 servings or more as part of a buffet

The addition of exotic saffron threads enhances the flavor of this simple tomato sauce without overpowering it. I like this sauce over pasta, meat loaf (try it on Mediterranean Twin Meat Loaves, page 233), and in any recipe that calls for tomato sauce.

I can't tell you how many pots I've used—and washed—to make a single batch of tomato sauce! Because tomato sauce burns easily and my keen nose signals when the bottom of the pot has started to burn, I would quickly transfer the sauce to another pan, leaving the burned bottom in the pot. One day Cindy, my right hand in the kitchen, told me that I'd used every pot and that if I got one more dirty, she would quit! From that point on, I baked my tomato sauces. Baking allows the sauce to reduce and eliminates the age-old problem of burning both the bottom of the sauce and the pan.

This is an excellent all-purpose tomato sauce. If you're using it as a base with other seasonings, you may want to omit the saffron.

For this recipe, I use Cindy's Best Baked Italian Sausages (next recipe). Sometimes I add chunks of sautéed boneless chicken breast. I like this dish for buffets and informal dinner parties when I don't have time for last-minute cooking.

Dust with freshly chopped flat-leaf parsley and serve over pasta or rice, or eat with crusty Italian bread.

Oven-Baked Tomato Sauce

2 tablespoons olive oil, approximately

2 large onions, chopped

6 cloves garlic, minced

1/2 teaspoon saffron threads

Three 28-ounce cans whole tomatoes in thick puree

3 tablespoons tomato paste

1/2 teaspoon dried thyme

2 teaspoons freshly ground black pepper

1/4 teaspoon red pepper flakes

¼ teaspoon sugar

Pinch of salt

5 cups Cindy's Best Baked Italian Sausages with their juices (page 246)

1. Preheat the oven to 350°F.

2. To prepare the Oven-Baked Tomato Sauce, heat the oil in a large, heavy flameproof casserole. Cook the onions over moderate heat until soft, about 6 to 8 minutes. Add the garlic, reduce the heat, and continue to cook until the garlic is soft and translucent, another 1 to 2 minutes. Add the saffron threads and cook until they become aromatic.

3. Stir in the tomatoes with puree, tomato paste, thyme, black pepper, red pepper flakes, sugar, and salt. Bring to a boil over moderate heat, stirring often to prevent burning. Cover, place in the oven, and bake until the sauce has thickened, about 30 to 40 minutes. Taste and correct the seasonings.

    The sauce can be stored in the refrigerator for 2 to 3 days or frozen for up to 1 month.

4. Add the sausages with their defatted juices and mix well. Bake until the sausages are hot and the sauce is bubbly, which will take about 30 minutes if you start with warm ingredients, 1 hour if they're cold from the refrigerator, and up to 1½ hours if the sausages are frozen.

CINDY'S BEST BAKED ITALIAN SAUSAGES

Makes enough for 12 servings over pasta or rice;
20 servings or more as part of a buffet

For nearly 10 years, Cindy Palombi, whose smile lit up my kitchen, was my assistant at Cooking With Class, Inc. She worked beside me at every class, handled scores of jobs in the kitchen, and kept me sane!

This method of cooking sausages comes from Cindy's grandmother, who owned a restaurant in the 1940s and '50s. First she pricked the sausage casing. Then she let the fat melt out of the sausages by boiling them in water flavored with garlic. Her next step is the secret to the best sausages I've ever eaten: she baked the bite-sized pieces of sausage in hearty red wine with yet another head of garlic. This renders out still more fat while the meat absorbs the garlic-scented wine.

I prefer long, slow baking for these sausages instead of my usual fast-forward. Once the sausages are cooked, I freeze them in zipper-lock bags for up to 4 or 5 months. They are ready to thaw for use in paella, on toothpicks for hors d'oeuvres, in a sauté of peppers, onions, and mushrooms, or in a sandwich.

2 pounds hot Italian sausages

2 pounds sweet Italian sausages

2 heads of garlic, cloves separated but unpeeled

1 bottle full-bodied red wine

1. Prick the sausages in several places with a fork and place them in a large stockpot. Add the cloves of 1 head of garlic and enough cold water to cover the sausages completely. Cover and bring to a boil. Reduce the heat and simmer for 30 to 40 minutes.

2. Preheat the oven to 350°F.

3. When the sausages are cooked, drain off the water. Prick the sausages again to release any fat that remains. Rinse the sausages with hot water and cut into 1-inch pieces.

4. Place the sausages, remaining cloves of garlic, and wine in a roasting pan. Cover loosely (the steam should be able to escape) with foil and bake for 30 minutes. Uncover and continue to bake, stirring occasionally, until the sausages are brown and crispy and have absorbed most of the wine, 45 minutes to 1¼ hours. If any juices are left in the pan, skim off the fat (see page 79) and reserve the juices.

chapter 7

DINNER SEQUELS

I've recently been thinking about leftovers and have concluded we don't give them the respect they deserve.

Let's take hash, the ultimate leftover. My great-grandmother made old-fashioned roast beef hash; my grandmother, my mother, I, and now my daughter, Paige, make almost the same hash. We've all served it proudly to family and friends.

What makes the ham served the third day inferior to the ham served the first night? How odd that if I cook a stew a day or two ahead of the night I serve it, it isn't a leftover; but if I eat part of that stew Sunday night, then on Tuesday the same dish is considered less praiseworthy than the original meal. The truth is the stew will probably taste even better on Tuesday night.

Let's declare that leftovers will no longer be the poor relations of cooking. *Voilà*! Dinner sequels!

In this chapter you'll find dishes to glorify the leftover. My Aristocratic Tapenade of Beef has served as an hors d'oeuvre at fine affairs. Is it a leftover? Mouth-watering Twice-Blessed Veal mixed with orzo and capers and olives— a leftover?

It's time to rid ourselves of the notion of leftovers as a hodgepodge of mediocre foods we're trying to use up. Let's view these previously cooked morsels instead as treasures waiting in our refrigerators for their brilliant encore. The only objection to leftovers was voiced by my good friend Linda, who grumbled, "But you still have to cook to serve leftovers."

sequels

MEAN ROAST BEEF HASH

COSMOPOLITAN HASH

ENCORE BEEF STEW

BLACK BEAN CHILI

1990s WILTED SALAD

BRISKET CAPONATA

ARISTOCRATIC TAPENADE OF BEEF

CONTEMPORARY BEEF AND BEETS

SHOPPING DAY FRICASSEE OF LAMB

RISING SUN SKILLET SUPPER

SEASIDE SUMMER SALAD

CALIFORNIA SALAD

WINTER SALAD

CHUNKY HAM HASH

HAM AND CABBAGE HEIDELBERG

HAM WITH WINTER FRUIT AND CURRIED SOUR CREAM DRESSING

THE NEW WESTERN OMELETTE

MINTED HAM AND PEA SALAD

SERENDIPITY SALAD

SAGE-SCENTED YAMS, ARTICHOKE HEARTS, AND VEAL

TWICE-BLESSED VEAL

MEAN ROAST BEEF HASH

Makes 6 servings

I grew up eating hash for breakfast. Sometimes it was adorned with a fried egg, sunny side up, and other times it was served just as it came from the skillet. Most times the basics were roast beef, boiled potatoes, onion, and milk or heavy cream. Sometimes the reserve team of ham, corned beef, or roast pork was sent in to substitute for the beef.

One of my guests complimented this as "a mean dish of hash" after I served it at a Super Bowl brunch. The secret strategy in making this dish is adding milk just before it's baked. The milk absorbs all the flavors and sneaks through the line of herbs, onions, and beef to pull off the play by evaporating into the potatoes!

2 tablespoons olive oil

1 teaspoon butter

2 to 3 medium-large onions, chopped

2 to 3 cups ¹/₂-inch cubes of roast beef

3 to 4 leftover boiled potatoes, peeled and cut in ¹/₂-inch cubes

¹/₂ teaspoon salt

1 teaspoon freshly ground black pepper

¹/₂ teaspoon dried savory

¹/₄ teaspoon dried rosemary, crushed

2 teaspoons fresh chopped parsley

¹/₂ to 1 cup low-fat milk, approximately

1. Preheat the oven to 350°F.

2. Heat the oil and butter over medium heat in a large cast-iron skillet. Add the onions and cook, stirring, until translucent. Add the beef and continue to cook for about 5 minutes, stirring often, until the beef begins to brown.

3. Add the potatoes, salt, pepper, savory, rosemary, and parsley. Cook for 3 to 5 minutes, stirring occasionally. Taste and correct the seasonings.

4. Pour enough milk over the meat and potatoes so that you can see the milk bubbling up from the bottom of the hot skillet. Place the skillet in the oven and bake until the meat and potatoes are brown and crusty. This will take from 30 minutes to 1 hour, depending on the size of the skillet.

COSMOPOLITAN HASH

Makes 6 servings

In this dish the soaking liquid from dried shiitake mushrooms replaces the milk or heavy cream traditionally used to pull hash together. The marvelous woodsy taste of mushroom and the hint of smokiness from the prosciutto impart a sophisticated flavor that makes this hash a hit for a late-night supper after the theater.

Make it before you go out and reheat it when you come home. Perfect with a green salad and a glass of red wine. Bravo!

6 dried shiitake mushrooms

2 cups hot water

2 tablespoons olive oil

3 medium Red Bliss potatoes, cut in 1 1/2-inch cubes

1 medium onion, chopped

2 to 3 ounces prosciutto, slivered

2 1/2 to 3 cups bite-size pieces of roast beef

Salt

Freshly ground black pepper

1. Cover the mushrooms with the hot water and allow them to soak for 20 minutes. Drain the mushrooms and remove and discard their stems. Strain the soaking water through a fine-mesh sieve and set aside. Pat the mushrooms dry and cut them into thin slices.

2. Preheat the oven to 350°F.

3. Heat the oil in a large cast-iron skillet. Cook the potatoes over medium heat, stirring occasionally, until well browned, about 10 minutes. Add the onion and continue to cook until the onion is soft. Add the mushrooms, prosciutto, and beef and cook, stirring occasionally, 5 minutes more. Add salt and pepper to taste.

4. Pour enough of the reserved mushroom soaking water over the meat and potatoes so that you can see it bubbling up from the bottom of the hot skillet. Place the skillet in the oven and bake until the meat and potatoes are brown and crusty, 25 to 30 minutes.

ENCORE BEEF STEW

Makes 8 servings

Borrowing the flavors of leftover roast beef and then adding a fragrant mélange of caraway seeds, sage, and coriander to sautéed vegetables results in an unpretentious stew that can be simmered on the stove or baked in the oven.

1 teaspoon olive oil

1 large onion, cut in chunks (2 cups)

2 cups baby carrots (about ¹/₂ pound)

4 medium zucchini, scrubbed, cut in ¹/₂-inch slices (3³/₄ cups)

4 cups 1-inch cubes of roast beef

¹/₂ teaspoon caraway seeds

1 teaspoon rubbed sage

¹/₂ teaspoon ground coriander

1¹/₂ cups beef broth (canned is fine)

¹/₄ cup full-bodied red wine (optional)

Salt

Freshly ground black pepper

1. Preheat the oven to 350°F.

2. Heat the oil in a large, heavy casserole over medium-high heat. Add onion, carrots, and zucchini and cook, stirring, for 2 to 3 minutes. Add the beef, caraway seeds, sage, coriander, broth, and wine if desired. Cover and bring to a boil.

3. Place the covered casserole in the oven and bake for 45 minutes. Add salt and pepper to taste.

Tasty Tip

The gravy in this stew is thin and clear, like a broth. If you prefer a thicker sauce, see page 80.

BLACK BEAN CHILI

Makes 4 to 6 servings

Rich, intense flavors with mild heat characterize this Mexican-inspired black bean chili.

Served on a bed of rice with vinegar-splashed bitter greens or a salad and a loaf of crusty bread, this can't be beat when the weather turns—you guessed it—chilly.

1 teaspoon olive oil

2 shallots, chopped

3 cloves garlic, minced

Two 14-ounce cans black beans, rinsed and drained

1 cup beef broth (canned is fine)

1¹/₂ to 2 cups American Beef Molé (page 86)

¹/₄ teaspoon ground allspice

¹/₄ teaspoon chili powder, or more to taste

1 bay leaf

1. Heat the oil in a heavy-bottomed saucepan over medium-high heat. Add the shallots and garlic and cook, stirring, until the shallots are soft, 4 to 5 minutes.

2. Add the beans, broth, and beef mole and bring to a boil over medium-high heat. Reduce the heat to medium-low and add the allspice, chili powder, and bay leaf. Cook, uncovered, at a quick simmer, stirring occasionally, until the sauce is thick, about 15 minutes. Taste and correct the seasonings.

1990s WILTED SALAD

Makes 4 servings

I'm glad to be living in the nineties, when wild mushrooms, mesclun, and sugar snap peas are available year round in nearly every large supermarket. If filet mignon isn't a staple in your refrigerator, substitute thin slices of left-over steak or roast beef.

The secret to this salad is to assemble everything except the mushrooms ahead of time. Just before serving, sauté the mushrooms in olive oil, toss with balsamic vinegar, and spoon the dressing over the salad.

Ideal for an important business lunch. Add crusty French bread and fresh berries for dessert.

> **4 to 6 cups mesclun (baby field greens) or shredded leaf lettuce, approximately**
>
> **12 to 16 ounces cooked beef tenderloin, steak, or roast beef, sliced into thin strips (about $1/4$ x $1/4$ x 3 inches)**
>
> **1 red onion, thinly sliced**
>
> **1 to $1 1/2$ cups sugar snap peas, blanched**
>
> **4 plum tomatoes, seeded and sliced lengthwise into strips**
>
> **4 oil-cured sun-dried tomatoes, drained and cut into strips**
>
> **4 teaspoons extra-virgin olive oil, approximately**
>
> **2 cups sliced fresh wild mushrooms (shiitake, portobello, or other)**
>
> **1 to 2 tablespoons balsamic vinegar**

1. Divide the mesclun or lettuce equally among 4 plates. Scatter the strips of beef, onion, sugar snap peas, plum tomatoes, and sun-dried tomatoes on top.

2. Heat the olive oil in a nonstick skillet over high heat. Add the mushrooms and sauté over high heat, stirring, until they "squeak," 3 to 4 minutes. Remove the pan from the heat. Add the balsamic vinegar to the mushrooms, toss, and spoon the mushrooms with their dressing over the salad.

BRISKET CAPONATA

Makes 4 servings in salads or sandwiches;
8 to 12 as part of a selection of hors d'oeuvres

One night when unexpected guests came over for drinks, I quickly made this up, using what I had on hand. We all liked it so much that I now cook brisket just to prepare this recipe.

The ingredients need to be chopped fine, but not so fine that they turn into a puree or paste, so I chop them by hand.

For canapés, fill spears of endive with the caponata or spread it on thin slices of sourdough bread. For a picnic, stuff pita pockets with a lettuce leaf, a slice of tomato, and the caponata.

1 1/2 cups finely chopped cold cooked brisket

1/2 cup finely chopped cooked mushrooms

1/2 cup finely chopped red onion

2 tablespoons chopped fresh basil

2 tablespoons finely chopped oil-cured sun-dried tomatoes, well drained

2 tablespoons brisket cooking liquid or beef broth

3 tablespoons homemade or bottled vinaigrette

3 tablespoons sweet pickle relish

Freshly ground black pepper to taste

Salt to taste

Combine all the ingredients and toss well.

ARISTOCRATIC TAPENADE OF BEEF

Makes about 3 cups, or 12 to 25 servings
as part of a selection of hors d'oeuvres

I always buy the whole filet and thriftily use every part. The filet trimmings are simmered into a broth to make a homemade glace-de-viande (see page 277). If you want to do this the easy way, however, substitute ready-made demi-glace (see page 282).

Recently at a cocktail party my waiters passed around doily-lined silver trays of the tapenade on toast points, garnished with capers and parsley.

If you prefer to serve this as a pâté, press the tapenade into a mold and refrigerate it for at least a few hours or up to 2 days, then unmold it on top a bed of lettuce and serve with crackers and apple slices.

**4 cups Homemade Beef Stock (page 276)
   or Homemade Veal Stock (page 281) or 1/2 cup
   demi-glace (page 273)**

1 pound well-trimmed leftover cooked beef, cubed

**1/3 cup chopped scallions (white and light green
   parts)**

1 rounded teaspoon black olive paste

2 tablespoons capers, drained

3 anchovy fillets, minced

1/2 cup mayonnaise

1/4 cup chopped fresh parsley

1 teaspoon fresh lemon juice

Freshly ground black pepper

Salt

1. Unless you are using demi-glace, boil the broth until it's reduced to 1/2 cup, about 20 minutes. Set aside.

2. Chop the beef in a food processor by pulsing on and off until the beef is a medium grind. Remove to a large bowl and add the scallions, olive paste, capers, and anchovies and toss. Add 1/3 cup of the reduced stock or demi-glace and stir well.

3. Add the mayonnaise, parsley, and lemon juice and stir again. If the mixture seems dry, add more of the reduced stock or demi-glace, a bit at a time, until you reach the consistency you like. (The meat should hold together on a spoon but be soft enough to spread.) Taste and correct the seasonings.

   Cover and refrigerate in a bowl or mold for at least a few hours or up to several days. (The flavor improves with age.)

CONTEMPORARY BEEF AND BEETS

Makes 8 servings

The familiar flavors of sweet beets and robust beef mingle in a snappy horse-radish dressing that acts as a quick marinade. The last-minute addition of crunchy snow peas completes this up-to-the-minute salad.

I serve this salad on a bed of red leaf lettuce as part of a buffet dinner menu. For a light supper, simply add hot crusty bread.

If you don't have any leftover beef, you can buy 1½ pounds of roast beef cut in ¼-inch-thick slices at your local deli.

Vinaigrette

½ cup olive oil

3 tablespoons fresh lemon juice

1 tablespoon red wine vinegar

1 tablespoon bottled horseradish

1 clove garlic, minced

1½ to 2 pounds rare roast beef, julienned

8 ounces canned whole beets, drained and julienned

5 to 6 shallots, chopped

Freshly ground black pepper

12 ounces snow peas, strings removed

Chiffonade of romaine lettuce

1. To prepare the vinaigrette, combine the olive oil, lemon juice, vinegar, horseradish, and garlic. Either shake in a tightly covered jar or whisk well.

2. Toss the roast beef, beets, and shallots together in a large bowl. Season with pepper to taste. Add as much of the vinaigrette to the roast beef mixture as needed to coat the ingredients and toss well. Refrigerate for 1 to 2 hours. Remove the roast beef from the refrigerator 30 minutes before serving.

3. Shortly before serving, blanch the snow peas by dropping them into boiling water for 30 to 45 seconds. Drain and run under cold water. Pat them dry with paper towels. Set aside a few of the snow peas for garnish and toss the rest with the roast beef mixture.

4. Make a bed of lettuce on a large serving platter or on individual plates and mound the roast beef and beet salad on top. Decorate with the reserved snow peas.

To make a chiffonade of romaine lettuce, roll 2 or 3 leaves together as you would a newspaper. With a sharp knife cut into very thin slices. Fluff the lettuce to separate the leaves and place on plates.

SHOPPING DAY FRICASSEE OF LAMB

Makes 8 to 10 servings

I spent Thanksgiving weekend with my adopted family, the Hoefeldts, in Connecticut. The entire family, all 29, were there.

We had traditional turkey with all the trimmings, roast suckling pig, and baby lamb stuffed with fresh mint and rosemary and grilled on an outdoor spit. There was enough food for a hundred.

The next day Albert cubed the leftover roast lamb. While Abbey browned it in a skillet, he sautéed onions, garlic, and carrots in a big stockpot, after which he added potatoes, the meat, red wine, and beef broth. Margo seasoned the concoction with tarragon and a cinnamon stick.

We ladies went shopping and the men played cards while this fricassee simmered. We added the peas during the last hour and served it for dinner with a mushroom and barley pilaf. There were no leftovers that evening.

3 tablespoons olive oil, approximately

6 cups cubed leftover roast lamb

3 large onions, chopped

3 cloves garlic, minced

8 carrots, peeled and chopped

8 to 10 baking potatoes, peeled and chopped

1/2 teaspoon salt, approximately

1 teaspoon freshly ground black pepper

2 teaspoons dried tarragon

1/2 cup chopped fresh parsley

2 cups full-bodied red wine

One 4-inch cinnamon stick

2 to 3 cups beef broth (canned is fine), or more as needed

Two 10-ounce packages frozen green peas

1. Film a large nonstick skillet with olive oil. Brown the lamb in batches for 2 to 3 minutes over high heat. Remove the lamb from the skillet as it browns and set aside.

2. Heat 2 to 3 tablespoons of oil in a heavy flameproof casserole over medium-high heat. Cook the onions and garlic together, stirring, until the onions soften, 4 to 5 minutes. Add the carrots and potatoes and sauté for a couple of minutes longer. Season with salt, pepper, tarragon, and parsley.

3. Add the lamb, wine, cinnamon stick, and enough broth to come up to about 1 inch from the top of the lamb. Cover and bring to a boil. Reduce the heat and simmer slowly for 4 to 5 hours. Stir occasionally and look to see if the stew needs more broth. Add the peas about 1 hour before serving.

RISING SUN SKILLET SUPPER

Makes 4 servings

If you have a tenderloin of pork left over, roast a tenderloin, as I often do, to make this dish. The crunchy broccoli stems and peppery daikon (a large white radish used in Japanese cooking, found in many supermarkets) add a sharp contrast to the tender pork and sweet carrots.

1 to 2 tablespoons olive oil

1 small onion, sliced

One 3-inch daikon radish, julienned

1/2 cup broccoli stems, peeled and sliced into 1/2-inch strips

1 cup cooked sliced carrots

1 cup cooked broccoli florets

1 roasted pork tenderloin, sliced 1/4 inch thick and cut in half

1/3 cup chicken broth

1 teaspoon chopped pickled ginger

Pinch of freshly ground black pepper

Sauce

2 tablespoons hot-pepper jelly or currant jelly plus 1/4 teaspoon red pepper flakes

2 teaspoons soy sauce

1. Heat the oil in a skillet over high heat. Sauté the onion, daikon, and broccoli stems, stirring, until the onion begins to brown, 4 to 5 minutes. Add the carrots, broccoli florets, and pork and sauté, stirring, for a few minutes.

2. Add the chicken broth and ginger and cook over medium-high heat until the vegetables are tender and the broth is reduced. Remove the pork and vegetables from the skillet. (I spoon them directly over cooked rice.)

3. In the same skillet, quickly cook the hot-pepper jelly and soy sauce until the jelly melts. Drizzle this sauce over the pork and vegetables.

SEASIDE SUMMER SALAD

Makes 4 servings

This salad conjures up sunny summer Saturdays at the beach when we'd take a bike ride to pick up local fresh corn from the farm stand. We'd walk to the beach for a swim in the afternoon and bring home a bucket of sea water with which to soak the corn while the lamb marinated.

I always grilled extra Mint-Marinated Lamb on a Stick (page 204) and more ears of corn than we could eat so that the next day I could fix this salad for guests.

Vinaigrette

1 tablespoon Dijon mustard

2 tablespoons sherry wine vinegar

6 tablespoons olive oil

Freshly ground black pepper

4 cups salad greens, approximately

1 onion, sliced

4 tomatoes, chopped

2 cups cubed roasted lamb, approximately

2 to 3 ears roasted corn, kernels removed (about 1 1/2 cups)

1. To prepare the vinaigrette, combine the mustard, vinegar, oil, and pepper. Either shake in a tightly covered jar or whisk well.

2. Divide the salad greens among 4 plates. Arrange the onion, tomatoes, and lamb on top. Spoon the corn over the lamb and drizzle with vinaigrette.

CALIFORNIA SALAD

Makes 4 servings

Serve this flavorful salad outdoors on a cool and breezy patio or porch. Sweet ripe avocado, slivers of Southwestern Grilled Pork Tenderloin (page 184), and fresh tomatoes are sprinkled with crunchy sunflower seeds and savory capers to make a terrific lunch or light dinner with the flavors of the West Coast. No dressing is necessary; simply drizzle olive oil and balsamic vinegar on top.

4 cups mesclun (baby field greens) or shredded leaf lettuce

1 cup thin strips of roasted pork tenderloin or loin

2 tomatoes, cut in 1-inch chunks

1 avocado, cut in 1-inch chunks

2 tablespoons snipped chives

2 tablespoons toasted sunflower seeds (see Tasty Tip below)

2 tablespoons capers

1 tablespoon extra-virgin olive oil, approximately

1 tablespoon balsamic vinegar, approximately

Freshly ground black pepper

Divide the mesclun or lettuce equally among 4 plates. Top with the pork, tomatoes, and avocado. Sprinkle the chives, sunflower seeds, and capers over the salads. Drizzle olive oil and balsamic vinegar over all and top with a generous grinding of pepper.

Tasty Tip

The easiest way to toast seeds and nuts is in a dry skillet. Be sure to shake the pan constantly. Depending on their size, seeds and nuts take just 1 to 3 minutes over medium heat to toast. When they're fragrant, they're done.

WINTER SALAD

Makes 4 servings

Sometimes during the winter I feel like having a salad for lunch. Tender roast loin of pork, seedless green grapes, and red onion dressed with apple-cider vinaigrette is often my choice.

I especially like this salad made with Roast Loin of Pork with Orange-Cranberry Stuffing (page 52). If some of the stuffing is available, add it too. Serve with a mug of hot mulled apple cider and toasted whole wheat bread.

4 cups mesclun (baby field greens) or mixture of romaine and red leaf lettuce torn into bite-size pieces

½ red onion, thinly sliced

2 cups strips of roasted pork loin or tenderloin

1 cup seedless green grapes

Freshly ground black pepper to taste

Vinaigrette

1 teaspoon grainy Dijon mustard

2 tablespoons apple cider vinegar

3 tablespoons olive oil

1. Toss the mesclun or lettuce with the sliced onion and arrange attractively on a serving platter. Place the pork strips and grapes on top of the greens. Season with pepper.

2. Prepare the vinaigrette by combining the mustard, vinegar, and olive oil. Either shake in a tightly covered jar or whisk well. Drizzle over the salad.

CHUNKY HAM HASH

Makes 6 servings

A hash should not look or taste like a hodgepodge of leftovers carelessly thrown together. Here herbes de Provence *combine with parsley to season chunks of potato and ham sautéed with onion to form a new creation that's more than the sum of its parts.*

Serve the hash with any green vegetable. For dessert I suggest baked apples.

2 tablespoons olive oil

6 large boiled or baked potatoes, cut in ¹/₂-inch cubes

1 Spanish onion, chopped

¹/₂ teaspoon freshly ground black pepper

¹/₂ cup chopped fresh parsley

1 teaspoons dried *herbes de Provence*

3 to 4 cups ¹/₂-inch cubes of ham

¹/₂ cup low-fat milk or low-sodium chicken broth, approximately

1. Preheat the oven to 375°F.

2. Heat the oil in a large cast-iron skillet over high heat. Add the potatoes and sauté, stirring occasionally, until they begin to brown, 4 to 5 minutes. Reduce the heat to medium-high and add the onion and pepper and cook, stirring occasionally, until the onion begins to soften, 4 to 5 minutes.

3. Chop the parsley and *herbes de Provence* together. Add them to the skillet, toss, and cook, stirring, for another 1 to 2 minutes. Add the ham and cook, stirring occasionally, until it begins to brown, about 5 minutes longer. Taste and correct the seasonings.

4. Add just enough milk or chicken broth to the skillet so that you can see it bubbling up from the bottom of the hot skillet.

5. Place the skillet in the oven and bake for about 20 minutes, until the top is browned and crisp and the potatoes are cooked through.

HAM AND CABBAGE HEIDELBERG

Makes 6 servings

My great-great-grandmother Broadwater, born in Heidelberg, served, as I was told she put it, "some sort of" cabbage with ham. Nearly 175 years later, the flavors are still comforting as well as exciting in this dish of stir-fried cabbage, onion, sauerkraut, and ham seasoned with juniper berries, beer, and caraway.

For a hearty dinner, serve with a frosty glass of dark ale, boiled potatoes, and black bread.

1 tablespoon olive oil

1 very small head (approximately $\frac{1}{2}$ medium head) or 6 cups $\frac{1}{3}$-inch-wide slices green cabbage

1 Spanish onion, cut lengthwise into $\frac{1}{3}$-inch slices

8 juniper berries, crushed

1 cup beer or apple cider, approximately

4 cups $\frac{1}{2}$-inch cubes of ham

1 cup good-quality sauerkraut

1$\frac{1}{2}$ teaspoons caraway seeds, lightly crushed

Generous grinding of black pepper

1. Heat the oil in a wok or large skillet and stir-fry the cabbage, onion, and juniper berries over medium-high heat until the vegetables are soft and translucent, 5 to 6 minutes.

2. Add 1 cup of beer or apple cider and cover. Cook for 7 or 8 minutes, until the cabbage is almost cooked through. Add the ham, sauerkraut, caraway seeds, and pepper and cook, covered, about 5 minutes, until the ham is heated through and the cabbage is cooked as you like it. Check once or twice and add a bit more beer or apple cider if the liquid dries out.

HAM WITH WINTER FRUIT AND CURRIED SOUR CREAM DRESSING

Makes 4 generous servings

Curry dressing with a touch of mace and cardamom gives this salad a mysterious Indian flavor.

Curried Sour Cream Dressing

¹/₃ cup light sour cream

1 tablespoon mayonnaise

1 tablespoon apple cider vinegar

Scant ¹/₄ teaspoon ground mace

¹/₄ teaspoon ground cardamom

¹/₄ teaspoon curry powder

Pinch of salt

¹/₄ teaspoon white pepper

1¹/₂ cups 1¹/₂-inch cubes of ham

1 cup green and red seedless grapes cut in half

2 tablespoons raisins

1 firm large apple (I like Gala and Granny Smith in particular)

Juice of ¹/₂ lemon

Chiffonade of romaine lettuce

Toasted pecans for garnish (see Tasty Tip, page 262)

1. To prepare the dressing, combine the sour cream, mayonnaise, vinegar, mace, cardamom, curry powder, salt, and pepper. Set aside.

2. In a separate bowl, mix together the ham, grapes, and raisins. Set aside.

3. Chop the apple in ¹/₂-inch cubes and combine with the lemon juice. Add the apples to the ham mixture and toss. Add the dressing and toss again.

4. Make a bed of lettuce on a large serving platter or on individual plates and mound the ham and fruit salad on top. Sprinkle with pecans.

THE NEW WESTERN OMELETTE

Makes 2 servings

After every Christmas program at the nursery school my daughter, Paige, attended, the two of us would eat a celebration lunch at Madame Romaine de Lyon's in Manhattan. This restaurant still makes the best omelettes and serves them with a croissant and a simple salad of escarole and romaine lettuce dressed with a classic mustard vinaigrette. Their Omelette Book, offering more than 300 extraordinary egg dishes, is handwritten. These days, naturally, you can order an omelette without the yolks.

In this breakfast, brunch, or supper omelette, egg whites are substituted for the extra egg.

$1/2$ teaspoon butter

$3/4$ cup chopped ham

1 small onion, chopped

$1/2$ green bell pepper, chopped

2 whole eggs

2 egg whites

1 tablespoon cold water

Freshly ground black pepper

1. Heat the butter in a nonstick skillet. Sauté the ham over high heat, stirring, until browned, about 2 minutes. Add the onion, lower the heat to medium, and cook, stirring occasionally, for another 2 to 3 minutes. Add the green pepper and cook, stirring occasionally, 2 minutes more.

2. Whisk the whole eggs, egg whites, water, and black pepper together with a fork.

3. Add the eggs to the skillet and cook, stirring occasionally with a fork, until done according to personal preference.

MINTED HAM AND PEA SALAD

Makes 4 servings

At the first sign of a tiny leaf of spearmint poking through the stones at the end of my driveway, I think of making this delightfully fresh-tasting salad. If your garden produces sweet peas and snow peas, so much the better. But usually I rely on extra-fancy tiny peas from the freezer section of the supermarket.

Serve with coarse-grained country rye bread and fresh fruit for a company luncheon on the porch.

Vinaigrette

1 tablespoon champagne vinegar or white wine vinegar

3 to 4 tablespoons olive oil

1/2 tablespoon Dijon mustard

Freshly ground black pepper

1/2 cup frozen baby green peas (*petit pois*)

2 cups julienned ham

1 bunch scallions, chopped (white and light green parts)

1 yellow bell pepper, julienned

1/4 cup chopped fresh mint

1 cup blanched, julienned snow peas

Red leaf lettuce

1. Prepare the vinaigrette by combining the vinegar, oil, mustard, and black pepper. Either shake in a tightly covered jar or whisk well. Set aside.

2. Place the peas in a strainer and run very hot water over them for 1 to 2 minutes, until they are heated through. Drain well.

3. Combine the ham, scallions, yellow pepper, mint, snow peas, and baby green peas. Add the vinaigrette and toss well.

4. Make a bed of the red leaf lettuce on a serving platter. Place the ham salad on top.

SERENDIPITY SALAD

Makes 4 servings

Some of my favorite dishes are created serendipitously. I threw this salad together with what I had on hand one summer morning when Diane and I were working on this book. One bite and she said, "Janeen, go write this down before you forget what you did." I did, and here it is.

Refreshing melon and rich, smooth avocado slices form a complement to the salty smokiness of ham, sun-dried tomatoes, and Calamata olives. Simply scatter the ingredients and sprinkle with oil and vinegar.

3 cups leaf lettuce torn into bite-size pieces

1 cup mesclun (baby field greens) or additional torn leaf lettuce

4 to 6 thin slices red onion

½ cantaloupe, cubed

½ avocado, cubed and tossed with lemon juice

5 oil-packed sun-dried tomatoes, drained and snipped

12 Calamata olives, pitted and sliced

1 to 1¼ cups julienned ham

1 to 2 tablespoons sesame seeds, toasted (see Tasty Tip, page 262)

Freshly ground black pepper

1 tablespoon extra-virgin olive oil, approximately

1 tablespoon balsamic vinegar, approximately

Place the lettuce and baby field greens on a serving platter. Scatter the onion rings, cantaloupe, avocado, sun-dried tomatoes, olives, and ham on top. Sprinkle with sesame seeds and freshly ground black pepper. Drizzle oil and vinegar over the whole salad.

SAGE-SCENTED YAMS, ARTICHOKE HEARTS, AND VEAL

Makes 4 servings

The unlikely combination of sweet yams, tart artichoke hearts, and tender roasted veal with lemon-accented sage and onion creates a yin-yang delight of contrasting tastes and colors. The sliced yams, usually cooked until they're mushy, are sautéed only until they are just tender.

Serve with steamed green beans and a crisp white wine.

1 to 2 teaspoons olive oil

1 medium onion, chopped

2 large yams, peeled, sliced, and cut in quarters

Pinch of salt

1 teaspoon rubbed sage

1/2 teaspoon freshly ground black pepper

One 13-ounce can artichoke hearts, drained and quartered

2 cups strips of leftover roasted veal

1 to 1 1/2 cups beef broth (canned is fine)

1. Heat the oil in a nonstick skillet over medium-high heat. Cook the onion and yams, stirring, until the onion is translucent. Season with salt, sage, and pepper.

2. Add the artichoke hearts, veal, and broth. Bring to a boil, then reduce the heat and simmer for approximately 15 minutes, or until the yams are tender and the liquid reduced.

TWICE-BLESSED VEAL

Makes 6 servings

When a deadline draws close, my friend and co-author, Diane Porter, works 15-hour days. She locks herself in her home office during the day, emerges to eat a quick dinner with her family, and returns to her office to work through the evening.

Diane confesses that during those weeks her husband and two daughters endure pizza, Chinese take-out, and uninspired leftovers. At one such dinner, when veal was making its third appearance along with leftover rice and beans, all four eyed the tired dishes with distaste.

As they do every night, the family held hands and bowed their heads to say grace. "Dear Lord," her long-suffering husband intoned, "please bless this food, even though it's been blessed many times before."

Last summer while we were working on this book, I created this exuber-ant dish with Diane in mind. Mixing orzo, the tiny rice-shaped pasta, with strips of cold roast veal, scallions, black olives, toasted pine nuts, capers, and an anchovy-flavored vinaigrette creates a mouth-watering lunch or dinner dish. Serve with steamed asparagus and sliced tomatoes, and a lemon tart.

Vinaigrette

3 to 4 anchovy fillets, mashed

1 clove garlic, minced

1 teaspoon dried oregano

3 tablespoons fresh lemon juice

6 tablespoons olive oil

3 to 4 cups cooked orzo

2½ to 3 cups thin strips of roasted veal

½ cup black olives, pitted

1 bunch scallions, sliced (white and light green parts)

2 tablespoons drained capers

2 to 3 tablespoons pine nuts, toasted (see Tasty Tip, page 262)

Salt and freshly ground black pepper

8 to 10 leaves romaine lettuce

Fresh chopped parsley for garnish

1. To make the vinaigrette, combine the anchovies with the garlic, oregano, and lemon juice in a small bowl. Slowly whisk in the olive oil.

2. Toss the orzo with the veal strips, black olives, scallions, capers, and pine nuts. Add salt and pepper to taste. Add the vinaigrette and toss.

3. Line a large serving bowl or platter with the lettuce leaves and spoon the orzo on top. Garnish with parsley and serve at room temperature.

chapter 8

STOCKS AND BROTHS

INDEED, STOCK IS EVERYTHING IN COOKING, AT LEAST IN
FRENCH COOKING. WITHOUT IT, NOTHING CAN BE DONE.
IF ONE'S STOCK IS GOOD, WHAT REMAINS OF THE WORK IS
EASY; IF, ON THE OTHER HAND, IT IS BAD OR MERELY
MEDIOCRE, IT IS QUITE HOPELESS TO EXPECT ANYTHING
APPROACHING A SATISFACTORY RESULT.

—*A. Escoffier,* The Escoffier Cook Book

*E*scoffier says it all. This is how chefs have historically seen stocks. Today, however, time constraints force us to improvise.

Let's begin with the word itself. Stock is the liquid that results from the cooking of meat, poultry, fish, or vegetables in water. But then *broth* and *bouillon* mean the same thing. Traditionally we use the word *stock* for the liquid used as the base for soups, stews, and sauces. Most cooks assume a stock will be unsalted so it can be reduced and seasoned.

The word *broth* commonly indicates the thin liquid of a soup. *Bouillon* usually refers to a thin, clear soup without solid pieces. Basically, all three are the same, their main difference being how a cook plans to use them. In this book I call the traditional, time-consuming beef and veal stocks that have been the mainstay of French cooking "stocks" and the other recipes in this section "broths."

In some of these recipes you can use canned broth without losing any of the flavor in the final dish. In many I recommend either my Homemade Beef Stock (page 276) or Doctored Beef Broth (page 279). A few require only an unsalted stock like the Homemade Veal Stock (page 281) or Homemade Beef Stock (page 276), particularly when the stock will be greatly reduced to form a sauce or glaze. In these situations there's the option of using purchased demi-glace, which I discuss below. In other words, you don't have to go through the work of making a homemade stock to be a smashingly good cook.

If you're unwilling—as I often am—to take the time to make a veal stock, low-sodium chicken broth, either canned or homemade, is preferable to beef stock for a number of the veal dishes. Each recipe includes my recommendations.

For most purposes my Doctored Beef Broth (page 279) is a fine compromise between a stock that takes days to make and using ordinary broth from a can. With Doctored Beef Broth I obtain most of the flavor of homemade stock with only a fraction of the work. Remember, though, that Doctored Beef Broth is made with salty canned broth and should never be used to make demi-glace or glace-de-viande.

Technically, glace-de-viande is a reduction of beef stock, veal stock, or a stock made with a combination of beef and veal bones. Demi-glace is made from a reduction of that same stock, a classic espagnole sauce, and Madeira wine or sherry.

My students describe in mouth-watering terms the rich, dark brown sauces served over steaks and chops at high-priced restaurants. You know— the intense, meaty sauces you've no earthly idea how to re-create at home. Well, they're usually made from little more than demi-glace or glace-de-viande (which I use interchangeably) added to the meat's pan drippings, along with shallots and a sweet wine like Madeira or port. And yes, you too can make them easily.

In this chapter are recipes for a classic stock made with beef bones and another made with veal bones, a flavorful broth from leftovers, and a simple broth made with the trimmings you can accumulate in your freezer. (I find lamb and pork too strong for the all-purpose stocks I keep on hand.)

The Homemade Beef Stock (page 276) and Homemade Veal Stock (page 281) are ideal for making reductions to use in sauces. Remember not to make these with canned broth, as they would be overpoweringly salty.

It's not difficult these days to find good-quality stocks, demi-glaces, and sauces sold in specialty shops and through mail order (see page 282). Along with many other chefs and caterers, I have recently discovered Demi-Glace Gold (see page 282), a fine product that eliminates most of the work in making an excellent sauce.

Stocks

BEEF BROTH FROM TRIMMINGS

HOMEMADE BEEF STOCK

GLACE-DE-VIANDE

SIMPLE BROTH FROM FILET

DOCTORED BEEF BROTH

BEEF AND MUSHROOM BROTH

HOMEMADE VEAL STOCK

BEEF BROTH FROM TRIMMINGS

Makes about 6 cups

If you have trouble finding soup bones, it's possible to make a good broth by using only the trimmings from beef and veal. The trimmings include the fat, bones, gristle, and small pieces of raw meat that are cut away and usually discarded. I accumulate trimmings from steaks, chops, stew meat, and roasts and keep them in a bag in my freezer. When I have about 3 pounds, I make this broth.

While this broth won't be as intensely flavored as one made with soup bones, it can be used successfully in place of Homemade Beef Stock in any recipe.

3 pounds (approximately) beef trimmings, including fat, gristle, and bones

Salt

Freshly ground black pepper

5 to 6 celery stalks, coarsely chopped

3 carrots, coarsely chopped

2 onions, coarsely chopped

1 tablespoon black peppercorns

3 quarts water, approximately

1. Season the beef trimmings with salt and pepper and brown them in a large stockpot over high heat. (There's usually enough fat in the trimmings so that it's unnecessary to film the pot with oil.) Add the celery, carrots, onions, peppercorns, and enough water to cover the ingredients by 2 inches.

2. Cover the pot and bring to a boil. Reduce the heat and simmer, with the cover ajar, for 3 to 4 hours. Remove the broth from the heat and allow it to cool in the pot. Put pot in a large bowl of cold water and ice (to prevent souring). Remove the solids and discard them.

3. Refrigerate the broth overnight, then remove the fat from the top. Simmer the broth until reduced to 6 cups, 20 to 30 minutes. Strain through a fine-mesh sieve.

HOMEMADE BEEF STOCK

Makes about 8 to 10 cups

This is my basic stock. I use it to make glace-de-viande (recipe follows), stews, soups, and sauces.

Generally, if I go through the effort of making a homemade stock like this one, I "clarify" it by boiling a couple of egg shells and egg whites in the stock at the end of the cooking time, a process that removes the bits that can cloud the liquid. Then I can use the stock for any purpose, and it will be clear and free of any specks of vegetable or meat.

5 to 6 pounds beef bones and trimmings

Flour (about ½ cup)

Salt

Freshly ground black pepper

1 medium onion, coarsely chopped

4 quarts water

1 small onion, unpeeled

2 to 3 carrots, coarsely chopped

1 to 2 stalks celery, coarsely chopped

4 to 5 cloves garlic, unpeeled

2 to 3 bay leaves

1 teaspoon dried thyme

1 to 2 egg whites and shells (optional)

1. Preheat the oven to 450°F.

2. Place the beef bones and trimmings in a large roasting pan and dust them with flour, salt, and pepper. Scatter the chopped onion around the pan. Roast, stirring occasionally, until the meat browns, about 1 hour.

3. Transfer the bones and chopped onion to a stockpot. Over high heat, deglaze the roasting pan by adding ½ cup of the water and scraping up any bits of meat stuck to the bottom of the pan. Add these pan juices to the stockpot. Add the unpeeled onion, carrots, celery, garlic, bay leaves, thyme, and remaining water. Cover and bring to a boil. Reduce the heat and set the cover ajar. Simmer for 4 to 5 hours. Allow the stock to cool in the pot.

4. Strain the stock through a cheesecloth-lined strainer and discard the solids. If you have the time, chill for several hours or overnight. If not, let it rest for a few minutes. Skim the fat from the top or use a gravy strainer to remove the fat.

5. If you choose to clarify the stock, bring it to a boil over high heat. Add the egg whites and shells. Stir, reduce the heat, and let the stock simmer, uncovered, for 5 to 6 minutes. Strain through a dampened cotton tea towel or cheesecloth.

The stock can be refrigerated for 2 to 3 weeks or frozen for up to 3 months.

The unpeeled ordinary onion adds a rich, brown color to liquids. I frequently add one to my stocks and broths.

GLACE-DE-VIANDE

Glace-de-viande is a fancy name for reduced beef stock. Use it to enrich stews, sauces, and soups. It can be used in place of demi-glace.

I make up a large batch of Homemade Beef Stock, reduce it, and keep it stored in the refrigerator as glace-de-viande until I need it. Add water to return it to a stock.

2 cups Homemade Beef Stock (page 276) or Homemade Veal Stock (page 281)

In a small saucepan, boil the stock over high heat for 15 to 20 minutes, until it's reduced to about $1/4$ cup. You want a glaze thick enough to coat the back of a spoon. Watch carefully once the stock is reduced to $1/2$ cup so that it doesn't boil away.

SIMPLE BROTH FROM FILET

Makes about 1 to 1½ cups

I grew up on the theory of "waste not, want not," and it still affects the way I cook today. When I make filet of beef for a party I'm catering, I cook the side pieces (see Basic Roast Filet of Beef, page 22) to make a broth from which I create the sauce for the filet. Any leftover broth can be used as you would Homemade Beef Stock.

I use the cooked meat in Aristocratic Tapenade of Beef (page 254). Or if my assistants and I are going to eat, I add onions, potatoes, and carrots to the cooking water. In addition to the broth to make a sauce, we end up with a tasty "New England Boiled Beef" meal. (Each side piece—there's one on each filet—feeds two.)

Side strip from 1 whole filet of beef, cut in chunks

1 onion, chopped

1 carrot, chopped

1 celery stalk, chopped

Water to cover

Salt

Freshly ground black pepper

1. In a heavy flameproof casserole, brown the meat over high heat, turning frequently, for 5 to 6 minutes. (There's enough fat on it so that no oil is needed.) Add onion, carrot, and celery. Cover the meat with cold water. Bring the water to a boil, reduce the heat, and simmer for 35 to 45 minutes, or until the meat is tender and the broth is flavorful.

2. Strain out the meat and vegetables and eat or discard. Season the broth with salt and pepper. Place the broth in a gravy strainer and let it stand for 5 to 10 minutes to allow the fat to come to the top. Skim off and discard the fat.

DOCTORED BEEF BROTH

Makes about 5 to 6 cups

While I like to keep a good homemade beef broth on hand, like most of today's working women, I don't always have the time to make it. This is the broth I fall back on. It's an excellent compromise, with most of the flavor of a good homemade broth but with only a fraction of the work.

I find the results are best using Campbell's beef broth, but if you are on a low-sodium diet, replace the broth and water with 7½ cups of a low-sodium beef broth. With the current emphasis on reducing our salt intake, I hope that there will soon be more low-sodium broths in the supermarket.

Three 10½-ounce cans Campbell's beef broth

2 cans water

1 soup can full-bodied red wine

3 to 4 carrots, chopped

2 to 3 stalks celery, chopped

1 medium onion, chopped

4 to 5 cloves of garlic, unpeeled

1 bay leaf

1 tablespoon peppercorns

1 potato, diced (optional)

1. In an uncovered large saucepan, bring all the ingredients to a boil. Reduce the heat and simmer for 1 hour. Taste the broth as you cook. If it's too salty for your taste, add the potato. (Definitely add the potato to absorb the salt if you are going to reduce the broth for use in a sauce.)

2. Strain to remove the solids. The broth can be refrigerated for 2 to 3 weeks or frozen for up to 3 months.

Tasty Tip

I don't peel the garlic clove when I'm going to remove it from the final dish and want just a hint of garlic flavor.

BEEF AND MUSHROOM BROTH

Makes 2½ cups

To make this frugal broth, I save the soaking water from dried mushrooms (shiitake, porcini, and others), parsley stems, and the bones from a standing rib roast. It's the ideal broth to use in any stew or pasta dish that includes mushrooms. I love the idea that I can have a woodsy-tasting, rich, earthy broth that has not cost me an extra penny to make.

When I need a mushroom-flavored broth, but don't have a standing rib roast to hand, I doctor my Doctored Beef Broth (page 279) by replacing 1 cup of water with 1 cup of dried-mushroom soaking water.

2 leftover standing rib roast bones

5 to 6 parsley stems (see Tasty Tip below)

1 quart cold water

1²/₃ cups dried-mushroom soaking water

Salt

Freshly ground black pepper to taste

1. In a large saucepan, cover the bones and parsley stems with cold water. Bring to a boil, reduce the heat, and simmer, uncovered, for 2 hours.

2. Strain the broth and discard the solids. Let the broth stand for 15 minutes. Remove the fat that rises to the surface.

3. Return the defatted broth to a clean saucepan and boil for 10 minutes to reduce slightly. Add the mushroom soaking water and return the broth to a boil. Reduce the heat and simmer, uncovered, for 30 minutes. Add salt and pepper to taste.

Tasty Tip

Parsley stems add parsley flavor without discoloring the liquid. I use the stems instead of the leaves in broths and some sauces—wherever they're to be cooked long and can be strained out—as the leaves give the liquid a grayish, cloudy tinge.

HOMEMADE VEAL STOCK

Makes about 4 cups

I don't usually bother to make veal stock, finding Homemade Beef Stock (page 276) or canned low-sodium chicken broth adequate substitutes in most dishes.

However, if I'm catering a fancy affair or making a special dinner for guests, I prefer to use this classic veal stock for sauces for veal scallops or chops and in fine veal stews, like Black-Tie Veal Ragout (page 114).

3 to 4 pounds veal bones and trimmings

Salt

Freshly ground black pepper

1 onion, coarsely chopped

1½ cups full-bodied red wine

1 or 2 carrots

1 or 2 stalks celery

4 or 5 parsley stems

2 sprigs fresh thyme or 1 teaspoon dried

2 bay leaves

2 quarts cold water

1. Preheat the oven to 450°F.

2. Place the veal bones and trimmings in a large roasting pan and sprinkle them with salt and pepper. Scatter the chopped onion around the pan. Roast, stirring occasionally, until the veal browns, about 1 hour.

3. Place the bones and onion in a stockpot. Over high heat deglaze the roasting pan by adding ½ cup of the wine and scraping up bits of meat that are stuck to the bottom of the pan. Add these pan juices to the stockpot. Add the carrot, celery, parsley, thyme, bay leaves, water, and remaining wine.

4. Bring the stock to a boil and skim off the scum that rises to the top. Reduce the heat and simmer for 3 hours.

5. Strain the stock through a fine sieve. Rinse the stockpot and pour in the strained stock. Let broth stand for 15 minutes. Remove the fat that rises to the surface. Return the stock to a boil and reduce it by half.

MAIL-ORDER SOURCES

Asian Ingredients

For a complete selection of Asian ingredients:

Oriental Food Market and Cooking School
2801 W. Howard St.
Chicago, Illinois 60645
(312) 274-2826
(catalog costs $2.00)

Most ingredients used in Chinese cooking are now available in supermarkets and specialty stores, but if you're having trouble finding an item like "tree ears," you can order from:

The Oriental Pantry
423 Great Road
Acton, Massachusetts 01720
(800) 828-0368
(508) 263-6922
(free catalog)

For Japanese ingredients and utensils, it's hard to beat:

Katagiri and Co.
224 East 59th Street
New York, New York 10022
(212) 755-3566
(free catalog)

Demi-Glace

Demi-Glace Gold is excellent. Follow the company's directions for diluting this highly concentrated product to create demi-glace. The 1-pound container will give you many months of cooking pleasure. Thanks to its 18-month sealed shelf life and 12-month refrigerator life after opening, you don't have to worry about it going bad.

Demi-Glace Gold
More Than Gourmet
115 West Bartges Street
Akron, Ohio 44311
(800) 860-9392

Mushrooms

For first-class quality fresh and dried mushrooms shipped overnight:

Aux Délices Des Bois Inc.
14 Leonard Street
New York, New York 10013
(800) 666-1232
(212) 334-1230
Fax: (212) 334-1231
(free catalog)

Something for Everyone

Zabar's is the ultimate Manhattan food store, specializing in gourmet foods and kitchenware at discounted prices. It accepts both phone and fax orders:

Zabar's & Co., Inc.
2245 Broadway
New York, New York 10024
(212) 496-1234
Fax: (212) 580-4477
(free catalog)

Spices

This company has every kind of seasoning you can imagine at reasonable prices:

Penzey's Ltd.
1921 S. West Ave.
Waukesha, Wisconsin 53186
(414) 574-0277
Fax: (414) 574-0278
(free catalog)

BIBLIOGRAPHY

The following are the books and organizations I consulted while writing this book.

Child, Julia. *The Way to Cook*. Knopf, 1989.

Escoffier, A. *The Escoffier Cook Book*. Crown Publishers, 1941.

Escoffier, A. *Le Guide Culinaire*. Mayflower Books, 1921.

Herbst, Sharon Tyler. *Food Lover's Companion*. Barrons, 1990.

Hillman, Howard. *Kitchen Science*. Rev. Ed. Houghton Mifflin Company, 1989.

Margen, Sheldon, M.D. *The Wellness Encyclopedia of Food and Nutrition* by The University of California at Berkeley. Rebus, 1992.

National Live Stock and Meat Board, 444 North Michigan Avenue, Chicago, Illinois 60611

National Pork Producers Council, P.O. Box 10383, Des Moines, Iowa 50306 (800) 937-7675

*The Corinne T. Netzer Encyclopedia of Food Value*s. Dell Publishing, 1992.

Pépin, Jacques. *La Technique*. Quadrangle–New York Times Book Company, Inc., 1976.

Schmidt, Stephen. *Master Recipes*. Fawcett Columbine, 1987.

U.S. Department of Agriculture, Food Safety and Inspection Service, (800) 535-4555

INDEX

C